OFF THE
BEATEN TRACK
ENGLAND
& WALES

CONWAY
Bloomsbury Publishing Plc
50 Bedford Square, London, WC1B 3DP, UK
29 Earlsfort Terrace, Dublin 2, Ireland

BLOOMSBURY, CONWAY and the Conway logo are
trademarks of Bloomsbury Publishing Plc

First published in Great Britain 2022

A catalogue record for this book is available from the British Library
Library of Congress Cataloguing-in-Publication data has been applied for

ISBN: PB: 978-1-8448-6611-3; ePub: 978-1-8448-6609-0; ePDF: 978-1-8448-6610-6

2 4 6 8 10 9 7 5 3 1

Typeset in Aestetico
Designed by Austin Taylor
Printed and bound in China by C&C Offset Printing Co

To find out more about our authors and books visit www.bloomsbury.com
and sign up for our newsletters

OFF THE
BEATEN TRACK
ENGLAND
& WALES

Wild drives and offbeat adventures
by camper van and motorhome

MARTIN
DOREY

C✦NWAY
LONDON · OXFORD · NEW YORK · NEW DELHI · SYDNEY

CONTENTS

Author's Preface 6

About this book 8

Introducing England 9

Introducing Wales 11

How to get to England
and Wales 12

Where and how to stay overnight
in England and Wales 14

Your essential kit 17

Travel, climate and the mess
we make 20

ENGLAND 22

The South-west

01 Wessex Wandering 25

02 The East Lyn River 39

03 Bude's Lost Waterway 49

04 The River Avon 61

05 The Jurassic Undercliff 73

06 Devon Coast to Coast 83

The South and South-east

07 The Wight Chines 97

08 The River Test 109

09 Goring to Maidenhead 121

10 Dungeness Desolation 133

11 Kent's Pilgrims' Way 147

East Anglia

12 The Suffolk Coast **159**

The North

13 Spurn Head and
    the Humber **171**
14 The North York Moors **183**
15 Stanhope to Newcastle **197**
16 The Northumberland
    Coast **207**
17 The Otterburn Ranges **219**

The North-west

18 The Tweed Valley **229**
19 The Solway Firth **241**
20 The Western Lakes **249**
21 The Forest of Bowland **259**

WALES **270**

22 Cwm Bychan and the
    Roman Steps **273**
23 The Pass of The Cross **283**
24 The Teifi **291**
25 The Brecon Beacons **303**

Index **316**
Acknowledgements **320**

AUTHOR'S PREFACE

I WAS SUPPOSED TO BEGIN this book in the autumn of 2020. However, a series of lockdowns delayed the start until I was able to get out, finally, in May 2021. Having spent lockdown walking Bude's hinterland, finding calm just a few miles from home, I set off, with a new van and a new hunger to get away from it all and find out if it was still possible to get 'off the beaten track' in England and Wales.

The summer of 2021 was busy. Foreign travel became restricted and difficult and this meant finding another way. My home town, Bude in North Cornwall, itself on the edge of the map, welcomed record numbers of visitors, many of whom might have otherwise been in Spain, France or further afield. The beaches were full and the pubs and restaurants heaving with people desperate for a table and, to a certain extent, normality.

I therefore wanted to see if I could find peace and solitude elsewhere. I didn't manage to cover the whole of England and Wales by any means, regretfully, but I did manage to find some glorious moments of calm in the places I did get to. I swam on empty beaches, kayaked down quiet rivers, walked along ancient pathways, cycled up mountains and down disused railways, fished famous, lazy rivers and desolate lakes, crossed lonely moors

and drove to places that are off the map, literally and figuratively. Mostly I only had my travelling companions and nature for company. At other times I was completely alone.

If you seek similar, this book will show you how. I loved every minute of it and hope that you will too.

When anyone tells you England is 'full', don't believe them. Our infrastructure may be stretched, but we aren't full. Not by a long way. There are vast areas of England and Wales with fewer than ten people per square kilometre. That's good news for those of you who are looking for something else from your time off. Anyone can go to those places and find their space. It isn't that far.

My final journey, to walk Bude's forgotten canal, took me deep into the heartlands of North Devon and to Cornwall's forgotten corner. It was a journey I started during lockdown and never quite completed. Then, as now, it is a silent, beautiful, lost highway, with bits missing and stretches that have disappeared under the plough. Walking that path – a glorious tramp through history, the Tamar watershed and some of the emptiest countryside in the West Country – brought me home, at the start of the winter, to a beautiful, isolated place that sits at the edge of the Atlantic, far from hospitals and rail connections, at the end of a long and winding road.

I finished where I had started: off the beaten track.

ABOUT THIS BOOK

HELLO.

Welcome.

In 2017, I wrote *Take the Slow Road: England and Wales*. In it, I found what I hoped would be the very best driving routes for motorhomes and camper vans.

This book goes a step further with a whole bunch of ideas for getting 'off the beaten track'. Almost every inch of England and Wales has been mapped, logged, covered and covered again. And in 2021, the year we all had to stay home for our summer holidays, there were people everywhere.

The answer, I found, was to work a little harder, get up earlier, stray a little further and try to see things from a different perspective. In the times when I left the van behind at the campsite and walked, cycled, kayaked or SUPed, I found as many moments of utter joy, peace and tranquillity as I have on the road. I discovered them in places where I imagined there would be none, too.

England and Wales might appear to be full if you choose to sit on overcrowded beaches, head for tourist traps or follow the crowd. But if you take the lesser trodden path, there is more than enough space for all of us.

You might even find yourself in places where you are moved by history, nature and landscape and that you might describe as 'thin', magical or even otherworldly. What you make of them is up to you, but I have to say that in criss-crossing this ancient land I have found it to be, at times, moving and beautiful and ultimately, a deeply fulfilling place to travel.

I hope you'll come with me and share my adventures.

For each journey, I've given you options to do it the hard or the easy way. So even if you don't feel you can cycle up a mountain, you can still enjoy the experience of being 'in the mountains'. That's what matters.

Pack up the van and head off. You never know what you might find.

INTRODUCING ENGLAND

IF YOU BELIEVE THE RHETORIC, you might be fooled into thinking England is a country with Spitfires patrolling the skies, Vera Lynn singing on every gramophone and great statesmen giving wise counsel in the House of Commons.

It isn't.

Our politics and politicians are generally grubby, our class system outdated and much of our press is unchecked and malevolent. Since the 1980s, we've worshipped money and become selfish and greedy and our royal family, though much loved, is irrelevant – a glittering symbol of our failure to have a decent revolution. At least that's my view.

That said, people in England and Wales, especially away from the stockbroker belt, are nice. They are friendly and helpful, although you might find that some of them won't thank you for reversing in a country lane. We're over that already.

England is owned by the Crown, the aristocracy, private individuals and various corporations. Oh, and the government. The model is based on the system put in place by William the Conqueror when he gave all the best bits to himself and rewarded his knights with vast swathes of what was left.

Some of England has been preserved by legacies from little old ladies and aristocrats who can't pay their death duties, while other bits are managed as national parks. We have ten of them, as well as more than 30 Areas of Outstanding Natural Beauty (AONBs) and almost 400 lakes that are more than 5 hectares (538,200 sq ft) in size.

England is my home. I might not like the way it's been of late and how it's come on in the last 2,000 years, but there is little doubt that it can be beautiful. It has moments of utter brilliance, if you know where to look. The

skies, when not leaden with rain, are huge. The seas, although once richer, are still rich. Our monuments, great houses and Stone Age wonders are magnificent, especially those that don't celebrate slave owners. Our history is, well, interesting, and has a lot to answer for. Our cathedrals, mesmerising.

Thank goodness there's more, much more, to England than lying politicians and faded memories of bygone glory.

We have champion trees. We have desolate moors. We have picture-perfect villages. We have Farrow & Ball paint (although it's no longer owned by us). We have huge, spectacular earthworks and Roman roads. We have mighty rivers and world-famous fly fishing streams. We have seas, beaches and cliffs. We have mountains, albeit smaller than those you might find elsewhere. We also have bits that have been left behind and forgotten, that have dropped off the map or that people don't bother with much these days. And you are free to go and find them.

We also have a couple of hairpin bends, a tiny valley in Cornwall that reeks of the otherworld and a coast where you can skinny dip in the middle of August with no one else there to enjoy the view.

It's a funny little country, this England.

I hope you like it.

INTRODUCING WALES

IN TERMS OF 'off the beaten track'-ness, Wales has a lot going for it. It might have 3.17 million people calling it home, but it enjoys some of the lowest population density in the British Isles. Most of the 3.17 million are crammed into the south or the far north-east of the country, leaving the middle bit relatively empty.

Wales is a great country. It has a sensible government, it seems, and people who still value community and caring above cash and corporations. It has pockets of inspiring people in towns like St David's, Crickhowell and Hay-on-Wye and has produced some world-beating musicians, writers and actors. It also has a real sense of adventure and pride. North Wales has reinvented itself as the adrenaline capital of the UK and now has an inland surf lake and the world's fastest zip wire. St David's, the diminutive city, is the place that invented coasteering and produced a saint deemed worthy of representing the whole of Wales.

Wales also has England and Wales' tallest mountain, Yr Wyddfa (aka Snowdon). It's also one of the most popular climbs, the Llanberis Path, so that means I haven't visited it for this book.

In terms of driving, Wales has a lot of great roads. It's even got one the locals call 'the *Top Gear* road'. That probably tells you all you need to know. Check for understeer. Because of the terrain, many of the main routes pass through incredible countryside and should never be discounted. Wales is like Scotland in that respect. Wherever you point your vehicle, you are bound to hit gold sooner or later.

I love Wales.

HOW TO GET TO ENGLAND AND WALES

ENGLAND AND WALES are countries that make up a part of the United Kingdom of Great Britain and Northern Ireland. They sit in the main land mass of a series of islands (the British Isles) in the North Atlantic off north-west Europe that also includes Ireland. England is connected to Wales and Scotland.

The English Channel separates England from Europe, while the Irish Sea separates Wales and England from Ireland, and the Atlantic Ocean separates us from the Americas. The North Sea separates England from Scandinavia and north-eastern Europe. England straddles the International Date Line at Greenwich, which gives us Greenwich Mean Time, and lies between 50 and 55 degrees north of the equator.

Getting to England and Wales is relatively easy. Honestly.

BY AIR

England and Wales are well served by plenty of of airports, with Heathrow being a hub airport for world travel. There are lots of other regional airports, including major hubs at Manchester, Birmingham and Gatwick. Wales has a few very small airports, including Cardiff.

BY RAIL

The Channel Tunnel links Folkestone in Kent to Calais in France for road traffic on board the Eurotunnel Shuttle. It takes just about 35 minutes and there are four trains per hour. The train links up with the major French and English motorway networks.

www.eurotunnel.com

The Eurostar uses the Channel Tunnel but is for foot passengers only, travelling from London to Paris, Brussels, the Alps or the South of France. There are connections in London for all English and Welsh railway stations and the same is true for Paris and Brussels in Europe.

www.eurostar.com

BY SEA

Ferries run to Europe from all major south coast ports and to Ireland from Holyhead, Pembroke Dock and Milford Haven in Wales.

www.ferries.co.uk

BY ROAD

As stated, you can drive to England via the Channel Tunnel. If you're coming from Scotland, the major route is the M74, which links Glasgow and Edinburgh with Carlisle and the English motorway network. Alternative routes exist on the A68 and the A1 via Berwick-upon-Tweed. There are other smaller roads, too.

VISA AND ENTRY

Despite the fiasco that is Brexit, it is still possible for EU, EEA and Swiss citizens to visit the UK without a visa, but you cannot travel on your ID card. Instead, you will need a passport.

Irish citizens can continue to work, live and visit the UK.

For countries outside the EU and EEA, check the visa requirements to enter the UK.

WHERE AND HOW TO STAY OVERNIGHT IN ENGLAND AND WALES

ENGLAND AND WALES have plenty of campsites, but you are not limited to them by any means. You can stay at Certificated Locations (CLs), on private land (with permission), in pub car parks, motorhome overnight stops and even some council car parks.

Here's the lowdown.

FINDING SOMEWHERE TO STAY

Gone are the days of turning up at a campsite and expecting them to find a pitch for you. In 2020 and 2021, things changed forever as more and more people saw #vanlife as their way out of lockdown. The van is the perfect, self-contained escape pod. It means, if you have on-board facilities such as a loo and shower, that you can be truly self-reliant and unrestrained. Indeed, in 2021, lots of campsites weren't accepting tents, only camper vans and motorhomes. It was our time to shine.

However, it did mean we had to book ahead, be a little more prepared and courteous. Planning has become de rigueur if you want to guarantee a good night's sleep or an electric hook-up.

In 2021, I used an app called Search for Sites more than I have done in previous years. On many nights it saved me. It marks locations such as campsites, CLs, stopovers and some wild spots and gives websites and details so you can book ahead. It also marks car parks that can be used by motorhomes and camper vans during the day, which is especially useful in places where we are 'welcomed' with height barriers or unhelpful anti-moho bylaws.

Search for Sites supports the work of Campra, a pressure group doing great work to extend the network of motorhome stopovers in the UK.

It costs £5.99 a year to use the app, but the website is free.

www.searchforsites.co.uk

TOURING PARKS AND CAMPSITES

England and Wales have a lot of campsites. From tiny sites to high-density touring parks and large Caravan and Motorhome Club or Camping and Caravanning Club sites, you have an awful lot of choice. Joining a club will get you a discounted rate at their sites. By contrast, a lot of the old-fashioned farmer's field sites may not have a website, never mind online booking.

So, you can play it any way you want to. My suggestion would be to book the first couple of nights on a big site and then shop around when you get there – if you can't find something that's right for you before you get there.

There are lots of great online resources for finding sites too.

www.caravanclub.co.uk
www.campingandcaravanningclub.co.uk
www.pitchup.com
www.coolcamping.com
www.campsited.com

CERTIFICATED LOCATIONS/CERTIFICATED SITES

These are small sites with a limited number of pitches. You can locate them with the handbook provided by the Caravan and Motorhome Club or the Camping and Caravanning Club or simply chance upon them as you drive. Either way, they offer a chance to camp in out-of-the-way sites, often in interesting locations. Commonly, what they lack in terms of facilities (some may not even have loos or showers) they make up for in location.

www.caravanclub.co.uk
www.campingandcaravanningclub.co.uk

BRIT STOPS

Based on the France Passion scheme, Brit Stops have been working hard to put growers, pub and restaurant owners, beauty spots, activity centres and farmers in touch with motorhomers by offering free overnight stops in exchange for nothing more than a smile and a wave, and hopefully, some business. There are hundreds of them all over England and Wales. It's a great scheme and worthy of your money – you'll make it back in no time.

The guidebook currently costs £28 and thereafter camping is free – just follow the code of conduct.

www.britstops.com

'WILD CAMPING' SPOTS

Wild camping is illegal in most of England and Wales. So that means you can't just turn up and expect a warm welcome. This is because most of the land is owned by someone, and to camp on it without permission is to cause a civil offence. Even with the 'right to roam' and open access land in National Parks you do not have the right to park up where you please and camp overnight. On Dartmoor, where you can wild camp (in a tent) you cannot wild camp in a van or motorhome. Likewise in the Lake District, where lightweight camping above the treeline is OK – but your camper won't go up there.

But – and it is a big but – it is possible to wild camp (park) in England and Wales if you know the right spot, are responsible and don't mind moving on if you have to. I have stayed overnight in my van in all kinds of places – lay-bys, motorway services, fields, lanes, beach car parks and remote parking areas – and never had any problem. But that doesn't mean it will be the same for you.

I usually check with the landowner if I can find them, talk to people in the area to find out if it's OK and generally try to tidy up when I arrive and before I leave. This is one way of answering the critics before they get started. People are afraid you'll stay for ages and will leave a mess. And everyone who does that ruins it for the rest of us. So, to mitigate, we try to change hearts and minds by being nice, sensible, well-intentioned campers.

Don't ignore 'no overnight parking' signs. Be respectful.

MOTORHOME STOPOVERS

Some councils and private individuals realise that motorhomers can be good for business. UK Motorhomes lists places where motorhomes can park up overnight in car parks, pubs and public spaces.

www.ukmotorhomes.net/uk-stopovers

Motorhome stopover is a scheme, not dissimilar to Brit Stops, that puts motorhomers together with pub and car park owners.

www.motorhomestopover.co.uk

YOUR ESSENTIAL KIT

THINK OF THIS SECTION AS A NUDGE. It's your cue to make a list before you go. You might not need everything that's on this list – like firelighters if your campsite doesn't allow fires – but there are some things that are essential if you want to guarantee a good night's sleep, a full tank of water and an empty, sweet-smelling loo.

HOSES AND UNIVERSAL ADAPTORS

Water is essential, but it's not always easy to get it from the tap to the van. Carrying jerrycans is easy, but even so, a length of hose can get you out of all sorts of trouble. If you have a Porta Potti or on-board toilet, a short length of hose can help you to clean it out. Keep it separately from the freshwater hose. A set of Hozelock tap adaptors and a universal adaptor will make sure you can always fill up.

- 10m (33ft) of flexible freshwater fill-up hose
- set of universal tap-to-hose adaptors
- 1m (3.3ft) length of hose for slopping out toilets

LEVELLING WEDGES AND SPIRIT LEVEL

Some people can sleep on a slope, but I can't. So I *always* carry my levelling wedges. Recently, I have acquired a mini two-plane spirit level that sits on the dashboard and tells me when I am getting close to level, but really a glass of water on a flat surface will do. And if you forget your wedges, a few copies of this book will do just as well.

- 1 x set of Level Up levelling wedges
- 1 x spirit level

ELECTRIC CABLES AND EXTENSIONS

If you have electric hook-up then you'll need a C Form or 16 amp cable to go with it. Around 25m (82ft) is usually enough to reach any pitch. It may also be a good idea to carry a 13 amp plug adaptor too, as well as a 13 amp socket if your campsite doesn't have a 16 amp socket (but it should!).

- 25m (82ft) 16 amp cable
- 13 amp plug adaptor
- 13 amp socket (to 16 amp)
- extension lead (for charging laptops, e-bikes and the like)
- charging cables for phones, etc.

SPARE GAS

Camping shops can be few and far between in some parts, so take a spare gas cylinder or two if you can. If you are running on LPG, fill up *before* you head into the wild. Some stations do not supply it or may not have the right nozzle adaptor in the more remote corners of England or Wales.

- Use the mylpg.eu app to find service stations that supply LPG
- Carry spare connectors to match your on-board tank to the UK nozzle

MAPS MAPS MAPS

I always carry a map for route planning, as well as large-scale maps of the specific areas I am visiting – so I can get into the heart of the landscape.

OS Explorer maps offer 1:25000 scale and OS Landranger maps offer 1:50000 scale.

OS have an app that has the complete set of maps, for a modest annual fee.

TOILET KIT

If you have an on-board loo, you'll need:

- eco liquid to add to your waste (stops it stinking)
- cheap loo paper (it breaks down easily)

If you don't carry a Porta Potti then sooner or later you may have to indulge in a nature wee (or worse). Do not urinate within 30m (33 yards) of

any open waterways, rivers or streams. If you do have to defecate, do it as far as possible from rivers, streams, buildings and animals. Dig a hole and bury it. Carry a trowel or folding spade.

- trowel
- cheap toilet paper (it tends to break down easier)

WIND-UP TORCHES AND LAMPS

Wind-up torches are incredibly useful because they don't need any maintenance and don't create any waste. Some lanterns will charge up from the 12v socket in the van, so can always be kept topped up at no cost. Always useful if you have to do a midnight loo stop.

AXE AND FIRELIGHTING EQUIPMENT

You may not always get the chance to have a fire, but it's always worth carrying the kit to make it happen if the need arises. Just remember to avoid lighting fires in sensitive areas or on grass or where there is a danger of it spreading. If possible, take a fire pit too, then you can light up safely without damaging turf.

- axe
- firelighters/matches/fire steel
- firepit/wood/kindling

IF YOU ARE RENTING A VAN

If you are renting a van or motorhome for your trip to England and Wales then you'll be limited by what you can carry in your luggage or by what you can cram into your car. However, do try to remember not to pack everything and the kitchen sink, especially when it comes to clothes. Space in camper vans can be limited, motorhomes less so, but they aren't unlimited in cupboard space.

Some essentials will be provided by the rental company so do check with them what they provide and what you'll need.

TRAVEL, CLIMATE AND THE MESS WE MAKE

GIVEN WHAT WE NOW KNOW about climate change and the state of our planet, we really need to take a new look at how we travel. Of course, travelling in a van or motorhome, from a CO_2 point of view, is better than travelling by plane, but the problem with hitting the road is the sheer numbers of us doing it. When you look at the carbon footprint of transport, only around 2 per cent of it is from aviation. Road transport accounts for about 75 per cent. In the UK, vans (mostly delivery vans and trades, to be fair) account for about 17 per cent.

The upshot? We still need to be vigilant about how we drive and how much we drive. You know the score here: accelerate gently, drive more slowly and don't carry too much stuff or travel with full water and waste tanks.

While e-campers are available now (Nissan's e-NV200 is a good example) and the Ducato is now available as an e-model, along with the VW T6 Transporter, prices start (at the time of writing) at £47,000 and £42,000 respectively. It seems that e-campers for all are a way off just yet. Which is a shame.

Also, it will take a while for campsites to adjust to charging e-vehicles and for the charging infrastructure to be put in place. It will also take time for all electricity to come from renewables, which is the elephant in the room for e-vehicles, isn't it?

So, while we wait, we have little choice but to continue with the fossil fuels, unfortunately, and will have to adapt to lessen our impact as much as possible.

Touring from place to place day after day is wasteful and unhelpful, from a planetary point of view, so stay a couple of nights (or more) in one place and give the van a break. Doing excursions on foot, or by bike, kayak or SUP is always going to deliver you more fun, a more genuine experience and more contact with the planet and the local community anyway.

So park up, pull on your boots and get out there.

However, it's not all plain sailing.

In 2020 and 2021, beauty spots around the UK were under enormous pressure because so many of us had no choice but to holiday at home. Oversubscribed places, whether through negligence, irresponsible behaviour or just sheer weight of numbers, suffer through littering, erosion and damage to flora and fauna. I live in Cornwall and we've had it all, from littering and bin fires to insensitive behaviour and lack of parking, stress and frayed tempers. But it doesn't have to be that way.

This book is about taking the path lesser trod and trying to find your own way. However you do it, the rewards can be great. Just remember:

- Smile and be kind.
- Don't park anywhere you are not supposed to.
- Take your litter home with you.
- Clear up your pitch when you arrive and before you leave. If necessary, clean up other people's rubbish too.
- Take the pressure off the hotspots by going out of peak times or not at all.
- Do not empty grey waste tanks anywhere you are not permitted to.
- NEVER empty black waste anywhere but at an approved Elsan point.

How you can lessen your impact once on site

- Shop locally to reduce food miles and contribute to the local economy.
- Eat in local restaurants.
- Walk or cycle. Contribute to eco projects, join beach cleans or volunteer for conservation projects.
- Offset your miles by planting trees.

ENGLAND

BEST FOR Walkers, cyclists and map readers

START Maiden Castle, Dorchester

END Winchester Cathedral, Winchester

TAKES IN Drove roads, the Roman road, Badbury Rings, Old Sarum, Dorset Cursus

DISTANCE By van: 62 miles (100km)

From Bake Farm to Win Green by bike: 31 miles (50km)

ROUTE 01

WESSEX WANDERING

FINDING ENGLAND'S HIGHWAYS, JUNE 2021

This journey took us from Maiden Castle to Winchester Cathedral in search of the old routes, drove roads and, of course, solitude. On the way, we found what Hardy called Wessex, a place where reality and imagination intertwine, populated by earthworks, ancient routes, perfect villages and beautiful chalk downland.

THE ALARM WENT OFF at 4.30 a.m. That was torment enough in itself. But what lay beyond the confines of my cosy bed in the van was worse. Yesterday had been sunny and clear, with a beautiful sunset, but this morning, if you could call it that, was misty, damp and dense. The gloom would certainly obscure what I had anticipated would be a dazzling dawn. But never mind. Lizzy and I dressed quietly, pulled on our walking boots and set out. Somewhere beyond the campsite lay Maiden Castle.

We knew where it was, of course, because yesterday we had been able to glimpse it as we arrived.

We walked along a lane out of the hamlet towards a path we hoped would take us up the ramparts. Despite the mist on the hills above us, the vibrant green of late spring shoots glowed enough for us to enjoy the hedgerows, the snails climbing cow parsley and fields of wheat swaying in waves against the breeze as the chorus of birdsong swelled in the hedgerows. We crossed a stile, walked through a steep field of wet grass and arrived at the boundary fence of Maiden Castle, a truly ancient feature of the Dorset landscape.

From Maiden Castle, we hoped to be able to see the sun rise in the north-east and to give us a rough bearing for our journey into Wessex, following the Roman road as closely as we could. Unlike other routes, which today still follow the rough lines of the old Roman roads, the route between Dorchester, Salisbury and Winchester, as marked on the OS map, only has a handful of places where you can drive its previous course. Our aim for this journey was to drive those that we could. It would take us to Badbury Rings, another important hill fort and major road junction during Roman times, then on to Old Sarum, another junction, before taking us to Winchester. It would bring us to ancient sites, cathedrals, museums and across the Dorset Cursus, a 6.2-mile (10km)-long earthworks, most of which has been

lost to agriculture. We also hoped to reach – via the old Ox Drove – another important site, Win Green, the highest point on our journey and a Bronze Age barrow with commanding views over southern England.

So this wasn't looking like the very best start.

As we walked around the huge dykes of the castle it started to feel, perhaps, as if we may have lucked out after all. The mist, reducing our visibility to tens of metres, emphasised the depth of the ditches and the scale of the enclosures. It lent something of the otherworld to the morning, as if we'd slipped through to another age by setting our alarm for that indistinct, lost time between night and day. As we entered the ramparts from the eastern end we saw how confusing and convoluted the complex entrances were. Anyone hoping to find an easy way in would have struggled. We walked across the huge enclosure and then out on to the southern ramparts. From here, we followed a path along the top of the ramparts, looking down the steep banks into the ditches. The only company we had, in our grassy island peaks cast adrift in a sea of mist, were freshly sheared sheep. Dew hung on the cobwebbed thistles and on the stems of the long grasses.

The bottoms of our trousers became soaked.
We named a few of the plants: yellow rattle,
bird's-foot trefoil and dwarf milkwort, resorting
to looking at the detail since the greater picture
– the picture we had most wanted
to see – was obscured by early fog.

I looked up, to the inner ramparts, and saw
a figure peering down at us through the mist.
I thought it was maybe a dog walker. When
I glanced back again, the figure had gone.

The Roman road from Dorchester took us
out of town on the B3150 on a dead straight
and tantalising section until it disappeared into Puddletown
Forest, home of Thomas Hardy's house. The road led us along the rather
lovely Rhododendron Mile, far from the madding crowd, crossing the Roman
road halfway through.

From there, following its rough course as closely as we could, the road
led us to 'chocolate box' villages with thatched roofs and roses around the

door, a picture-perfect vision of Hardy's imagined England, if ever there was one. We went through Tolpuddle, across the Piddle and on to the Stour at Spetisbury, and then into Shapwick before cruising a further section of dead-straight tarmac before Badbury Rings. The mist had been replaced with humid June sunshine by now, which brought the meadows around the fort to life. We walked the ramparts but saw no otherworldly figures except a few dog walkers and runners.

From here, we navigated tiny lanes through Gussage All Saints and Wimborne St Giles before crossing the almost unfathomable dykes of the cursus that covers 6.2 miles (10km) between Cashmoor and Martin Down. If we hadn't been looking for them we would have simply passed by. We stopped and could just make out the low mounds running in parallel. It's all that's left of one of England's largest Neolithic sites. The rest, presumably, lost to the plough.

The cursus runs parallel to the A354, which also runs parallel, more or less, with the Roman road for a while and, in one place, follows its course for a short stretch before getting to Coombe Bissett and the outskirts of Salisbury.

We camped at Bake Farm, just outside Salisbury, and took to our bikes

to discover a road that may well be even older than the Roman road. The Old Shaftesbury Drove is an ancient ridgeway path that gets its name from the medieval drovers who used it to take cattle to Portsmouth. However, it is believed that this route has been used for thousands of years: the drovers came later. It offers an elevated view of the surrounding countryside and, presumably, some kind of safety for the ancient traveller.

The first section was deeply disappointing. We passed piles of fly-tipped building materials, bathrooms and bags of rubble at the back of Salisbury Racecourse. Even a Scrabble set. The further from the city we got, the less litter we found on the path, presumably because lazy builders and fly-tippers can't be bothered to go that far. We felt, again, like we could be slipping back in time. Parts of the road were asphalted, while on other sections we endured deep, muddy ruts caused by off-roaders. Often, we cycled in the trees, through carpets of hawthorn blossom, beside viburnum, whitebeam, oak and yew in the ancient hedgerows. We scared rabbits, hares and the occasional squirrel as we cruised along. The day was perfect: sunny but not too hot, with a gentle breeze.

We stopped at gateways to look at the views as the downs became more pronounced and the road felt more and more like a ridgeway, the land dropping away steeply towards the north and the old A30 and into a series of steep-sided valleys to the south. At White Sheet Hill, we took a left turn into a meadow of buttercups and clover and headed down a steep track into Berwick St John, a dreamy village of thatch and cream-coloured stone houses, losing a hundred metres of vertical height in a few minutes on a steep bridleway between chalky banks bobbing with wildflowers.

Getting to Win Green took us back up to 277m (909ft) above sea level via a steep and deeply rutted path that we could barely pedal. Most of it had to be pushed. However, it brought us out at another drove road, the Ox Drove, which would lead us back to the campsite on the opposite side of the valley from the Shaftesbury Drove. We followed it up to the barrow and stand of beech at Win Green and lay among the wildflowers, counting butterflies (and attempting to take pictures of them), and stocking up on bananas and water for the ride back.

A sign at the trig point showed us the sites of interest on the horizon and their distance from us. Up here, at the highest point in Cranborne Chase and the Wiltshire Area of Outstanding Natural Beauty (AONB), we saw a few people who had arrived by car and some who had come on foot.

Check it out on the way

MAIDEN CASTLE, DORCHESTER A fabulous, huge earthworks near Dorchester. It's one of the most complex in Europe. www.english-heritage.org.uk/visit/places/maiden-castle

DORCHESTER MUSEUM, DORCHESTER This magnificent museum has been newly refurbished and now houses four floors of art, books, Hardy memorabilia, artefacts and fossils from Dorset. Truly lovely. It's also the only place in Britain where you can walk on an original Roman mosaic. www.dorsetmuseum.org

OLD SARUM The site of Salisbury's original cathedral and of Roman, Saxon and Norman occupation. www.english-heritage.org.uk/visit/places/old-sarum

BADBURY RINGS, BLANDFORD FORUM One of Dorset's finest Iron Age hill forts. Great views. National Trust owned. www.nationaltrust.org.uk/kingston-lacy/features/badbury-rings

WIN GREEN, DONHEAD HOLLOW A Bronze Age fort topped by a clump of beech trees. Great views. The highest point in Cranborne Chase. www.nationaltrust.org.uk/win-green

SALISBURY CATHEDRAL, SALISBURY Pointy and lovely, dating back to 1220. One of only four copies of the Magna Carta is located here, too. www.salisburycathedral.org.uk

WINCHESTER CATHEDRAL, WINCHESTER No spire on this one, but hey, it was the seat of Alfred the Great, Wessex's greatest Anglo-Saxon. He's buried here, along with King Cnut and William Rufus, the Conqueror's son. www.winchester-cathedral.org.uk

On the heatmap of population density, Win Green is at the centre of a vast, empty area: a space for cooling off away from the heat of Salisbury traffic or A303 snarl-ups. It does well on the Campaign to Protect Rural Britain (CPRB) tranquillity map too, scoring highly on all counts: air quality, biodiversity, lack of noise and light pollution. As I walked around the trees and looked out across the chalk hills I could easily believe it. The only annoyance was light air traffic from Salisbury airfield.

The route back to the campsite took us along the Ox Drove and on a spectacular downhill through East Combe Wood that brought us out on the valley floor and the River Ebble at Ebbesbourne Wake, another dreamy English village where wisteria battled with roses

for prime position at the door and a chalk stream ran gently through the back gardens. I loved the peace and quiet on these narrow, little-used lanes. Where possible, we took back roads and bridleways to avoid traffic and found farms with stone follies, village greens surrounded by cottages and tiny bridges crossing the chalk streams. If ever that half-imagined rural idyll of Wessex created by Thomas Hardy existed today, it was here beneath the ancient bridleways. We passed a half-open garage where a man was hand-making furniture. A couple strolled on to a grassy riverbank hand in hand to share a picnic. An elderly gent, smartly dressed in a Panama, pink shirt and Oxfords, shuffled to the local pub, grumbling as we passed him.

Just before Coombe Bissett, we found our way back to the campsite along the final section of Roman road, a tiny section at Stratford Tony that led us over a stile and into a forgotten path that was so overgrown we had to endure stinging nettles brushing our fingers as we rode. It crossed the Shaftesbury Drove and brought us neatly back to Bake Farm and the van, our legs and fingers fizzing with nettle stings and the happiness of a good day's ride.

The route to Winchester started at another huge earthworks, Old Sarum, the place where more Roman roads converged. This time, in the bright sunshine, I could see our route ahead clearly: a straight-as-an-arrow B road heading west towards Winchester. Once again, we followed it closely, through idyllic villages and diverting only for a coffee stop at Stockbridge, the place that could easily pass for the HQ of Hardy's Wessex PLC.

The Roman road led us along the southern edge of Farley Mount Country Park and into the heart of Winchester. We pitched up and cycled into the city, parking our bikes against a railing in the cathedral close and parking our bums on seats outside The Old Vine. It seemed the world had converged on the cathedral grounds. All the madding crowd was here: artists painted while families sat on the grass, kids ran around, lovers shared blankets and a busker played on a beautiful white Gretsch guitar. We supped our pints, enjoying the noise, the life and the company. Here we were, in the capital of King Alfred's Wessex, having arrived by the old routes, descending on the city like thirsty drovers, slaking our thirst in the sunshine. I doubt if it could have felt more like a dream of England if it tried.

DO IT THE HARD WAY

The Roman roads are marked on Ordnance Survey maps and can be easily followed with the help of a good navigator. Map reading skills are essential on this journey, if only to be able to find the places where the road should be. On your map, draw a line between Maiden Castle, Badbury Ring, Old Sarum and Winchester Cathedral ... after that it's up to you! You can drive on some of the sections, but not that many. When you do find them, it's fascinating to see how time has kept these thoroughfares in use. When you can't, you'll discover that there are lots of opportunities for wandering down pathways that still follow the course of the road, especially in Puddletown Forest. It's invigorating and exciting to look down a line of trees and follow it the way that the Romans did 2,000 years ago. Keep your eyes out, too, for features in the landscape: the cursus is here, along with Grim's Ditch and Bokerley Ditch and lots of barrows and burial mounds.

You will need:
- a bike (to cycle the drove rodes)
- OS maps

CAMPING

Dick's Field, Dorchester: A field adjoining a Caravan and Motorhome Club Certificated Location, adjacent to Maiden Castle. https://searchforsites.co.uk/marker.php?id=35843

Morn Hill Caravan Club Site, Winchester: It's a mile or so from the centre of Winchester, but it's easy to get to on a bike or on the bus. A pleasant, standard Caravan Club site with nice staff. www.caravanclub.co.uk/club-sites/england/southern-england/hampshire/morn-hill-caravan-club-site

Salisbury Campsite at Bake Farm, Salisbury: A newly opened site with really helpful owners and a cold shower. Handy for Salisbury, with direct access to the Old Drove Road. www.salisburycampsite.co.uk

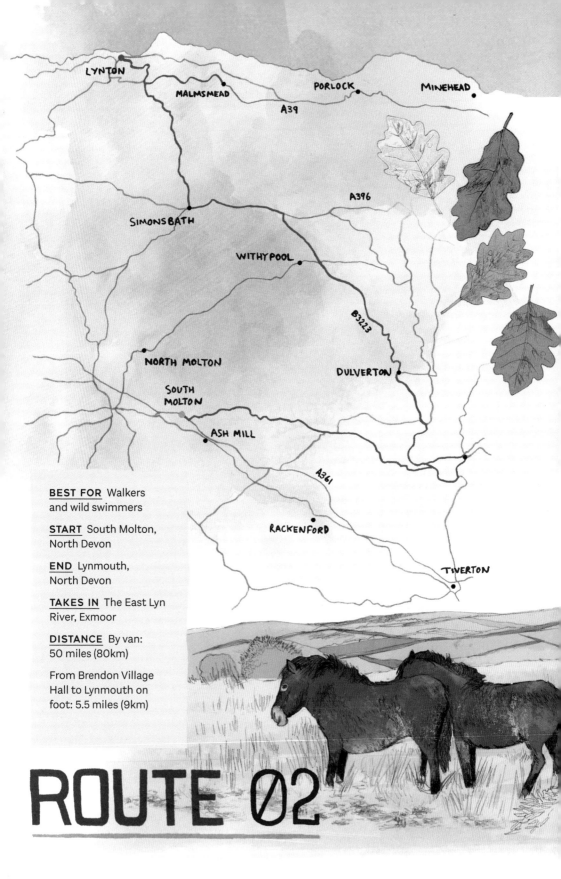

LYNTON

MALMSMEAD

PORLOCK

MINEHEAD

A39

A396

SIMONSBATH

WITHYPOOL

B3223

NORTH MOLTON

DULVERTON

SOUTH
MOLTON

ASH MILL

A361

RACKENFORD

TIVERTON

BEST FOR Walkers
and wild swimmers

START South Molton,
North Devon

END Lynmouth,
North Devon

TAKES IN The East Lyn
River, Exmoor

DISTANCE By van:
50 miles (80km)

From Brendon Village
Hall to Lynmouth on
foot: 5.5 miles (9km)

ROUTE 02

THE EAST LYN RIVER

THE EXMOOR ALPS, 21 NOVEMBER 2021

Pull on your boots and experience a corner of Devon that feels like it belongs somewhere else. With twisted oaks, water rushing over boulders into plunge pools, and paths that climb high above a deep ravine, it's more like the Alps than Exmoor. But Exmoor it is. And, of course, being on Exmoor, England's smallest National Park, makes it very special indeed.

WHENEVER LIZZY GETS TO A BRIDGE, any bridge, she goes to the middle and looks over the side at the water below. She leans out as far as she can and peers into the depths to see if any fish are lying in the shadows. It's a habit she's formed over many years. This time though, it was different.

'Looks deep enough to me,' she said.

'Are you thinking of swimming?' I asked. 'It would make a great photo from up here,' I said as I looked over the edge of the bridge, too.

We had been discussing the prospect of finding a deep pool in dappled light as we walked along the narrow pathway that follows the East Lyn River from Brendon to Lynmouth. So far, a few had offered something, but not everything, and more often than not, no comforting sunlight.

The sun, low in the sky because of the time of the year, was barely penetrating the valley. Despite the deep-blue sky above us, much of the valley bottom lay in shade. Bright patches of sunlight illuminated the remaining leaves on the trees on the upper slopes of the gorge, making them glow in rich autumnal colours high above us: orange, brown, yellow and red.

From time to time, as we walked along the winding, leaf-strewn pathway, we would turn a corner and find that the angle of the valley made it possible for the sun, skimming the trees at the top of the gorge, to find its way to us. Here, the light was piercing and bright, creating dark shadows and glowing patches of the kind of dappled light we had been talking about. Leaves, falling from the highest branches, caught the light as they fell, glinting in the sun

like gold. On these stretches, we'd be travelling roughly from south to north so the sun was behind us, creating long shadows that walked on ahead. When I turned to look back at where we'd been, I noticed the backlit trees, the sun sparkling off the river and shafts of sunlight flashing through the swaying branches of the trees above us.

The wind, coming from the north, brought us a dry but cold day, with great visibility. When we had been driving across the moor to get to Brendon we'd been able to see for miles to the green hills of Devon to the south and to Wales in the north. Every time I got out of the van to take photos or admire the views I would be beaten back by the cold wind.

It reminded me of winter and travelling in the dry cold of Europe. The light was incredible, but the temperatures forced me back to the van hurriedly.

Down in the valley, once we had pulled on our walking boots, locked up the van in the Village Hall car park at Brendon, dropped £2 in the honesty box, layered up and set off to walk the 5 or so miles (8km) to Lynmouth, the wind had lost its bite. We were in shelter but also the shade. If I looked up, I could see the treetops waving, dropping their leaves on us as we walked.

The East Lyn River is spectacular. It rises on open country and then follows a short but turbulent course to Lynmouth, on Exmoor's north-facing coast. The valley is deep and steep sided, which means that it has been saved from agriculture, leaving natural woodland of native trees and plants, an understorey of ferns and bracken, and lichens, mosses and epiphytes growing on the mature and gnarled oaks. There are hazel, oak, huge beeches, ash and chestnut in the valley, as well as pines and larch. It's ancient and natural, making it a very special and protected place. The roads are narrow and the access is difficult, making it quieter than further down the valley. A lot of people walk on Exmoor, of course, but few of the day trippers make is as far upstream as this.

Lynmouth has long been a tourist destination so it's not exactly off the map. It once had a mineral water works, mining, lime kilns and even

Check it out on the way

LYNTON AND LYNMOUTH CLIFF RAILWAY, LYNTON
The world's steepest and longest water-powered funicular railway.
www.cliffrailwaylynton.co.uk

VALLEY OF THE ROCKS, LYNTON A spectacular valley with
equally spectacular cliffs above Lynmouth and just outside Lynton,
the town at the top of the hill. www.visit-exmoor.co.uk/things-to-do/
natural-attractions/valley-of-rocks

GLEN LYN GORGE A tourist attraction on the West Lyn River
with information about the 1950s' flood and hydroelectric power.
www.theglenlyngorge.co.uk/Glen_Lyn_Gorge.htm

EXMOOR NATIONAL PARK There's more to Exmoor than just
Lynmouth and the East Lyn. www.exmoor-nationalpark.gov.uk

TARR STEPS, EXMOOR This ancient clapper bridge on the River
Barle is around 1,000 years old and is worth a walk. www.visit-exmoor.
co.uk/things-to-do/natural-attractions/tarr-steps

DOONE VALLEY The valley made famous by RD Blackmore in
his novel can be explored in all its beautiful, fictional reality.
www.nationaltrust.org.uk/lorna-doone-valley

hydroelectric power (it still does). Even so, the deep gorges and the fast-flowing rivers retain a feel of being wild and untamed. In places, it seems like another country and not sleepy Devon. The area, discovered as it was by the romantic poets of the 18th century, became known as 'Little Switzerland' because of its difficult alpine landscapes. English tourists, thwarted by the Napoleonic wars, came here in droves, first on steamers, then by train, because it reminded them of Europe. My grandfather came here in the 1920s to paint.

The East Lyn River path is part of the Coleridge Way, a 51-mile (82km) waymarked route that takes in a number of places associated with the poet. It begins in the Quantocks and ends at Lynmouth.

Parts of the path we walked were paved and lined by mossy walls with

overgrown hazels growing out of them. They felt like ancient routes, similar to the trods of Yorkshire or the drove roads of Salisbury. Many people had walked here before me. Between Brendon and Lynmouth we passed just a couple of cottages on the west side of the river, joined to the villages opposite by wooden bridges. Outside one, a white cottage that had its pathway swept recently, an old man washed his rake in the river below us. I thought what a hard life he must have: everything would have to be brought across the river on the wooden bridge. At least it would be quiet.

As we walked, I was moved by the landscape. It was delivering everything I have ever wanted from a walk. There was always something to look at, whether it was a sharp bend in the river, a set of falls, a heron or a wagtail. I liked travelling on the narrow paths with steep hillsides above me. I liked it when the woods opened out and a stand of tall beech trees created a

clearing. I loved imagining swimming in the pools below the falls. Finding shots that would best represent the walk became, as always, an obsession and I snapped away at the trees, the path and the river, hoping to get the feel in just one image. But with a changing, twisting, undulating track leading us downstream it seemed impossible.

Then we came to Ash Bridge, just before Watersmeet. Lizzy peered into the water and decided she would become the fish she always looks for. I looked downstream. The river was straight and ran deep for about 45m (50 yards). There was an easy way in and an easy way out. Beneath the bridge, the river narrowed between two rocks, creating a fast-flowing, deep channel. It would be an easy swim. Above the bridge, the sun was making its bright and breezy way through the trees, lighting up the water and providing a beautiful backlight. The sky, a ribbon of blue above the gorge, was reflected on the surface of the dark, swiftly moving water.

Lizzy stripped off and changed into her swimming costume (we always pack our togs for times like this – even on winter days), then, without hesitating, strode into the water and began to swim. The current took her quickly towards the bridge and under it as I took photos. She climbed out and walked back up the path, through the fallen leaves. When I asked her to do it again so I could get a few more photos she obliged and walked straight in again without a murmur. If it were me, I'd have made such a lot of fuss. This is something I admire in Lizzy. When she got out of the water she had a look of serenity on her face, as if she knew a happy secret. Wild swimming in cold water does this to her. Something in the cold and the water and the unexpectedness of swimming, without a care, in a wild spot gives her a resilience, a wildness and an aura of peace. As we walked downstream towards Watersmeet I felt I had missed out on something very special but knew that maybe my childish complaining would have spoiled the moment.

Between Ash Bridge and Watersmeet the footpath climbed high above the river to avoid a deep gorge below. As the sound of the rushing water faded away from us, the path wound its way through gnarled, bare oaks.

I was back in my element, tramping quiet paths in a beautiful landscape, trying my best to capture the essence of it with my camera.

We walked on. At Watersmeet, a 19th-century fishing lodge and now National Trust cafe, we encountered more people than we had in the miles before. For many, it is the apex of a walk from Lynmouth up one side of the valley and down the other. For us, it was the halfway mark. Once again, the path took a turn upwards and skirted us around another section of gorge through thick woodland in autumnal colours. We walked through patches of sun and places where the path was orange with fallen beech leaves. Below us, the river tumbled down a series of falls over huge mossy boulders.

A couple of miles later, we arrived in Lynmouth. The north wind whipped across the Bristol Channel and hit us full in the face as we sat on the sea wall eating our lunch. Looking back up the river towards the gorge we could see the depth and steepness of the valley. Victorian hotels looked down on us from above. The water rushed into the sea behind us.

'Maybe we'll come back in the summer and swim,' I offered.

'That would be nice,' Lizzy replied.

'Warmer, too,' I said.

Lizzy smiled.

DO IT THE HARD WAY

There are a couple of fantastic campsites along the East Lyn River from which it is easy to find the Coleridge Way on the north side of the river. It is also possible to park at Brendon Village Hall, as we did, for a very reasonable £2 in the honesty box. There is a loo here too.

We drove from the A361 at South Molton on the B3227, a fantastic road with great views that meets the A396 at the River Exe Valley. This follows the river north to Exebridge, where the B3222 and then the B3223 take you on to Dulverton and then Simonsbath over open moorland. After Simonsbath, the B3223 takes you to the junction with the road to Brendon past the Church of St Brendon. It's a fantastic drive.

Walking from Brendon or Malmsmead to Lynmouth will take a couple of hours, more if you stop and swim. You can either walk back along the south side of the river, crossing over again at Watersmeet, or retrace your steps. For a more challenging walk you can follow the coast path out of Lynmouth to Countisbury and then drop down the valley to Watersmeet.

You will need:
- walking boots
- swimming gear
- packed lunch/water

CAMPING

Doone Valley Camping, Malmsmead: A great site on the river that's back to basics. Fires are allowed. Book ahead. www.doonevalleycamping.co.uk

Leeford Farm Riverside Camping, Lynton: This is another brilliantly situated site, right on the river. Call Ray on 01598 741231.

DO IT THE EASY WAY

Walk from Brendon and then take a taxi back with Riverside Taxis: 01598 753442.

Alternatively, park in Lynmouth and then walk upstream to Watersmeet, cross over the river and walk back down the other side.

ROUTE 03

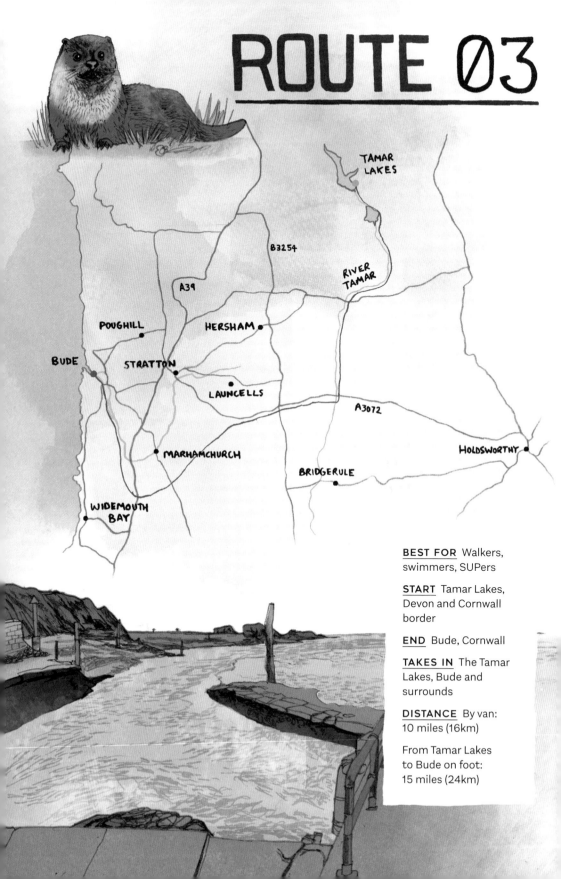

TAMAR LAKES

B3254

RIVER TAMAR

A39

POUGHILL

HERSHAM

BUDE

STRATTON

LAUNCELLS

A3072

HOLDSWORTHY

MARHAMCHURCH

BRIDGERULE

WIDEMOUTH BAY

BEST FOR Walkers, swimmers, SUPers

START Tamar Lakes, Devon and Cornwall border

END Bude, Cornwall

TAKES IN The Tamar Lakes, Bude and surrounds

DISTANCE By van: 10 miles (16km)

From Tamar Lakes to Bude on foot: 15 miles (24km)

03

BUDE'S LOST WATERWAY

FOLLOWING THE CANAL, 17 NOVEMBER 2021

Most people have heard of Bude. But its position, on the edge of the Atlantic, surrounded by a green desert of pasture and far away from cities, motorways, railway stations and hospitals, makes it one of the most isolated places in England. Thousands might flock to the beaches here in the summer, but it still has its secrets. And one of them – Bude's lost canal – will lead you right to the heart and soul of the action.

BUDE IS MY HOME. It's the place I went when I was looking for empty surf in my 20s and the place that I return to time after time. It's on the edge of the North Atlantic, battered – and held to ransom – by relentless seas. It sits in a crucible formed by the cliffs of Morwenstow to the north, Milook to the south and Bodmin Moor and Holsworthy to the east. Beyond that lie hundreds of square miles of farmland, most of which is dairy. It's a green desert, punctuated by the occasional plantation or, in areas where the plough couldn't reach, snippets of Celtic rainforest. The town is 36 miles (58km) from the nearest A&E department, 28 miles (45km) from the nearest mainline train station (making it the furthest town in the UK from a mainline station) and 47 miles (76km) from the nearest motorway.

In short, Bude is about as 'off the beaten track' as it's possible to be in England. It's what makes the place special and gives it a fantastic community and a strong sense of independence. Suspended between ocean and earth, breathing clean, ozone-rich air and yet under constant assault from weather and the outside world, it's a rare gem.

Bude's unusual canal has one of just two working sea locks in Great Britain. They connect the hinterland to the sea in dramatic fashion, opening on to Bude's beautiful Summerleaze Beach. The canal basin is the heart of the

town, now providing a lively place to grab an ice cream or coffee and watch the pedalos and rowing boats go by. But head a little inland and you'll find a story of neglect and assimilation that has left the canal dried up and empty, ploughed into the fields, fragmented by time and carelessness.

In the lockdown of early 2020, I walked much of the canal's path between the

Tamar Lakes where it ended and Bude, doing my best to link up the restored sections with those that have been lost. During those walks, I rarely saw another soul as I passed through those hundreds of square miles of nothing in search of my town's history. It seemed natural to walk the path again for this book. I wanted to come home, finishing at the beach I surf most often and to swim in the sea pool that I use regularly throughout the year.

I set off on a day that had real promise. Light cloud and a gentle westerly wind meant it was cool, but wouldn't be all day. If the sun burned through I would be treated to a rare, calm day when the yellowed leaves would be crisp under my feet and the morning dew would rise in steam as it evaporated under a still-warm autumn sun. A good day for putting one foot in front of the other.

Lizzy dropped me at Upper Tamar Lake, the reservoir that was created

in the 1970s. It's very near the source
of the river that forms the border
between Devon and Cornwall and
that runs south for 61 miles (98km)
instead of heading straight to the
sea just about 2.5 miles (4km) away.
It makes Cornwall almost an island
and a place that's separate, both
physically and culturally. To cross the
Tamar is to head into another place,
where cream comes first on a scone
and pasties are crimped to the side.
In these parts, these things matter.

I walked south, following the
Tamar to the Lower Tamar Lake, another, older reservoir
that was built to service the Bude Canal. At its southern end I walked over
the dam and across the wooden bridge leading to the towpath.

I saw a few early morning dog walkers at the lake, but once I walked on to
the towpath I was completely alone. As it turned out, I wouldn't see another
person for almost three hours. As the infant Tamar snaked away from me,
the towpath took a straight line south, on the Devon side, leading me under

a canopy of overgrown hazel and willow, bent over to form half an arch by the prevailing westerlies. Between the branches I could see the river below in soggy fields of marsh grass and died-back bracken. Across the shallow, damp canal – it was never very deep or wide – I could see open fields on the eastern side. Sheep stared at me through the branches. Pied wagtails and finches flitted about in the branches, while the occasional fat squirrel scampered away from me up one of the oak trees that grew out of the canal's forgotten banks.

The canal was abandoned over a number of years and was sold off by the local council in the 1960s, although sections of it have been bought back by Bude Canal Trust. The remainder of it is in private hands, with limited access in some places. In a lot of places, it has all but dried up, while in others, reeds and rushes grow out of the still, murky water.

I was determined to follow the course of the canal as closely as I could, but at Brendon, some 4.5 miles (7.2km) in, I had to take to the lanes. High Devon banks, topped by beech and hazel, towered over the road and grass grew down the middle as it drew me out of the countryside and towards the Tamar and the A3072. A hump-backed bridge brought me over the river and dropped me unceremoniously at the main road. This is the road that leads from Holsworthy to Bude. It's one of the main arteries into Bude and is almost always busy. I walked along the verges for a couple of miles, dodging trucks as they sped towards me, crossing the road several times to avoid blind bends. I can't say it was pleasant, but I was determined.

At the lay-by just outside of Hobbacott Down I walked through a gate on to a track that crossed open farmland with a fantastic view of the coast to the south, Dizzard Point a hazy mass in the background. As I was about to close the gate, a car pulled in and the driver, the landowner, chatted to me about the canal.

I walked past the house that was once the planekeeper's cottage and down the permissive path to the inclined plane, a steep incline up which the canal's unique tub boats on wheels were hauled by chains on to rails. From the top, I could see across the valley and to the sea. I walked down the inclined plane and down into the valley, where there is still some of the dock left. I followed the towpath as best I could, but much of it has been lost here and all I could do was trace the course of the now-closed Planekeepers Path, a route that has since been abandoned by Cornwall Council because of the cost of repair. I crossed a number of broken boardwalks, waded through a deeply muddy section and inched across a dangerously rickety bridge.

Finding the towpath once more in the woods, I followed it to a gate, where it stopped abruptly in a field with a ram who stared at me. I crossed the field, avoiding the ram, and found the canal again, following it into a field full of curious bullocks feeding on a pile of rotting silage. I hopped over a gate and landed on the road into Marhamchurch. Opposite me, the canal continued along another short section past Cann Orchard and on to another quiet lane. This led me into Marhamchurch and then on to the first of the canal's incline planes down the steep hill to Hele Bridge and the restored canal basin.

I was now on the part of the canal that's been tended and restored. It's owned by Cornwall Council and was part of a big restoration project in the 1980s so it's tidy, well kept and much loved by locals and visitors. I have heard there are otters here, too. It was a completely different world from where I'd just been. I felt disappointed that the canal has only been restored up to a point. So much of it has been lost to the plough, to private hands or roads that I fear it will never be joined up again.

Instead of mud and tree roots I now had the pleasure of walking along a tarmac towpath next to a canal that actually had water in it. People were walking their dogs or pushing prams, wishing me a good day or simple hello as they passed. A mother and daughter paddled past in a blow-up kayak. The sun was as high in the sky as it was going to get considering the time of the year, and it warmed my back as I headed north to Bude. The water on the canal was like a sheet of glass, except in a few places where the wind ruffled the surface around a bend

Check it out on the way

BUDE SEA POOL, BUDE Saved from demolition by a group of local saints, Bude Sea Pool is tidal so it gets washed out once a day. It is loved by all and swum in year round. www.budeseapool.org

TAMAR LAKES WATER PARK There is sailing and angling, as well as kayaking and SUPing on the Upper Tamar Lake. It also has a popular 3-mile (4.8km) path around it. The Lower Tamar Lake is popular with twitchers and anglers. www.swlakestrust.org.uk/tamar

KAYAKING ON THE CANAL, BUDE Shoreline run all kinds of outdoor activities in Bude, including kayaking on the canal. Hire a kayak or get some tuition. www.shorelineactivities.co.uk

THE BARREL AT BUDE, BUDE The outspoken landlord of this real-ale-boozer-in-miniature is not the only reason people come to drink here: they come for the beer, too, which is all from Cornwall. It's my second-favourite watering hole. www.thebarrelatbude.com

THE WEIR, BUDE A restaurant and pond adjacent to the weir at the furthest navigable point on the canal. Cycle trails take you out to Widemouth and back. Good food. www.weir-restaurant-bude.co.uk

or where the trees opened out. Fishermen sat under brollies on the banks, patiently waiting their lives away with the best excuse in the world. In the marshes on the valley floor, sheep grazed silently.

The smell of salt from the waves in Summerleaze Bay told me I was almost at the end of my walk and I picked up the pace a little. I crossed Rodd's Bridge and walked the final few hundred metres through gaggles of geese and ambling herds of dog walkers on to the wharf, where Lizzy was waiting for me with the van.

We walked to the end of the canal, past the huge green oak lock gates and down the steps on to the sand. Having enjoyed the luxury of tarmac for the last few miles, walking on the soft sand made my legs feel tired and made me realise how much my feet were hurting after 15 miles (24km) of walking.

When we reached the sea pool, I took off my boots, changed into my swim shorts and walked into the cool water. I swam a few strokes out into the pool and then returned to the poolside. I didn't feel much like swimming but didn't want to get out of the water just yet, so I walked down the steps that led from the pool's concrete walls to the sand and ran into the sea. Lizzy followed me into the sea, wading out into the breakers.

I waited for her to catch me up so we could immerse ourselves together. A wall of white water roared towards us. We looked at each other and dived into it, body surfing back towards the beach. I ran up the sand to my towel and clothes. Across the beach, I could see the entrance to the canal and the huge, open lock gates. We'd better hurry or we'd get cut off by the tide, I thought. I didn't want to have to walk through town instead of across the beach to get back to the van.

I didn't hang about. I'd done enough walking for the day.

DO IT THE HARD WAY

Walking from the Tamar Lakes to Bude along the old canal sounds like it would be easy. However, since lots of it has been lost, ploughed over or is simply inaccessible because it's on private land, it's not so straightforward. Walking from the Tamar Lakes will take you along the towpath for 5.5 miles (9km) and over the aqueduct, through the heart of the border country. The Tamar will be close by most of the time. When you reach Vealand you have the option to carry on for another mile and then turn back, or walk away from the canal and take the road.

If you decide to walk along the A3072 then please BE CAREFUL as it can be busy and at times has very narrow verges. That means you'll have to cross over occasionally to avoid walking around blind bends. Always walk in single file and wear bright clothes so you can be seen. This stretch is 2 miles (3.2km) long and ends at the lay-by on the left-hand side. The alternative is to head back to the Tamar Lakes.

At the lay-by, a gate leads to Hobbacott Down and then on to the inclined plane. Look out for the signs to the Planekeepers Path. Some parts of the path have been closed due to damage to bridges, but there is an alternative route via a footpath if you don't want to follow the canal and risk the path at this point. This crosses the valley and ends up, more or less, in the same place on the road to Marhamchurch. Once in Marhamchurch, take a right down Hele Road after the school and this will lead you down the inclined plane and on to the restored sections of the canal and into Bude.

You will need:
- decent walking boots
- weather-appropriate clothing
- picnic or snacks
- OS maps

DO IT THE EASY WAY

If you're camping at the Tamar Lakes then it's easy to wander down to Lower Tamar Lake and then carry on along the Aqueduct Trail, a walk that's 5.5 miles (9km) to Burmsdon Bridge. Alternatively, you could walk around the Tamar Lakes (3 miles/4.8km).

If you're staying in Bude, it's a great walk to follow the canal out of town, head up the inclined plane at Marhamchurch and do your best to follow the canal to the second inclined plane at Hobbacott. Be careful though – some of the paths are very muddy, bridges are rickety and broken and walkways are rotten.

Failing that, rent a kayak or take your SUP for a spin on the canal at Bude as far as the locks after Rodd's Bridge or portage the locks and go as far as the inclined plane at Hele Bridge or the weir.

CAMPING

Efford Camping, Bude: A great little site that's as close to Bude as you can get. Small vans only though as the lane is tight. It's a very short walk to the canal. https://effordcamping.co.uk

Wooda Farm Holiday Park, Bude: A big, well-organised, family-run touring site. It's a little out of town, but there are some great cycle routes to get to the canal and beaches. www.wooda.co.uk

By The Byre Caravan Site CL, Bagbury Byre: Great location adjacent to the cycle path and just a stone's throw from the canal. There are only five pitches, so book early. www.caravanclub.co.uk/certificated-locations/england/cornwall/bude/By-The-Byre-Caravan-Site

Tamar Lakes: South West Lakes trust run a number of campsites at their lakes. The Upper Tamar is one of them. www.swlakestrust.org.uk/tamar-campsite

ROUTE 04

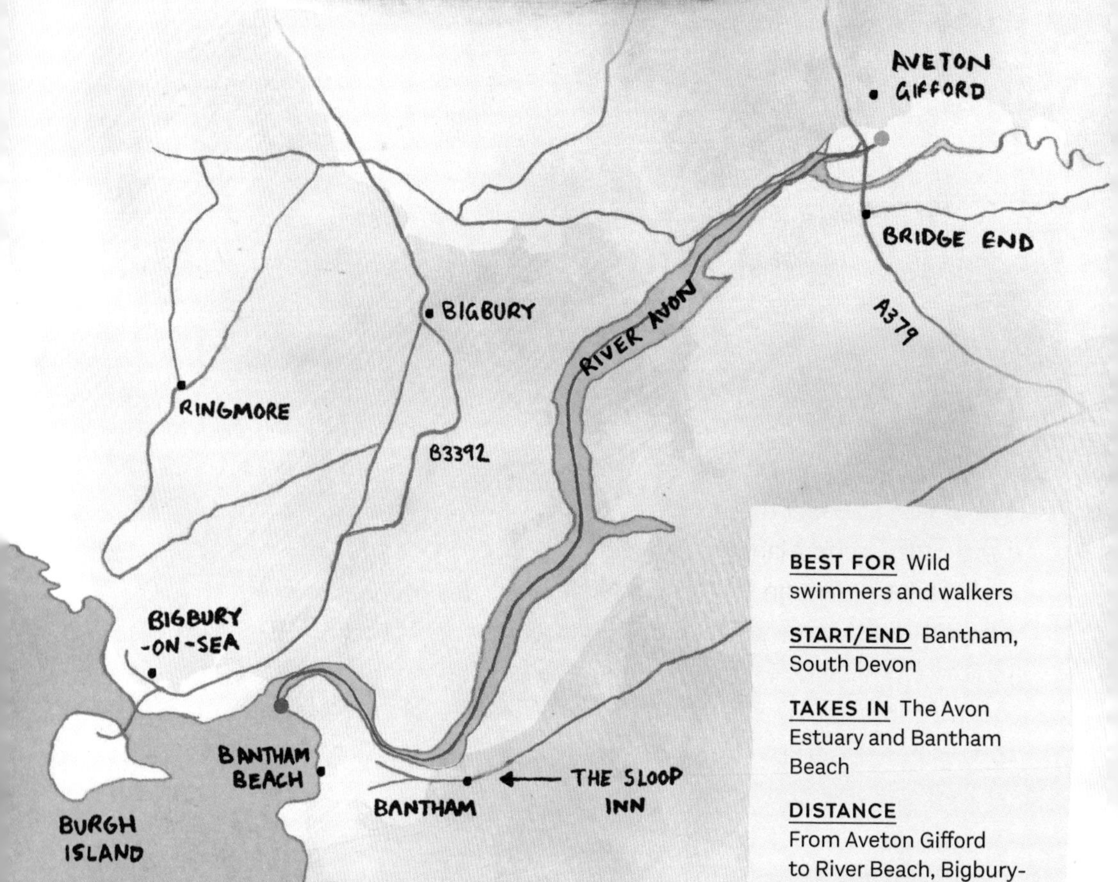

AVETON GIFFORD

BRIDGE END

A379

RIVER AVON

BIGBURY

RINGMORE

B3392

BIGBURY -ON-SEA

BANTHAM BEACH

BURGH ISLAND

BANTHAM

← THE SLOOP INN

BEST FOR Wild swimmers and walkers

START/END Bantham, South Devon

TAKES IN The Avon Estuary and Bantham Beach

DISTANCE
From Aveton Gifford to River Beach, Bigbury-on-Sea swimming: 3.7 miles (6km)

From Bantham to Aveton Gifford on foot: 1.2/3.7 miles (2km/6km)

From Bantham to Aveton Gifford by bike: 3.7 miles (6km)

From the River Beach to Bantham on foot: 1.55 miles (2.5km)

THE RIVER AVON

The shortest journey in this book takes us down a mesmerising, secluded estuary on a magical, tide-pulled swim to one of Devon's favourite beaches. With no other company save the cormorants and ducks – and the odd boatman – it's a wild and beautiful swim with a glorious, out-of-control swoosh at the end.

GEOGRAPHICALLY SPEAKING, Bantham could hardly be considered off the map or under the radar. As long as you don't mind making your way down a few winding lanes and over a couple of narrow bridges, it's not hard to reach. The only reason that Bantham is tough to get to these days is the bank holiday traffic. Posh visitors driving oversized urban off-roaders, with barely a tail-flick of mud on them, who seemingly refuse to acknowledge the rules of country driving, cause snarl-ups that drive the locals potty and temperatures to rise.

Despite this, Bantham is still a glorious place to visit and it's easy to see why it's popular. The dune-backed beach is a haven for wildlife and wild flowers, the water is clear, the surf is often good and the pub is great. A bucket-and-spade type destination, but with a gilded edge, on Devon's wealthiest stretch of coast, Bantham is forever genteel and well heeled, a cause that is helped by the ever-present backdrop of Burgh Island's famous art deco hotel across the golden sands of the bay.

Traffic aside, I have loved Bantham for a very long time and have visited regularly since going there on holiday with my parents sometime in the 1970s. Before their jet-set vanity discovered the Algarve, we were transported down the lanes in a Vauxhall Viva to go camping, stay in musty rented cottages or, sometimes, at a hotel they couldn't afford in nearby Thurlestone.

During one of these summer trips, I saw something that changed the course of my life. I can remember it as if it were days, not decades, ago. I was building sandcastles on the beach. I looked up across the sweep of sand towards Burgh Island and Bigbury-on-Sea and saw, in the middle of the bay, backlit by the sun, a surfer riding a wave. The water sparkled silver as the silhouetted figure cruised the shimmering wave for a moment, then fell off.

For me, a freckly faced and jug-eared inland kid with smash-and-grab hair, this was the greatest thing I had ever seen. At the campsite that night, I counted my ice cream pennies and negotiated with my parents to let me buy a surfboard. I have since made it my life's work to be in, on or near the ocean whenever I can.

When the time came to learn to surf properly (just days after passing my driving test), Bantham was the place I headed. I went there often, to camp with friends, to celebrate the end of school, to stop off on trips to the ferry at Plymouth and to grasp those moments of glory on the water. Every year, for

many years, I made the pilgrimage to Bantham, to catch a few waves and pay homage to a simple, happy time during which a gawky kid finds surfing and alters the trajectory of his life.

Lizzy, during the early days of our relationship, persuaded me to go back to Bantham to have a go at the Pub to Pub swim. It's a race from The Pilchard Inn on Burgh Island, up the river with the oncoming tide, to The Sloop Inn, with a pasty and a pint as reward. It was my first big open water swim and I was nervous, but it gave me a taste for the pull of the tide, something I feared as a surfer. I lay on my back and let the current carry me towards the finish line on the village slipway.

Later, I heard about the other local, but more difficult, open water swim, the Bantham Swoosh. Run for a few years by the Outdoor Swimming Society, it takes you downriver to the sea with the outgoing tide. The 'swoosh' bit is the final 91m (100 yards). Where the channel narrows, between a pink boathouse and a spit of sand on the opposite bank, the outgoing tide is forced into a race through the gap. The resulting push projects swimmers very quickly towards the beach and the open sea. Each year, the Swoosh

welcomes more than 600 swimmers to Bantham in a well-organised event that sells out in minutes.

The Swoosh had been an itch that I hadn't been able to scratch. I secured press tickets one year but couldn't make it and had to give away my place at the last minute. Somehow, the years went by and I never did it. Over time, the idea of swimming the Swoosh became symbolic for everything I wanted in my life, so when I had the idea for this book, my thoughts immediately turned to Bantham, its thatched cottages and the sand-bottomed estuary. I wondered if I could put together a trip that would take me back to the source, from the hinterland to the sea in one gloriously momentous and magical swoosh. As a side bonus, I'd get an evening in The Sloop Inn and a few nights under the stars, too. This wouldn't be an organised swim. Far from it. We'd swim alone, on an early spring tide, taking our time, experiencing this very special place, perhaps rather selfishly, with no one else to sully our solitude.

Lizzy and I waded down the tidal road at Aveton Gifford until the water reached our chests. By a road sign depicting a child taking the hand of a parent, we pulled on our goggles and pushed off into the murky, brackish water. It was early, about 7 a.m., and a light frost clung on to the banks where they remained in shade. A mist rose from the water, lit up by the low sun. We  had watched the water creep up the tidal road until it reached its apex and then set out. We had chosen a big spring tide so the extra water in the river would make the flow faster as we descended.

I shivered a little as the water entered my wetsuit. My face felt a little chill as I immersed myself fully for the first time, but it wasn't that stinging, aching cold you get in the winter. The air was warming quickly, no doubt helping to amplify the smell of seaweed coming from the muddy riverbanks. I stopped swimming for a moment and put my foot down to check the depth. My toes sank into the silky mud briefly, and then, like the child on the road sign, the current pulled me downstream as if it had an urgent message. 'Come with me!' it called, sweeping me towards the sea, a little over 3.4 miles (5.5km) away.

It took me a while to get into a good swimming rhythm, partly because I was anxious that I wouldn't have the strength to complete the swim

and partly because I wanted to enjoy every moment of being on the river. I alternated my stroke between crawl and breaststroke, with periods of floating on my back. We drifted past boats and moorings, alongside bits of debris and next to an island of muddy reeds noisy with nesting swans. Cormorants warmed themselves in the sun, their wings slightly outstretched. As the river pulled and we swam and drifted, we saw no one else, except for a man chugging towards us in an old clinker-built boat.

We rounded the first bend and came to a stretch with steep wooded banks topped by fields of bright green hay. Here, the water began to taste more like the sea. The clarity improved and we could see the bottom for

Check it out on the way

BIGBURY-ON-SEA AND BURGH ISLAND Island made famous by Enid Blyton and now a posh hotel. www.burghisland.com
THE SLOOP INN, BANTHAM A cracking 14th-century pub with nice food and a friendly atmosphere. https://thesloop.co.uk

the first time. I put my head down and swam with a slight roll, one arm sharply bent while the other stretched out, fingers searching the water in front of me. As the sandy bottom passed by beneath me it felt more like flying than swimming.

The more I swam, the more I became mesmerised. I began to drift into a dream-like state, allowing the rhythm to take over, not really thinking but allowing my mind to wander gently between boats, over the bottom, into the gullies and the creeks and with the tiny shoals of sand eels. The sea was pulling me, as it has always done. The only things that mattered were breathing and being. I half heard the water rush past and felt the cold on my face. I saw the contours of the bottom drifting by as if in a film, tasted the salty water and smelled the sea. Nothing else mattered. I felt no pain, no thirst or hunger or longing or need. It was just the swim, the water, the rhythm and my wonderful, strongly beating heart keeping me moving.

I've never been too much of an open water swimmer, partly due to being a surfer. If you surf, swimming in the open sea means your board is lost and you are in trouble. Before I met Lizzy, I spent ten days in hospital, awaiting tests for a possible heart attack, following one such long and cold swim (it wasn't). Since then, and with Lizzy's help, I have overcome my fear and have come to love open water and the distraction swimming gives me. Like the moments

when you are gliding across a wave on a surfboard, there is nothing else. Life's laundry can sit in a pile and wait for all you care. Being in nature trumps my meaningless niggles any day.

We stopped at a buoy in the middle of the river to clear our goggles and drifted past it, the current pulling us faster. Treading water, but still moving quickly, we let the scenery flow by. We saw big, quiet houses overlooking

the river. An elaborate weathervane squeaked gently. A kayak, stashed on a wooded bank, waited for its owner. A dog yapped on a balcony. But still we saw no one. We were completely alone on the river.

The village came into view as we rounded the next bend. Aiming in a diagonal, we swam between two boats to get closer to the slipway and line ourselves up for the swoosh. From the water, looking at the village from a completely new perspective, it was possible to make out the way it had developed. Most of the cottages sat on the crest of the cliff, while a few tumbled down to the river alongside a steep lane. At the bottom lay the quayside, where boat houses huddled at the water's edge. I took out my camera and tried to take pictures, but the current carried me too quickly towards 'the Pink House', the landmark where the flow begins to run fast and deep.

Flying still, we entered the last stages, travelling quickly past seaweed-covered banks and more boat houses. I noticed a parrot in the window of one, a dilapidated blue shack. It made me smile but was soon gone. The calmness of the river changed. Swell from the open sea travelled up to meet the tide, colliding to make a series of rolling, unbroken waves like river rapids. There was no point in fighting now, the pull of the ocean was too great. There never is. Better to let it carry us. I stopped swimming and gave myself entirely to the current as it swept me, faster and faster, up and down, getting closer and closer to the end that I didn't want to come.

We rounded a small, rocky headland revealing Burgh Island, the beach and a vast blue sky to the south. Lizzy, now quite cold, began to swim towards the sandbar we had decided would be our exit point. To leave it any later would be to risk being swept into the open sea. She reached it, crawled up its steep bank on all fours and lay in the sun, shivering. I followed and stood on the beach, disappointed that the spell of the swoosh had to be broken but replaying it in my mind to secure its memory. Behind me, waves broke on the seaward side of the sandbar.

It took Lizzy a while to warm up on the walk back to the campsite. The sun was already high enough in the sky to make a difference and its warmth heated our black wetsuits quickly. Smiles, momentarily disfigured into gurning, lock-jawed grimaces by the cold, returned quickly. At the campsite we boiled a kettle, peeled off our wetsuits, dressed and settled down to breakfast. It was 9 a.m.

We stretched a blanket out on the grass and slept until noon.

DO IT THE HARD WAY

Leave the van at the campsite (or leave bikes at the campsite and take the van). Cycle (or walk, following the Avon Estuary walk) to the beginning of the tidal road to Bigbury at Aveton Gifford. The cycle is downhill all the way. Enter the water just after high tide on a spring tide and swim with the tidal pull as the tide draws out. On busy summer days, beware of ski boats and watercraft on the estuary. However, if you swim on spring tides early in the morning, it should be quiet.

When you approach Bigbury, try to favour the left-hand bank to prepare for the swoosh (which starts at the pink house) and to exit the water. Get out of the water at River Beach before the current takes you out into the estuary.

From the beach, it's a 20-minute walk back to the campsite.

SAFETY NOTICE

Do not attempt this swim unless you are confident of being able to swim for an hour or more at a time, are happy in open water and can read tide tables.

You will need:
- a very good level of fitness and swimming skill and experience
- a good, warm wetsuit
- a bike or good footwear
- tide tables or an app for Bantham/Salcombe tide times

CAMPING

Aunemouth Camping, Bantham: Super chilled and relaxed back-to-basics camping with cold water showers and long drop loos. https://aunemouthcamping.co.uk

North Upton Camping, Bantham: Caravan and Motorhome Club Certificated Location with nice showers, electric hook-up (EHU) and waste facilities. www.northupton.org.uk

DO IT THE EASY WAY

The Avon can be travelled on any kind of craft, of course, and local companies will take you out on a guided tour of the river.

Go on a paddleboard tour with www.adventuresouth.co.uk/paddleboard-tour

Hire a SUP or kayak from https://banthamsurfingacademy.co.uk

You will need:
- a SUP or kayak
- a wetsuit
- transport to launch and retrieve kayaks or SUPs

DO IT THE REALLY EASY WAY

Swim just the last section, with the swoosh, on the dropping tide from the slipway, and get out at River Beach (left-hand side), just past the pink house. As usual, take care and don't do it if your swimming isn't up to it. You can also do the swoosh in reverse on the incoming tide, swimming from River Beach to the slipway at Bantham. Reward yourself with a pint at The Sloop Inn.

ROUTE 05

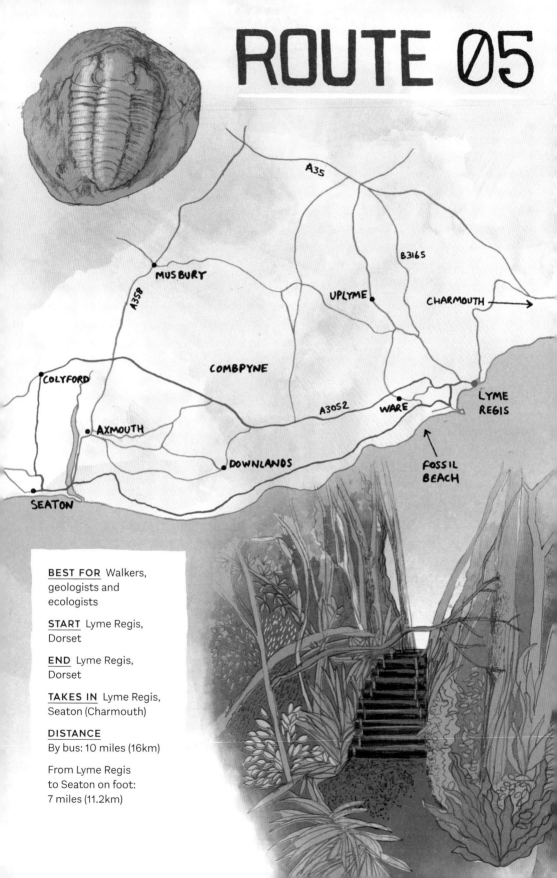

MUSBURY

A35

B3165

UPLYME

CHARMOUTH →

A358

COLYFORD

COMBPYNE

A3052

WARE

LYME REGIS

AXMOUTH

DOWNLANDS

FOSSIL BEACH

SEATON

BEST FOR Walkers, geologists and ecologists

START Lyme Regis, Dorset

END Lyme Regis, Dorset

TAKES IN Lyme Regis, Seaton (Charmouth)

DISTANCE
By bus: 10 miles (16km)

From Lyme Regis to Seaton on foot: 7 miles (11.2km)

05

THE JURASSIC UNDERCLIFF

Between Lyme Regis and Seaton, on Devon and Dorset's Jurassic Coast, you'll find an area where nature is untamed and that has been described as one of southern England's last true wildernesses. While the creation of the South West Coast Path – in 2016 – brings walkers here, a few minutes of walking will transport you into very possibly the nearest thing we have to pristine rainforest.

I PULLED ON MY BOOTS, slung my backpack across my back, grabbed my camera and set off up the steps leading me away from Lyme Regis and the warming autumn sunshine and up the cliff, between wooden chalets and into thick woodland. I stopped halfway up and looked back towards the sea and the harbour. My view was almost entirely concealed by dense foliage, even after just a minute or two of climbing. Save for the sound of the waves drawing back on the shingle beach and the brighter-than-usual light, it may as well not have been there.

I continued up the steps and began to enter another world.

Lyme Regis' Undercliffs is a National Nature Reserve. Formed by a series of landslips that happened as a result of chalk and limestone lying on softer clay, it is an area of land that was once farmed but that is now well beyond the reach of the plough. With cliffs below cutting it off from the sea and cliffs above cutting it off from the farms it once belonged to, it became useless as farmland. That allowed nature to take its course. Over the centuries, natural succession has allowed the site to be rewilded. A series of slips, some of which are recorded as having taken place in 1775, 1828, 1839 (this one was known as the 'Great Slip') and 1840, have further isolated the area, making it unreachable. Access is only possible from either end of the 7-mile (11.2km)

stretch, which means it's 'useless' as land and therefore remains untouched by the ravages of agriculture and exploitation.

The Undercliffs Reserve only recently became part of the South West Coast Path after landslips made passage impossible. In 2016, a new path was forged through the landscape. It must have been a huge task: the landslips have created a series of platforms, ridges, deep culverts and impassable hollows. It's a landscape that's unstable and really difficult, and now that the forest has grown wildly, almost impossible to navigate without a pathway.

At first, I passed a few dog walkers as the path took me through wooded sections and across slippery meadows. The last sign of modernity, an ultra-new glass and cedar holiday home, led me to an old lane and then a sign that warned me about the walking: it would be tough going and the terrain difficult. I liked that because I knew it would keep most people away. After that, I didn't see another soul for almost three hours.

I followed the old track through the thick woods and then, when it ran out, followed a narrow, muddy path that wound its way through the forest like a goat track. I walked through spiderwebs and beneath the tendrils of brambles growing overhead that looked more like vines growing from the canopy of a rainforest.

The forest was dense and seemingly impenetrable, with a ground covering of ivy and ferns, died-back bracken and wild iris. The path rose and fell as it led me through the landslip, sometimes going along the top of narrow ridges with huge chasms either side, at other times passing through steep gorges or skirting ponds in hollows. Steps, cut out of the earth and strengthened by planks of wood, allowed me to climb or descend the steeper sections.

I spent a lot of time looking at the muddy and slippery ground, making sure my footing was good – I didn't want to fall or trip and find myself face down in the mud. When I was an hour in and hadn't met anyone coming the other way, I realised that it would be a nightmare to break a leg out here. I didn't bother to check my phone for a signal but figured that, since it had been silent in my pocket for a while, it was unlikely a distress call would find its mark.

It would have been easy to feel hemmed in by the forest but, once I slowed down and looked up and around me, I felt completely at home. All I had to do was stick to the path.

Check it out on the way

CHARMOUTH HERITAGE COAST CENTRE, CHARMOUTH Charmouth is one of the best locations for fossil hunting on the Dorset coast. The fossils at the discovery centre will tell you all about it. https://charmouth.org/chcc

THE COBB, LYME REGIS Made famous by *The French Lieutenant's Woman* and Meryl Streep, the cobb is a curved sea defence that's beautifully made and quite spectacular. www.lymeregis.org/the-cobb.aspx

LYME REGIS MUSEUM, LYME REGIS It's right on the seafront and it's a favourite with hero fossil hunter David Attenborough. A gem of a building with a new wing. www.lymeregismuseum.co.uk/about-us

FOSSIL HUNTING AND WALKS The low-tide limestone slabs beneath the Undercliffs Reserve on Monmouth Beach (the ammonite pavement) are famous for producing some fantastic fossils. You can wander there yourself or you can take a guided fossil walk with experts to look for your own piece of Jurassic prehistory. www.lymeregismuseum.co.uk/events/category/walks/fossil-walks

LYME REGIS SCULPTURE TRAIL, LYME REGIS A relatively new attraction in Langmoor and Lister Gardens featuring work by local and national sculptors. www.lymeregis.org/sculpture-trail.aspx

The woods smelled of leaf mould and must, and the air damp and
moisture laden, but it still felt fresh and clean. While my boots trudged
through thick mud and slipped on tree roots and steps, I loved breathing in
the cool, sharp air. With an entire forest photosynthesising around me, I felt
lucky to breathe in the rich atmosphere. It would be worth coming here,
I thought, for the oxygen and the ozone alone. As I climbed and climbed again,
I felt beads of sweat form under the brim of my hat and roll down my face.

Pigeons rose from branches above me as I walked underneath, breaking
the silence and bringing my attention to the sound of the forest. It was quiet,
or so I thought, except for the distant sound of the sea sloshing at the base
of the cliffs and the chattering of distant birds. An occasional rustle from the
undergrowth might reveal a blackbird looking for grubs or a squirrel rushing
up a tree to get away from me. When I slowed enough to eavesdrop on the
wood I realised it was gently noisy, if I cared to listen, but easily drowned
out by the crass and classless noise of a distant aeroplane.

Where chestnuts were the dominant trees, I saw a lot of squirrels,
no doubt rushing to claim their autumnal cache before the winter sets in.
Unlike their suburban counterparts, they looked healthy and well fed – a
bonus I suppose of living under protection with few dangers.

I passed fungi that I've never seen before growing on rotting tree stumps
and on the steps, and bright orange berries in the understory. I saw the
delicate, dead flowers of wild honeysuckle and the deep, inky blue sloes of
the blackthorn. I tried to identify the trees, calling their names as I walked by,

occasionally reaching out to touch the largest trunks and offer my thanks to them for allowing me into their space: holm oaks, sycamore, holly, hazel, chestnut. My favourite, the huge, ancient beeches, did such a perfect job of keeping out the light that their presence formed glades of dappled shade and a floor of dark ivy with patches of bright brown fallen leaves.

I trudged on, the landscape changing constantly. I walked on a section paved with old bricks that petered out into a narrow path, became a boardwalk across a boggy brook, then led to a steep set of wooden steps up to a ridge. A sharp turn wound me around a fallen bough. I followed the path religiously but was occasionally tempted by the occasional track that led off into the forest. One took me to a gushing brook, another led me to a set of wooden walkways that seemed to go nowhere. Another down a steep ravine. It felt like the woods I grew up in. As a child, I lived in the Chiltern Hills and spent all my evenings and weekends exploring the beech woods around my home. Tracks through the undergrowth would always lead to adventure. I felt the same here in the Undercliffs, as if, given enough time, I could find a way down to the beach or into a part of the wood where no one ever goes.

I didn't allow my curiosity to get the better of me: I was never far from a sign that warned me of the dangers of landslips or cliff edges. When I rounded a bend and caught sight of Charton Bay I instantly regretted not following the track that led away towards the sea. But I reminded myself that I was still only halfway to Seaton and ought to get going. That was the grown-up in me talking like my grandmother would have.

Almost as quickly as the woods had engulfed me they threw me back out into the light at Goat Island, an area of grassland that was formed after the

'Great Slip' of 1839, an event that saw millions of tonnes of grassland slip
hundreds of feet towards the sea. The island is a perfect meadow leading
to sheer cliffs. In summer, as I understand it, it's alive with wildflowers and
insects. Today, all I saw was mushrooms, growing beneath stunted gorse.
Here, I met David, a coast path walker on day 55 and still delighted to be
there. We stopped and chatted about the path and the places we'd been. He
was the first person I'd spoken to for almost four hours, although I had been
passed by two couples a little earlier. I was glad to meet him and later looked
at his blog, which contains images of his extensive travels around the world.
He told me he was walking in memory of his wife, Lynne, who had passed
away three years previously. He gave me his card and took my photo, then we
parted. He headed for the woods and I started the long walk into Seaton.

The coast path took me along a bridleway, across a golf course and down
a steep hill to the Axe Valley. I followed the river to the sea and sat on the
shingle eating my lunch with the Undercliffs Reserve stretching off into the
distance to my left. I watched a cormorant fight for his favourite rock with
a couple of rooks and then made
my way along the promenade into
Seaton to find the bus back to Lyme
Regis. People sat on benches while
others strolled.

With mud on my boots and on
my trousers, I felt like an alien, as if
I'd come from another planet with
some kind of great message from the
Undercliffs. I wasn't really sure what
it was, but I was sure it was bursting
with life and fully oxygenated. What
did the Undercliffs need to tell us?

Something about the planet
perhaps? That nature – and
the Undercliffs Reserve – are
uncontainable, unconstrained and
unimaginably brilliant.

DO IT THE HARD WAY

The Undercliffs Reserve is about 7 miles (11.2km) long from end to end, although the complete walk is probably more like 8 miles (12.8km) once you've reached Seaton town centre. That said, it takes between three and four hours because of the difficulty. The path can be slippery, muddy, tricky and steep, with sections of precipitous steps and the occasional slippery slope. There are boardwalks and also some sections of old road that are wider, but it must be noted that there is no exit from the path once you have set off. The only way out is to turn around or carry on.

I walked from the Holmbush Car Park in Lyme Regis, through the town and down to the seafront, then climbed up to the coast path from the Monmouth Beach Car Park. It should be noted that motorhomes are not welcome in the Monmouth Car Park. The Holmbush Car Park has designated motorhome spaces.

You will need:
- decent walking boots
- weather-appropriate clothing
- a picnic or snacks
- a mobile phone

There is also a path that links it up with the coast path.

The Undercliffs Reserve can be walked from any direction. If you choose to walk from Axbridge, you start with a really steep climb up to the golf club and across the golf course, then on towards Goat Island. If you walk from Lyme Regis, you will enter the woods almost immediately.

The 9A bus runs between Lyme Regis and Seaton hourly (at the time of writing) and takes about 25 minutes to take you back to the start.

ROUTE
https://jurassiccoast.org/visit/attractions/the-undercliffs-reserve

CAMPING
Wood Farm Caravan Park, Charmouth: A popular holiday park with a pool and touring pitches near Charmouth. www.caravanclub.co.uk/club-sites/england/southern-england/dorset/wood-farm-caravan-park

DO IT THE EASY WAY

Park at the Holmbush Car Park in Lyme Regis and follow the signs for the Undercliffs Reserve and South West Coast Path. Go as far as you want, for as long as you want.

ROUTE 06

FREMINGTON QUAY BARNSTAPLE

A361

A39

TORRINGTON

A386

A377

HATHERLEIGH

CREDITON

M5

OKEHAMPTON

A30

A30

EXETER

LYDFORD

EXMOUTH

DARTMOOR NATIONAL PARK

A38

A380

TAVISTOCK

TEIGNMOUTH

NEWTON ABBOT

A381

A386

SALTASH

A385

TORQUAY

PLYMOUTH

TOTNES

DARTMOUTH

BEST FOR Two-wheeled adventurers and railway lovers

START/END
Barnstaple,
North Devon

TAKES IN Plymouth, Dartmoor, the Torridge and Taw valleys

DISTANCE
From Barnstaple to Plymouth by train: 80 miles (130km)

From Plymouth to Barnstaple by bike: 80 miles (130km)

DEVON COAST TO COAST

THE DAWN OF THE CUCKOO, 2 MAY 2021

A quiet, yet epic coast to coast (C2C) ride across Devon and Dartmoor, via one of the UK's best railway journeys, with options to tent it, ride just the wilder sections or go posh on the train for the very best views of Devon.

I WAS BROKEN by the time we got to Lydford, a small, pretty village on the western side of Dartmoor. I sheltered from the rain under a yew, astride my bike, breathing hard, staring through the water dripping off my cycle helmet. I wished I was back in the van, mostly prostrate and under a duvet, but it was 40 miles (65km) away, in Barnstaple, and the only way to get there was by pedal power.

While I was busy feeling very sorry for myself indeed, Lizzy, the expender of boundless energy, went off into the churchyard in search of a tap with which to fill our water bottles. Opposite me, and next to the church, stood Lydford Castle, a tall and square keep on a motte that glowed

with bright green grass and primrose, even in this dreary, post-storm light. To my right, a little further up the hail-covered lane, sitting between thatched cottages, I could see a pub. Even without its lights on it looked like a beacon of hope, but I knew that it was hopeless. It would be table service only in the garden. People were leaving with their coats above their heads.

A few minutes earlier we had been on open moorland, navigating our bikes over dried-up bog and granite, on a nearly-path that was signposted as being the 'summer route'. Until then, the cycling had been tough but glorious, between the showers, and it made me feel like I was on a 'Very Fine Spring Bank Holiday Adventure: The Temerarious Two Ride Coast to Coast'.

How different it soon became as we headed towards a dense and blackening sky. Checking the wind direction, I realised that it was only a matter of time before we got soaked. It was actually less than a matter of minutes. There were mere moments before the first fat and freezing drops crashed into the dusty soil and on to my face. They stung my eyes, then cascaded down my nose. I put my head down and cycled into the gusts, legs wanting to dismount and push and yet determined to get off the moor as quickly as possible. To our right, the giant scrub-covered granite hulks of Black Down and Gibbet Hill sat above us like the head of a fat, green toad. It felt as if its tongue could

sweep us away at any moment, like an irritating fly traversing its lips.

When we reached the safety of tarmac and tree cover, the road's margins were thick with hail. At least it hadn't landed on us when we were on the moorland. Instead, luckily, we'd had sleety rain. Luck, of course, is relative. Pedalling up the steep hill into Lydford was pointless and painful so we pushed and got even wetter. We passed the entrance to the gorge (closed) and continued on to the church where there was, as it turned out, no tap.

Legs reluctantly pushed on. Just outside the village, we refound the old railway line we had been following and slipped, once again, into a steady, slow rhythm against the slight gradient. The line, once the Great Western Railway between Tavistock and Launceston, is now known as the Granite Way and is a small section of the Route 27 Devon Coast to Coast National Cycle Network, from Plymouth Hoe to Ilfracombe. We had set off from Plymouth around six hours ago, from Smeaton's Tower – the displaced lighthouse on the Hoe – after another sudden storm left us sheltering, cold and a bit fed up, in a bus shelter. Epic trips like this one should surely be started in more auspicious circumstances. Until that point, we'd been excited and a bit giddy. Setting off from Barnstaple on the Tarka Line had been a jolly, bright affair with friendly conductors, old-fashioned signage, lovely views of the River Taw out of the window for much of the route, and a sense that a cream tea would never be too far away. Changing on to the Penzance train at Exeter offered us more glorious views of the Exe Estuary and the sea on what is one of Britain's loveliest railway sections. It's the bit that gets washed away regularly in winter storms. Today, it had been sunny and calm and full of promise.

With my backside feeling every bump, my legs laden with lactic acid and melancholy, we pedalled on slowly, scanning the verges for places to pitch our tent for the night. This section of the route passes closest to the area where

wild camping is permitted by the
Dartmoor authorities, and so it
would be our only option. The rain
stopped and the clouds began to
clear as we crunched our way over
the granite arches of Lake Viaduct.
Below us, we could see a few flat
areas of land where it might be
possible to pitch a tent. Freewheeling
down the steep ramp, passing
through a gate and pushing our bikes
(cycling is not permitted on open
moorland) over the grass and to the
banks of a tiny river, we decided there and then that this was it.

We would camp here. It was perfect. Funny how things can change in
an instant.

I wheeled my bike over the stream, up a shallow bank and on to a small,
flat area next to a mossy wall. An old five-bar gate separated the grass from
a patch of ancient forest containing huge, moss-covered oaks that towered
over a blanket of bluebells and primroses. Downstream, in the bottom of a
mini gorge, the river ran into a clear pool that looked inviting but not that
warm. I took off my damp cycling shorts, thought twice about taking a dip
and pulled on some long johns. I hung my wet coat on my bike's handlebars,
donned a couple more layers and set about putting up the tent, preparing
our supper and warming up. Lowering myself to sit, after such a long day in
the saddle, was something I put off, for fear of not being able to get up again.

As the light changed and with the sky cleared, I wandered over the moor
to watch the last of the sun between the arches of the viaduct. The huge
granite spans cast shadows across the hillside, arches of golden light beamed
on to the grass as if from stained glass windows on the floor of a cathedral. A
copper beech, as tall as the viaduct itself, burned fiery red in last light's glow.
Birdsong filled the air as I walked further up the moor to keep in line with the
shadows, growing taller and longer the lower the sun set.

From the moor, I could see our bikes and tent in a tiny corner of the landscape, an impermanent space for us below the granite arches, perched on the granite itself. Our mission had been to get as far off the beaten track as we could on this, a bank holiday weekend in the West Country, and I felt then that we had found what we wanted. With no one around and no one on the trail since I'd seen the stragglers leaving the pub in Lydford, we were truly on our own. Mission accomplished, save for getting back to Barnstaple in the morning – another 40 miles (65km) or so of pedalling and pushing.

The cold came quickly, forcing me inside before the birds had stopped singing. Lizzy and I shared a can of rum and coke and half a bar of white chocolate before falling asleep.

I woke in the night to find that my mattress had self-deflated, lowering me uncomfortably close to the granite. I felt it like an unwelcome presence in a creepy room. I wasn't cold, exactly, because my sleeping bag was warm, but I was very aware of the coldness beneath me. Granite never yields. Lizzy woke too, complaining that she was cold. She went outside to the loo and shouted to me that the stars were bright but there was a frost on the tent. I should have got up to look but didn't move. She came back inside, put on the rest of her clothes, pulled up the hood of her coat and disappeared inside her sleeping bag. I lay awake for a while listening to the brook next to my head. At times, the babbling sounded like people talking, then the hissing of a late-night TV show and then a deeper gurgling, like someone swallowing a huge pill. As I dozed, wondering if we'd be disturbed in the night, Lizzy's gentle snoring sounded like an engine starting up in a distant field.

My imagination heard a door slamming. A shotgun cocking. People whispering. Malignant and angry farmers creeping through the undergrowth, swishing bracken with their wellies. The brook babbled. I fell asleep.

I'm not sure if it was the birdsong, the cold or the light that woke me. I knew I wouldn't get back to sleep, despite my tiredness, so I lay on my back, feeling every bit of the moor beneath me, not wanting to get up, but not wanting to stay in bed either. The birdsong began to swell, like a rising tide around the tent, drowning us in sound. In the distance, a cuckoo, the first I'd heard for years. Dartmoor, I read later, is one of the last strongholds of this most elusive of declining summer visitors. The sound, travelling like a memory across space and time, through the woods, from a source unseen, reminded me of my grandfather's allotment. Another age.

'It's International Dawn Chorus Day today' Lizzy said, from beneath the covers.

'It certainly is. Good morning.'

'Hello. Is the sun up yet?'

'Almost,' I replied as I unzipped the tent and poked my head outside. 'It's frosty out there.'

'Cuckoo. Cuckoo.' It sounded like a taunt from the woods now, daring me to abandon my sleeping bag in favour of the morning.

'I'll get the kettle on then.'

Standing upright wasn't easy. It never is when you're rising from a small tent, but this morning it was particularly difficult. I made a mental note of aches and pains as I stretched a little. Chest and back? OK. Legs? Sore, but OK. Breathing? Clear and bright.

The first rays of sun were creeping up the side of the tent but had yet to defrost it. A few sheep were grazing above me on the slopes, their lambs warming up in the sunny nooks between bracken and stone walls. The sky, thin blue, with a hint of moon, free from the dark clouds of yesterday, promised greatness in the day ahead.

I lit the stove, scooped up a pan of water from the river, put it on to boil and went into the woods to pee. The old gate creaked as I teased it open. Passing from open moorland to ancient forest felt warmer and altogether safer. The air smelled damp, earthy, clean. The moss on the oaks, soft and dry to the touch. The golden rays of the early morning backlit the trees, making their young leaves glow vibrant green against the tough knuckles of their winter branches. I noticed a tiny oak sapling growing between the bluebells, the leaves a young-blooded red. Little sound above the birds but the dull, hollow crunching of my boots over the spongy earth.

And, of course, the cuckoo.

I wandered back to the tent to fetch my camera and turn off the now boiling water, noticing that Lizzy had already commandeered my sleeping bag.

Curled up inside it, while still inside her own, with just her eyes visible between the bag and her woollen hat, she watched me. I wasn't surprised and could see there'd be no point in turfing her out. From somewhere, the cuckoo taunted me. I smiled, glad she would be warm at last, safe in someone else's nest.

I photographed a patch of feathers where something had taken a pigeon, then a scattering of bones where a sheep had died. Tufts of wool hung from brambles above it. I caught foxgloves growing out of the moss of the ancient wall and tried my best to capture shoots in the warm light. A young rowan grew out of a bank, a lone tree among the unfurling bracken. Robins flitted about the hazels growing out of the old stone wall, while a grey wagtail flashed its yellow flanks at me from rocks in the brook. Steam rose from the

Check it out on the way

TINSIDE LIDO, PLYMOUTH Open air pool on the Hoe.
SALTRAM HOUSE, SALTRAM National Trust property and gardens on the banks of the River Plym. www.nationaltrust.org.uk/saltram
PLYM VALLEY RAILWAY, PLYMOUTH Heritage railway and museum. www.plymrail.co.uk
MELDON VIADUCT AND RESERVOIR, OKEHAMPTON Beautiful walks, plus ancient oak woodland at Black-a-Tor Copse.
PETER TAVY INN, TAVISTOCK Classic Dartmoor pub just before a delightful section of bridleway. www.petertavyinn.co.uk
LYDFORD GORGE Stunning gorge with Whitelady Waterfall and the Devil's Cauldron, a wild stretch of river. www.nationaltrust.org.uk/lydford-gorge
FREMINGTON QUAY CAFE, FREMINGTON The place to meet the public again after your trip to the wilds. Just outside Barnstaple. Great cakes. www.facebook.com/fremington.quay
YARDE ORCHARD CAFE, EAST YARDE Purveyors of fine local food and rest stops. www.yarde-orchard.co.uk

pan of water. If I'd remembered, I'd have pinched myself. I felt as if I'd woken in some otherworld, where cycle touring is easy and fun.

Lizzy and I sat in the sun taking in the warmth – like cormorants in long johns and puffer jackets – while we ate breakfast and sipped our tea. We watched the birds, identified the trees and plants and allowed the day's brightness to wash away the cold of the night. Camping's like that sometimes. One minute it's hell, the next it's heaven. Your fortunes can change on a sunbeam.

We were the earliest birds to cross Meldon Viaduct, the highest point on the C2C ride. Freewheeling for the first time in a while, we met a few day cyclists winding up the incline from Okehampton. As we wished everyone a good morning I felt like we'd navigated some kind of divide between the ordinary and the extraordinary, the normal world of sofas and TV and the off-grid world of wild camping and open spaces. We were now entering the land of the dog walker, the day tripper and the Sunday cyclist. And yet we'd been out in the wilderness of Dartmoor just an hour or so ago, sleeping on granite, side by side with the ancients and boiling our tea with water from the river. From the imaginings of a long, dark night we'd stepped into the sun. My inner monologue was painting me as a pioneer, pedalling towards home with news from distant lands: 'The cuckoos are here at last!' In reality, I may have been no more than a middle-aged man looking knackered, riding a bike as if it were a Spanish donkey.

From here to Barnstaple it would gradually get busier and busier, especially once we hit the Tarka Trail, the final 25 miles (40km) along the bed of the old railway. But first we had mid-Devon to ourselves as we rode the quiet backroads between Okehampton and Hatherleigh, enjoying views of the rolling hills below us. I occupied my mind with thoughts of the stops and cake at East Yarde and Fremington Quay for motivation. I was very pleased to reach Yarde Orchard Cafe, but by the time we got there the tables were full, the sun was high in the sky and people were arriving constantly. We left with a slice of soggy apple cake in tin foil and full water bottles, cruising into the 5-mile (8km) downhill to The Puffing Billy Trading Co. Takeaway and bike hire stop at Torrington. I slipped my bike into the big boy's gear and pedalled slowly and deliberately, enjoying every metre, feeling the rush of the wind on my face, the freedom of the fast and free-flowing trail through a beautiful valley of native woodland and pine plantations.

We sat in the sun on the warm concrete quay at Instow, watching the River Torridge and the ever-increasing cycle traffic on the trail flow by us, planning that cake stop at Fremington as a final luxury before loading up the van with bikes and panniers. When we got there, a queue was already well formed and snaked out of the door, down the ramp of the old platform and almost into the car park. I gave up on the idea of jam and scones or a pot of tea and unwrapped the apple cake from Yarde Orchard Cafe we'd saved, just in case our dreams were betrayed. Sitting on the grass among the other day trippers, we ate the apple cake, stared at the sky, at the river, at the people walking by, very much back among the hustle and bustle. Bundled ingloriously from the cosy, off-grid nest of our wandering.

Back at the van, I was both happy and sad. I unloaded the panniers, peeled off my cycling gear and prepared the bikes to go back on the rack. I was happy to be out of the saddle and that I had completed the ride, but also a little sad that I was back in the real world and that it was over. We had truly found our little slice of 'off the beaten track' silence, despite the cuckoo.

Before I put the bike on the rack, I rode around a little without panniers and all the trappings I'd had to carry for the last 80 miles (130km). My bike felt light, easy to manage, energised, free and ready to soar again.

'Where next?' I asked Lizzy.

DO IT THE HARD WAY

The Tarka Line will whisk you in old-fashioned branch line style to Exeter from Barnstaple (£11.00 off peak). From there, the Great Western Railway (you must book free bike spaces in advance) will take you through Devon's finest countryside and along the sea to Plymouth, where you disembark and cycle into the city and the Hoe.

At Smeaton's Tower, head to the left and follow the signs for Route 27. It is around 60 per cent off road, with 40 per cent on quiet backroads and country lanes. Cycle for 80 miles (130km), on the Plym Valley trail and the West Devon Way, stopping overnight on Dartmoor or at Sourton, where there is a campsite, cycle shop and pub adjacent to the Granite Way. Join up with the Tarka Trail at Meeth for the last sections to Barnstaple. Signposting is generally good, but be on your toes. Use the OS app and keep your phone battery alive.

You will need:
- food for two or three days
- a gravel or mountain bike (road bikes will struggle with some of the surfaces)
- lightweight camping equipment and panniers
- the OS app, at the very least, as you can view the route on the Cycle Network setting

ROUTE
www.sustrans.org.uk/find-a-route-on-the-national-cycle-network/devon-coast-to-coast

CAMPING
Bundu Camping and Caravan Park, Okehampton: Within the boundary of Dartmoor National Park. www.bundu.co.uk
Wild camping: Check the National Park's wild camping zone map. www.dartmoor.gov.uk/about-us/about-us-maps/camping-map
Motorhome Overnight Parking, Barnstaple. There's an emptying point (contact Simon on 07778 750748).

CYCLE HIRE

Devon Cycle Hire, Okehampton. https://devoncyclehire.co.uk
The Pump and Pedal, Okehampton. www.okecycles.co.uk/the-pump-and-pedal.html

DO IT THE EASY WAY

Rent a bike and cycle to quieter sections of the Tarka Trail or Granite Way.

CYCLE HIRE

Tarka Trail Cycle Hire, Barnstaple station. www.tarkabikes.co.uk
Biketrail, Fremington Quay Cafe. www.biketrail.co.uk
Granite Way Cycles for the Granite Way. www.granitewaycycles.co.uk

You will need:
- a bike or a rental bike
- a packed lunch
- a raincoat!

DO IT THE REALLY EASY WAY

Leave the van at Barnstaple station and take the train to and from Plymouth for the day. For the best views, sit on the left side when travelling out and the right side when coming home.

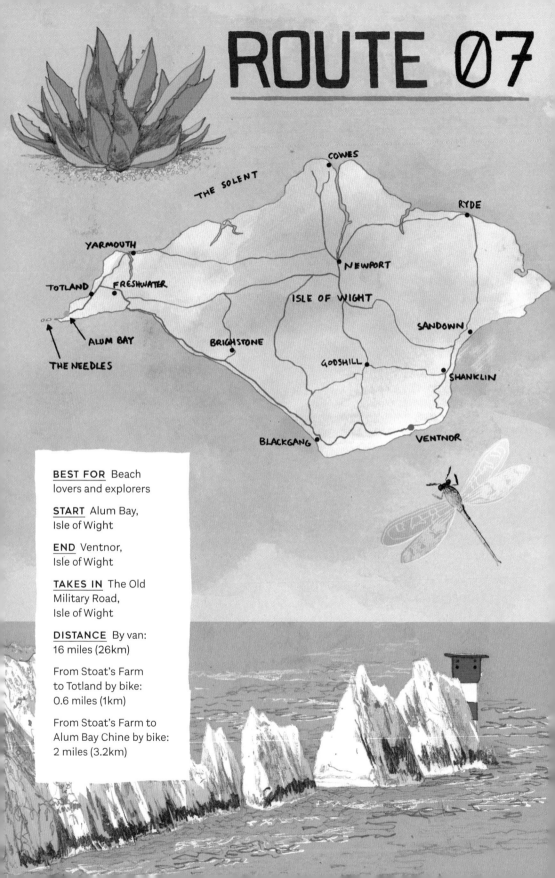

ROUTE 07

BEST FOR Beach
lovers and explorers

START Alum Bay,
Isle of Wight

END Ventnor,
Isle of Wight

TAKES IN The Old
Military Road,
Isle of Wight

DISTANCE By van:
16 miles (26km)

From Stoat's Farm
to Totland by bike:
0.6 miles (1km)

From Stoat's Farm to
Alum Bay Chine by bike:
2 miles (3.2km)

Map labels:
THE SOLENT
COWES
RYDE
YARMOUTH
NEWPORT
TOTLAND
FRESHWATER
ISLE OF WIGHT
SANDOWN
ALUM BAY
BRIGHSTONE
GODSHILL
SHANKLIN
THE NEEDLES
BLACKGANG
VENTNOR

07

THE WIGHT CHINES

ALONG THE OLD MILITARY ROAD, 15 JUNE 2021

The Isle of Wight is famous for its chines, a series of steep ravines that give access to otherwise inaccessible beaches. Some of them are wilder than others. Theme parks and attractions populate those in Alum Bay Chine and at Blackgang Chine, but there are still places where you can get away from it all. You might just have to make a little effort.

LOOKING AT THE PHOTO overleaf of Lizzy sitting on the bleached tree trunk, you'd have a hard time believing we were on the Isle of Wight. With the sun high in a deep blue sky and the Solent reflecting the colour beautifully, the mood was more Bahamas than English Channel. It suited us. We had just arrived on the island and cycled from our campsite at Stoats Farm to Totland. We walked west, along the sea wall, to the furthest corner

of the beach, where the chalky boulders began. Here, on fine sand and flint, we left our clothes and went for a dip, feeling more Robinson Crusoe than Cliff Michelmore. We swam out to the line of buoys marking the swimming area and looked back at the shore.

This would be all right.

I never got the chance to write about the Isle of Wight in my *Take the Slow Road* series, so I felt I owed it something. At least a second glance. But where would I find solitude on this popular holiday isle? The quieter, less-populated side of

the island seemed like an obvious place to start. The old Military Road runs along the entire length of the south-west-facing coast. It's extremely exposed and open and is a spectacular coastal drive in itself. The rapidly eroding and slipping cliffs here are punctuated by a series of chines – ravines created by streams – some of which give access to sandy and shingled beaches. In the winter, swells from the western channel, whipped up by Atlantic gales, erupt

on these beaches, exposing fossils and undermining the cliffs.

Surely, I hoped, somewhere, deep in a ravine, on a sunny summer's day, I would find that slice of sand and sea to call my own. I had high hopes. Totland had got us off to a good start, but, despite our best attempts at framing Caribbean photos, we were still within sight and sound of holidaying families, expensive boats over from the mainland and SUPing teens goofing about on the sparkling water.

We hit the road on a beautiful, hot and clear day, stopping at Freshwater to take photos. Paddleboarders and kayakers were setting up in the car park and launching from the shore, heading west towards the chalk cliffs and, presumably, the Needles. We drove on, towards the east, taking the Military Road out of the village, up the steep hill and on to the top of the chalk downs above the cliffs. We stopped at the top to take more photographs. I found lovely purple pyramidal orchids growing at the side of the road, as well as kidney vetch, yellow rattle and the occasional clump of bright blue echiums.

Looking east, we could see along the line of the coast and down Compton Beach, where a few people were already swimming in the milky water. The sandy beach, backed by crumbling cretaceous rock, looked beautiful, benign and very inviting. We stopped at the small National Trust car park and walked over the meadows of sea pinks, wild carrot and bird's-foot trefoil to the chine, a steep gash in the cliff where a stream trickled towards the beach. A rope, set into the rock, led down to the beach, with the last 2.4m (8ft) or so knotted

to allow a rough abseil on to the sand. It looked dangerous to me as I peered over the edge. I wouldn't be going down there today. We walked back to the van, puzzling at the sign that pointed to 'steps to beach' and wondering why we couldn't see them. We headed further along the Military Road towards the bigger, busier car park at Compton Beach, just over a kilometre away.

At Compton Beach, we walked away from the people, back towards the chine and the rope climb. Looking for a suitable spot to drop our kit and dip, we walked towards a place where the water looked clear and silt free and a sand bar was pushing up shapely little waves. We had the beach to ourselves, so we stripped down to our togs and dived in. The water was cold, of course, but not cold enough to stop us swimming and bodysurfing for a good half an hour. The sun was also hot enough to warm us and make the goosebumps disappear when we got out. The waves were perfect for bodysurfing: just steep enough to give you a push and not too dumpy that you'd get tumbled. As each wave approached, I timed my dive towards the beach as well as I could. The idea to be falling down the face of the wave just before it broke takes split-second timing. Once I had caught the wave, I put my arms out in front of me and used my hands like hydrofoils to give me lift. I raised my head from the water only at the point where I knew I was moving along with the wave. Any sooner and I'd sink. Any later and I'd miss the rush.

The beach was filling up so we decided to pack up and carry on. We continued to walk east, away from the van, in the hope that we'd find a path up the cliff. A little further on, we found the missing staircase, an elegant flight of 90 wooden steps. Built above a landslip that had slumped enough to allow a narrow path to get about halfway up, the steps made it possible to climb the near-vertical last section of the cliff. Below the steps, we found a pool surrounded by rushes and with lilies growing in the middle. Between the stems, neon blue dragonflies darted, settling for a second before flitting off again. Blue butterflies performed the same ritual on the sea pinks, buttercups and daisies growing around the pond. It was a glorious, shameless explosion of life, growing in spite of the scar where the cliff had collapsed, against the odds, for a small slice of time before the sea finally took it.

I knelt down in the grass with my camera, hoping to catch one of the dragonflies, listening to the sound of the crumbling waves, the sea breeze and call of the skylarks rising from the grass.

A group of smartly dressed women called time on the silence as they climbed down the flights of steps. We waited for them to descend and could hear their conversation as they got closer to us: 'Next time Margaret recommends a beach, remind me to ignore her. I thought it was going to be easy. This is mountaineering. How am I going to get down that cliff with these shoes?'

Check it out on the way

ST CATHERINE'S POINT, NITON This wild spot is at the southern tip of the island and is home to St Catherine's Lighthouse, a light built after 23 people died in a wreck at Blackgang Chine. It's on National Trust property and is a beautiful walk from Niton. www.trinityhouse. co.uk/lighthouses-and-lightvessels/st-catherines-lighthouse

VENTNOR BOTANIC GARDEN, VENTNOR A popular spot with themed areas and a VERY hot hothouse. www.botanic.co.uk

LONGSHOREMAN'S MUSEUM, VENTNOR This is one of those quirky little museums that you only find by poking about in the back of a souvenir shop. It provides a fascinating history of Ventnor. www.facebook.com/longshoremansmuseum

THE PIER, TOTLAND Having been saved from demolition and refurbished, this is now a top-notch cafe. The pier is worth a visit on a hot day just to swim. www.totlandpier.co.uk

DONALD MCGILL MUSEUM, RYDE Donald was the king of the saucy seaside postcard and created more than 12,000 of them. He ran into trouble with the censor in the 1950s and some of his designs were banned. Visit and see the banned cards, as well as thousands of others drawn by McGill. https://saucyseasidepostcards.com

We pushed on, with the feeling that getting off the beaten track, even on this less-busy part of the isle, might have to be taken as fleeting, grateful moments. We were determined to enjoy them, whatever they turned out to be, whenever we found them. It might be as simple as spending a few minutes watching dragonflies or bodysurfing.

Further on, we found an empty clifftop car park. We walked along the edge of a steep, brush-filled chine to the point where someone had tied ropes to a stake in the top of the cliff. The cliff looked near vertical, but as we peered over the edge we could spy a few rough steps and a narrow path leading very steeply down into the ravine – the first section of the route. Thereafter, it was obscured

by the steepness of the cliff. On the
opposite wall of the chine – a vertical
wall of layered sandstone – there
was a huge nest, presumably from a
peregrine falcon, along with the holes
made by sand martins.

The rope was teasing me. I felt
that it was our pathway to solitude,
our one genuine chance, so I
persuaded Lizzy to descend with
me to the beach below, which, I felt sure, would be deserted. A narrow path
led down the cliff to the first rope and the half-steps leading off into the
abyss. As I held the rope and inched my way towards the precipice I could
finally make out the whole route down. The first section would be difficult,
but after that it seemed relatively OK. Holding on to the rope, I bum-shuffled
to the edge and dropped down on to the second section where another
knotted rope was attached to a wobbly steel fencing stake. The steps were
worn and dry and covered in sand, rendering them slippery and difficult

and making it necessary to rely on the rope for stability. I sat on a step and swung my feet over a drop of a couple of feet and on to the final section of the steepest part. After that a short traverse on to another section of rudimentary steps, we were in the bottom of the chine, about 15m (50ft) feet below cliff top level. All we had to do then was make our way down the chine another 15m (50ft) or so, over boulders, across the river and down to the beach.

As we walked out on to the golden shingle I looked to the west and east. In the west, the shingle was backed by a long section of the muddy cliff, and beyond that the white of the chalky cliffs past Compton. To the east, all I could see was cliff, with the occasional slump, for a couple of miles. It seemed that the chine – and the precarious way down it – was the only access point on to this beach for miles. We saw no one else. I looked back up at the cliff, now towering above us, and stripped off. Lizzy, getting the idea, stripped off too and waded into the sea. A small swell churned up shingle at the shore and the sea was

otherwise calm. We swam for a few minutes and then dragged ourselves out and on to the beach. I lay on my back, feeling the warmth of the sun from the hot stones beneath me, allowing the gentle breeze to dry me off.

That evening, after eating at the campsite, we cycled over to Alum Bay Chine, the bay to the north of the Needles, the Isle of Wight's famous chalk sea stacks. It's the site of a 'Needles' theme park with rides and shops and a chairlift to the beach. By the time we got there it was 8 p.m. and the place was deserted, the rides silent, and the chairlift skeletal and without movement. We wandered down the steep steps to the beach as the sun was setting over the mainland, lighting up the white cliffs of Tennyson Down and the Needles with an orange glow. The cliff behind us, famous for multicoloured sand deposits in 21 shades of yellow, orange, red, brown and ochre, reflect the setting sun like fire.

Again, even here, at this really popular beach, we had found a little bit of solitude in which to watch the sunset. We might not have been off the map, but we certainly had the place to ourselves. And that was all that mattered.

DO IT THE HARD WAY

I'm not going to name the chine we descended, simply because I want you to either find it for yourself or do something safer. The climb isn't easy. So, park at Compton Chine and descend the beautiful staircase early in the morning. It's around 90 steps so it does keep all but the most hardy (except the misdirected) away. Enjoy the rare habitat of the calciferous maritime grassland and spend some time watching butterflies and dragonflies.

Better still, head down one of the chines to the east of Compton – try Chilton Chine or Shepherd's Chine and walk in either direction for your own section of secluded beach. Watch for the tides and time your exit.

SAFETY NOTICE

Do not attempt to climb down to beaches if you are not sure of your exit and if safety is called into question. There are lots of other safe alternatives.

CAMPING

There are a lot of campsites on
the Isle of Wight. This is the
one we used:

Stoats Farm, Totland: A lovely
peaceful site with a brand new toilet block and a great pub (The Highdown
Inn) opposite. Pitches with electricity are available. www.stoatsfarm.com;
https://highdowninn.com

> ### You will need:
> - good footwear
> - a tide table

DO IT THE EASY WAY

You don't have to descend a chine on a rickety rope to enjoy the Military
Road. Start out from Freshwater and head east, stopping at Compton Beach
to get the best views of Tennyson Downs. Head for Alum Bay to see the
Needles or strike out across Tennyson Downs to the Old and New Batteries
on the point for a bird's-eye view.

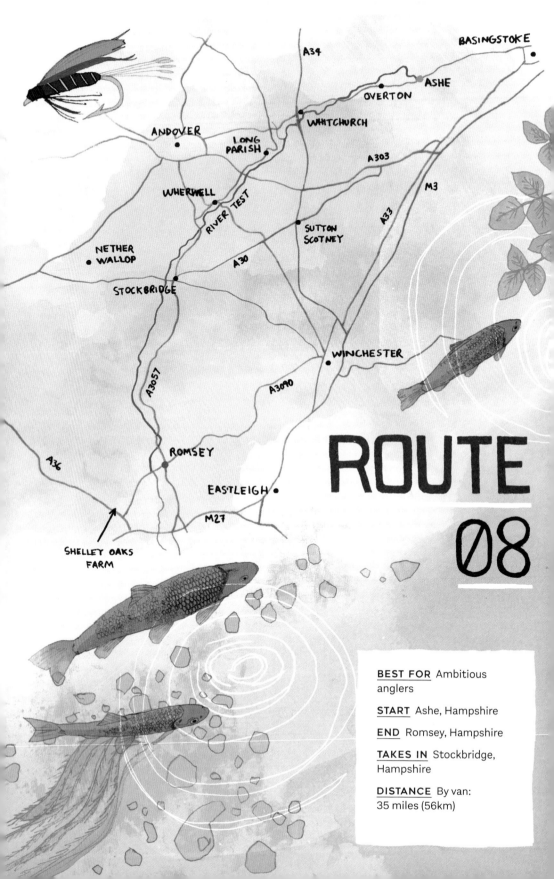

BASINGSTOKE

A34

ASHE
OVERTON

WHITCHURCH

ANDOVER
LONG PARISH

A303

M3

WHERWELL
RIVER TEST

A33

SUTTON SCOTNEY

NETHER WALLOP

A30

STOCKBRIDGE

A3057

WINCHESTER

A3090

ROMSEY

A36

EASTLEIGH

M27

SHELLEY OAKS FARM

ROUTE
08

BEST FOR Ambitious anglers

START Ashe, Hampshire

END Romsey, Hampshire

TAKES IN Stockbridge, Hampshire

DISTANCE By van: 35 miles (56km)

THE RIVER TEST

*The River Test is England's most famous
chalk stream. It runs through beautiful countryside
from its source near Basingstoke to the sea at Southampton.
Following it takes you to pretty villages and beautiful beats
and into the heart of prime fishing country. And if you are
going to follow the world's most famous rivers for fly fishing,
you might as well go and see what the fuss is all about.
The result? Excitement, a steep learning curve and
a whole lot of time to watch the water
– with no one else for company.*

OUR JOURNEY DOWN the Test began as near to its source as we could get: a bridge less than a mile downstream at Polhampton Farm. We parked the van in a lay-by and walked back to the small bridge to get our first proper look at this celebrated river.

My companion for this journey was my old friend Andy, a keen sea and coarse fisherman but novice fly fisherman. We looked over the sides of the bridge to the water below. The water was gin clear, fast running and beautiful, moving quickly over a shingle and gravel bottom between stands of deep green weed waving like tresses of a mermaid's hair. Below the bridge, a trout swam lazily, head pointed upstream, remaining stationary in the water. As our shadows cast over it the fish spooked and darted beneath more weed on the bank.

The idea of following the Test for this book came about because I wanted to learn to catch fish on the fly on England's foremost trout river and I wanted a journey to accompany it. We would begin at the source and then work our way down, learning as we went. This journey would be as much about travelling as it would be about picking up new skills, satisfying itches and seeing, at first hand, what's so special about England's finest and most famous chalk stream. I also wanted to experience a little of the quiet of the riverbank, of the peace of the angler and the lure of fly fishing for trout, even if you have to pay for it.

I got all that I had hoped for, and more.

The Test passes through some of Hampshire's prettiest villages. Following the course brought us into Overton, Freefolk, Whitchurch, Longparish and Wherwell before bringing us to Stockbridge, the tidy town that's busy with tea shops and fishing tackle specialists. We were stunned by the buildings we passed, built of brick and flint, often with thatched rooves, sometimes half-timbered, but more often than

not, Victorian cottages in neat rows. A lot of the buildings were picture perfect, with roses around the door or wisteria growing up the frontage. I'm not sure I've ever been anywhere that represents an idea of England as much as this. You might call it 'chocolate box' or 'vernacular', but the effect is the same. Do we shape this to an image of what we think is perfect or was it there already? It's hard to tell. But with a chalk stream running quick and clear at the end of the garden, why worry. Life is sweet in the Test Valley.

Much of the Test Valley is a Site of Special Scientific Interest (SSSI) and is protected, both for its water and its wildlife. The river has a huge amount of biodiversity and yet is almost wholly managed by man. Watercress beds, leats and channels cut out of the land by hand many years ago make the river convoluted and dispersed with lots of twists and turns. Driving it is greatly enjoyable, but doesn't take long. Which is why we felt this journey required some time on the banks.

At Stockbridge, we took a right turn to Nether Wallop Mill, a beautiful brick-built mill owned by Simon Cooper, author and owner of Fishing Breaks. There, by the side of a pond stocked with rainbow, tiger and blue trout, we learned about fly fishing from Bob, a hugely knowledgeable and personable fisherman who has clearly devoted his life to fish and fishing. Sitting outside the fishing hut, a thatched shack that I would happily move into, I felt as if I were in the presence of a giant. Despite our self-depreciation and comments about being duffers when it comes to fishing, he knew he could tease a bite or two out of us. Bob taught us about flies, casts and the history of fly fishing and the chalk streams. It was dizzying. And that was before we'd even picked up a rod. When we did, he got us casting bits of orange wool into hoops on the lawn, testing our accuracy.

The next day, wc were booked in to fish a stretch of water further downstream at Parsonage Mill. Bob told us about a beetle he had seen falling out of an alder tree that trout had been enjoying recently. He gave us each a fly that he had tied to mimic the beetle and said that we should try them and let him know how they went. It sounded like a fisherman's sure thing to me so I made a mental note of the details.

After lunch, Andy and I got to do what we had come for: to cast our flies. Bob loaded up our rods with nymphs and pieces of wool as indicators and let us loose on the water. The water was beautifully clear and deep and we could see the fish as they cruised the depths. At first, they seemed a little elusive, as if judging the quality of our casting with the bored, seen-it-all disdain of trout that really have seen it all. I worried that I would never get to experience the thrill of casting and catching for myself. But, of course, the experience is not meant to bring you down. It's designed to pick you up and make you feel like the complete angler, even in an afternoon. Andy hooked and almost landed a small rainbow, while I hooked and lost another. It taught us, very quickly, the need to keep the rod tip up or they get away. A harsh lesson after you've hooked your first fish on the fly.

A little while after this hurt I landed and kept what I thought was a huge rainbow trout, a whopper at 1.07kg (2lb 6oz), which was surpassed by Andy's 1.162kg (2lb 9oz) a little while after that. For the rest of the afternoon we caught about four or five each. The blues I liked the best. They fought hard and were absolutely beautiful in and out of the water, with a shimmering blue grey on their top half and silvery blue underneath. The tigers were prelly, too, with dappled markings that were more like those of a mackerel than a trout.

At the end of the day, we left with a fish each and big smiles. I had long dreamed of catching a fish on the fly and I had achieved it. Of course, it was like shooting them in a barrel really, as the lake was stocked and the fish, once we'd proved ourselves worthy, obliging. It would be different on the river I was sure. I had a beautiful rainbow trout to take home. Andy had decided not to take anything.

Andy's final cast changed his mind. As he wrestled the huge rainbow he shouted at me to get the landing net. I pushed it as far out into the water as I could, netting it after a few false starts. It was a stunning fish and had fought well. I laid the net down on the bank to get a good look at it before we dispatched it and put it in the van's fridge. The fish had other ideas. With one huge flip it bucked its way out of the net. I tried to grab it, but it bucked again, slipped out of my grasping hands and plopped back into the water.

We camped at Shelley Oaks Farm that night. Andy put up a pop-up tent to avoid my snoring. It was called the '20-seconds tent'. The next morning, he took about half an hour to work out how to put it down again, having to search for the instructions from the Decathlon website on his phone. I sat in the van, tea in hand, and enjoyed the spectacle, reminding myself why I love sleeping in vans so much.

Once packed away, we found ourselves driving down an overgrown and muddy track on the way to The Parsonage, a long stretch of river near Romsey. We unlocked the gate, drove over a narrow railway bridge and past a beautiful meadow before landing at a car park next to the fishing hut. Here, the water wasn't quite so clear as further upstream, but it was still

clear enough to see fish lying in the gravel patches between the weeds. Our fishing guide for the day, Ian, walked us down the bank before we put the kettle on and got any tackle out. What we had learned from the day before – that it pays to listen and learn first – became more

apparent as Ian showed us fish along the bank and under the trees that he said we'd come back to later. He was interested in our beetles from Bob and showed us one of his own that he'd tied for the very same purpose of attracting the trout that scoop up falling insects from the large alder at the far end of the beat.

We began casting out into the water pretty aimlessly, with no discernible target, to get into the rhythm of the day. My ability to cast went in waves. As soon as I thought I had got it I would fluff one into the trees or plop my line into the water in front of me. In between, while castigating myself for poor performance or taking a breath to keep my cool, I looked around at the surroundings. The banks were mown short, allowing for weed and plants to grow on at the river's edge. A few trees made casting difficult. Damselflies, bright blue and brilliant, flitted about. Dragonflies patrolled the margins. Behind the mown path there were trees, bushes and open fields. Geese and

swans cruised the river. Fish, elusive and jittery, swam at the edges of the patches of gravel. The only noise was the swishing of rods and the occasional chatter about fish. Everything else was of and from nature.

From that point of view I had achieved something special. We had found some quiet time on a remote stretch of the River Test and it was as peaceful and relaxing as I could have hoped for. Granted, we had to pay for it, but that's to be expected to get the place to yourselves, I suppose.

I spent an hour casting into three trout that were swimming on one patch of gravel. They were no more than a few metres away, but I couldn't seem to cast accurately enough to get their attention. Either that or they weren't hungry. Ian, our guide, tied on three or four different types of imitation nymph, but they showed very little interest, except for a quick look and a small chase every now and then. It was unbelievably frustrating and my casts got worse the more I tried, so I decided it was time for a break.

After lunch sitting outside the van in the sunshine, I hooked a brown trout but let it get away before we could get the net to it, which was a blow, to say the least. But at least my casting was getting better.

Ian and I walked the beat a little further upstream and spotted a trout lying under a small alder, rising occasionally to take insects on the surface.

Ian suggested we try one of Bob's beetles and put one on the line for me to cast. The fish was sitting in dark water, on the edge of the weeds and in partial shadow from the tree. I wasn't confident I could make the cast under the tree but gave it a go. I caught up in the tree. The more I cast, the worse it got. I caught the beetle in the trees, in the weeds and in the bank. Each time I fluffed it, the trout made to move but stayed, remaining, thankfully, unspooked. I felt so frustrated at my own ability. I couldn't cast near it. I couldn't cast without getting caught up in something. I couldn't cast at all!

The fish moved slightly, disappeared for a moment and then reappeared where it had been lying. I figured I'd give it one last cast. I pulled back, waited and whipped the rod forwards, coming to a stop the way Ian had taught me. The line landed a couple of feet in front of the fish and floated towards it. It was the best cast I'd done all day. The fish took it and made to dive. Ian, having just told me not to strike too early, held out an arm for a moment. I pulled the rod up and hooked it as it dived. It swam away and leapt out of the water, but I held the rod firm and high, desperate not to lose this one. It swam towards the weeds but remained hooked. The undergrowth between me and the river was deep so I walked the fish gently downstream a few

metres to meet Ian's net.

The fish was a beauty, a wild brown trout of about 900g (2lb) and the stuff of my wildest dreams, caught on the fly, with a little insider knowledge and some luck with casting. I was elated. I've fished (badly) for many years and this was easily the best fish I have ever caught. I gutted it and prepared to call it a day, while Andy went down to the big alder at the end of the beat. He put

on one of Ian's beetles and started to cast for a fish under the trees, casting backhand to avoid the foliage. After a few casts, he hooked it, and then netted it after a few minutes' fight. It was 1.35kg (3lb), another beautiful brown trout.

Andy was elated, too. He'd had a good day, having caught a grayling and a small brown and put them both back. But this one was for the smoker. We opted to call it a day. Our luck wouldn't get any better. Until the next time.

Check it out on the way

THE MAYFLY, STOCKBRIDGE A great boozer with great food that's right on the river. www.mayflyfullerton.co.uk

WALBURY HILL The highest point in South East England and the start of the Test Way.

STOCKBRIDGE A great town that's famous for fishing. It's posh and it's lovely and you can get a cup of tea and slice of cake and watch the world go by. Check out the huge trout swimming in the river along the high street.

MOTTISFONT ABBEY, MOTTISFONT A National Trust-owned house and gallery on the Test with extensive grounds, wetlands and a walled garden. www.nationaltrust.org.uk/mottisfont

DO IT THE HARD WAY

Fishing on the Test is strictly controlled and is divided into beats controlled by fishing companies, conglomerates or private individuals, so you can't just rock up and fish, more's the pity. However, if you want to try your hand at fly casting and want expert tuition, get in touch with Simon Cooper at Fishing Breaks. He can sort you out with everything you'll need, including guides

who come with everything you need for a day's fishing.

If you're a beginner, start at the Nether Wallop Mill, a stocked lake that is connected to one of the Test's tributaries. You are guaranteed to catch, almost.

Fishing Breaks have a number of beats and you can choose which you prefer. Of course, it isn't cheap to fish on the Test. However, I consider that it's worth it if you want to understand a little about the river. Spending the day with a guide will greatly improve your chances of catching anything. We chose to start upstream and work our way down to the Mill, then carried on downstream to The Parsonage. https://fishingbreaks.co.uk

You will need:
- a day fishing pass
- fishing tackle (if not taking a guide)
- an EA rod fishing licence

However, if you want to truly experience the Test, you can always walk the Test Way, a 44-mile (71km) footpath that runs from Inkpen on the Downs to Eling on Southampton Water.

CAMPING

Highview, Little Firs Farm: Situated right next to the Salisbury Caravan and Motorhome Club site, this Certified Location campsite has a lovely owner who also keeps bees. Great honey! www.caravanclub.co.uk/certificated-locations/england/wiltshire/salisbury/Highview
Shelley Oaks Farm, Romsey: A fantastic site with great loos and showers on a working farm near Romsey. Recommended. Very friendly and hospitable owners. www.shelleyoaksfarm.co.uk

DO IT THE EASY WAY

Without the fishing, the drive down the Test is nice for a few hours' fun and a bit of a navigational challenge. You'll need to bob and weave in and out of tiny villages and will cross over the Test a number of times.

ROUTE 09

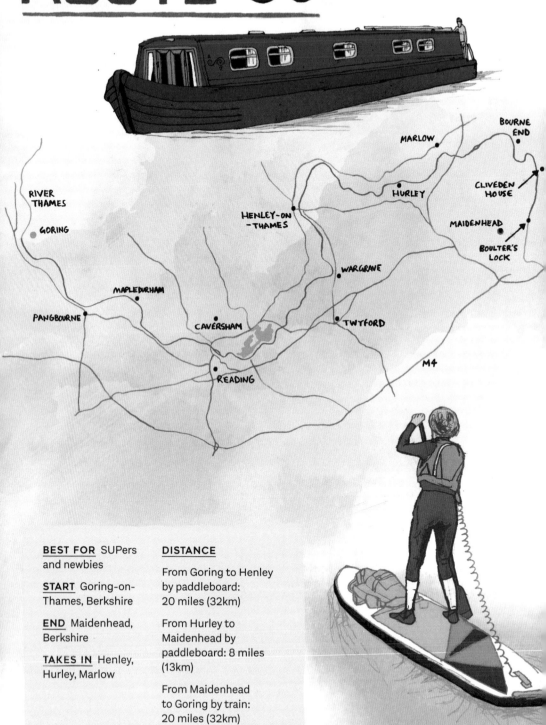

RIVER THAMES

GORING

BOURNE END

MARLOW

HURLEY

CLIVEDEN HOUSE

HENLEY-ON-THAMES

MAIDENHEAD

WARGRAVE

BOULTER'S LOCK

MAPLEDURHAM

PANGBOURNE

CAVERSHAM

TWYFORD

M4

READING

BEST FOR SUPers and newbies

START Goring-on-Thames, Berkshire

END Maidenhead, Berkshire

TAKES IN Henley, Hurley, Marlow

DISTANCE

From Goring to Henley by paddleboard: 20 miles (32km)

From Hurley to Maidenhead by paddleboard: 8 miles (13km)

From Maidenhead to Goring by train: 20 miles (32km)

GORING TO MAIDENHEAD

**THE VIEW FROM THE WATER,
6 AND 7 JULY 2021**

Seeing the Thames from the water gives you a brilliant new perspective on life. It forces you to slow down and go at the river's pace. And that means seeing wildlife, community and the river itself in a brand new, more relaxing way. Plus, of course, it's quieter on the water than off.

WHY IS IT THAT SO MANY of my tales of derring-do start with relentless, pissing rain? Maybe because it always turns up – like an unwanted guest – whenever I set out to do anything. It's as if the sky knows that I am about to do something I have not done before and is hell bent on making me even more nervous than I already am. As if I need the anxiety levels ramping up before setting out to paddleboard 33 miles (53km) down the Thames. As if I need reminding that water is unpredictable and dangerous

and that anything can happen or that I have only ever paddleboarded a few hundred metres. Maybe it's just because the weather in England, like water, is unpredictable at best, and we'd better just get used to it.

I lay in bed listening to the rain on the skylight. I reckon I was awake for most of the night but then I must have nodded off near dawn as the alarm woke me at 6.30 a.m. I leapt out of bed, my head filled with all kinds of prep we needed to do: make lunch, get our bags ready, eat breakfast, settle the nerves.

I wanted to paddleboard down the Thames because I wanted to see what it's like from the water and to travel along it under my own steam. I wanted to experience it from a different perspective. The Thames is England's second-longest river, running through much of England's Conservative heartlands. And yet it's often ignored, blocked in, hidden away behind flood defences and private gardens. We might get glimpses of it from trains or the car, walk along the embankment in London or enjoy a pint by its side in places like Henley-on-Thames or Caversham, but unless we live on the river or travel on it regularly, we rarely see it all.

We climbed in a taxi at the campsite and headed off to pick up our paddleboards. Tara, who had packed them up ready for us, tried to reassure us that the river wouldn't be too swollen, despite the night's rain and the fact that the river levels were going up, heading for amber status. She seemed a little nervous herself, too, especially when Lizzy said she'd not done much paddling. We loaded the boards and the chatty taxi driver – himself a swimmer and river lover – took us on to Maidenhead station where we caught the train bound for Goring.

As the train took us past Reading and into the open countryside we passed out under the cloud and into sunshine. When we alighted at Goring, the platform was still wet from the overnight deluge, but the sun stayed out. We walked through the village, admiring the hollyhocks and brick cottages and privet hedges, coming out at the river a little downstream from the lock. Seeing the water for the first time and having the first opportunity to size it up properly, I felt a huge amount of relief. I had expected a raging torrent, or at least a fast flow to unseat us, but it was calm and flat, moving steadily. I knew then that we'd be all right.

We walked further upstream to the lock to find somewhere suitable to cast off. Just below the lock gates, we found a set of steps leading to a spot where we could get the boards into the water easily. We pumped up the SUPs, changed into our wetsuits and pushed off into the current.

We passed a few boats moored up below the lock and under a bridge. Beyond that, the banks were tree lined and deep green. Tall trees – willows, ash, alder and sycamore – towered over us and whispered in the wind, the willows showing us their silvery undersides as they rustled. The wind, from the south-west and therefore a handy tailwind, was forecast to get stronger throughout the day, but for now was pushing us along nicely.

As we began to make progress, I remembered what I already knew about paddleboarding from experience on lakes and on the sea. It's not strenuous or particularly difficult if you already have some board skills and can balance on a moving platform. What some people find difficult are the constant adjustments you need to make to stay upright. It requires a lightness and an ability to be fluid, never quite locking knees and not standing up too stiffly that sudden movements unseat you. The first challenge to this came as a boat passed us, its wake forming several gentle, but close, swell lines. I paddled at it to hit it head-on, as I would do with a surfboard, and stayed as loose as I could to counter the movement. I didn't fall in. Dealing with wakes got easier the more we paddled, although I found it less tricky to cope with those from boats approaching us. Ones that overtook us brought wakes that both sped us up but also slowed us down. We almost surfed, but then got bogged down as the waves went underneath us.

I got into it quite soon after embarking and enjoyed the calm of being on the water, although I wished the current ran faster and offered more excitement. Progress was slow and steady, a little faster than walking pace. The constant paddling added a steady rhythm: each stroke sent me one way or the other so I had to change sides after three or four strokes to correct the trajectory. That was as complicated as it got.

I had been worried about the locks and the weirs that we'd have to navigate, naively concerned that we might find the current pulling us over the weir, but at Pangbourne Lock, where we cruised neatly into the lock and stopped at the sign showing us the way we needed to portage, my fears disappeared. I was more in danger of falling over when I hit the riverbank than I was of being sucked over the weir. Hauling the boards out and walking around the lock was the most strenuous bit (and became harder the longer that day dragged on).

After Pangbourne, we entered a long stretch of river with fields either side, encountering moored-up narrowboats and places where people had made a home on the river. There were pirates and artists, abandoned boats and boats that were half sunk, cockpits covered in tarpaulins and slime-covered tenders. We waved at the boats as they passed and at the people living on the shore, some of whom watched us silently as we paddled past them. After the next lock, Mapledurham, the railway came close to the river, running alongside for a short stretch at the top of a brick-built embankment. By a sign that said 'Welcome to Reading', a pair of winos waved cheerfully and skulled cans of beer.

Entering Reading didn't quite offer the cityscape I would have liked. We passed houses with back gardens that led down to the river – nothing too ostentatious – and a park before we passed under Caversham Bridge and portaged Caversham Lock. By this time, we'd completed about 10 miles (16km) and were three hours in. I was beginning to get tired and Lizzy was too, preferring quietness over chat, which I took to be a sign we had a tough afternoon ahead. We stopped to eat our lunch at the side of the lock and tried to work out how far we had to go to the campsite at Hurley and how much water we'd covered. We had a long way to go.

As red kites soared above us, we enjoyed the company of all kinds of ducks and geese, including mallards, tufted ducks, coots and moorhens, Canada geese and the strange-looking Egyptian goose. I swear I also saw a mandarin duck, but I can't be sure.

The long straight stretch past Reading Marina and on to Sonning Lock took an age. The stretch after Sonning Lock was open and wide and felt like it wasn't moving very quickly. We rounded a bend and hit a side wind. I could see the rippled water coming up where we left the shelter of the trees and shouted to Lizzy to go to her knees. She did, although the wind pushed her immediately into the bank just as it started to rain again. I dropped, too, and managed to avoid the bank until I decided to turn around and find out where Lizzy had gone. A gust hit me as well and I veered straight into the rushes. Lizzy covered the next section on her bum, sitting as if in a canoe, making herself as small as possible to avoid the wind taking her again. I stayed on my knees until we arrived at Shiplake Lock.

The rain poured down on us, throwing up droplets as it hit the water and leaving small bubbles wherever it landed. The lock keeper let us paddle into the lock instead of carrying our boards around and we sat on the boards, hanging gratefully on to the chains as the water drained out of the lock and the walls rose to their full height. We paddled out of the lock and into the last stretch: Wargrave, then Henley. The houses got bigger and further from the river the closer we got to Henley. Many had their own boathouses and boats moored up. Some looked like they hadn't been used for a while. Others were beautifully clean and shiny. There were a few exceptional wooden cruisers, but mostly big white river boats.

During the last mile before Henley we decided that the final stretch, 5 miles (8km) into Hurley, was too much for us. We'd been on the water for seven hours already and couldn't face another two so we disembarked at Henley and deflated the SUPs, wandered 46m (50 yards) up the road to the taxi rank and caught a lift home.

The next day, we launched from Hurley, meeting old friends Guy and Cath at Hurley Lock and paddling with them for the last 8 miles (13km) to Maidenhead. We passed by Bisham Abbey and the outdoor adventure centre where, as young Sea Scout, I'd ventured forth among the waves and failed to execute an Eskimo roll in a kayak.

As we passed under the beautiful white-painted bridge at Marlow and the four of us chatted away and caught up on news, it struck me that SUPing might be the perfect alternative to a pint or a coffee or even just a chat on the phone. It's an activity that you can do almost instinctively once you get the knack, which means that you have headspace to talk. I loved that. As we paddled downstream, the four of us drifted into pairs, talking all the time about our lives, kids and history. It was like on-the-water therapy or a coffee morning or a night at the pub for people who never get the time to go to the pub any more. I found out more about the important details of my friends' lives in a few hours than I would have in weeks of texts or calls. That was what made the time special.

We were also there for each other when the side wind hit, around Bourne End. The river changes course here and heads south for the first time. That meant we had to look for shelter, on our knees to keep our surface area to a minimum. It often meant getting really close to the bank and moving slowly past people's neatly clipped lawns, boathouses and garden offices. Some of the properties were incredible, huge and flamboyant, possibly even tax write-offs. We passed one floating 'TV pod' with brand-new white leather sofas that still had the plastic wrapping on. And yet the

Check it out on the way

CLIVEDEN HOUSE GARDENS, MAIDENHEAD Formal gardens overlooking the Thames run by The National Trust. Posh views of the river for sure. www.nationaltrust.org.uk/cliveden

THE ANGEL ON THE BRIDGE, HENLEY-ON-THAMES Riverside pub with great views and great food. Outside tables right on the river. www.theangelhenley.com

pod, despite being new, had clearly been in the water for long enough to develop algae at the waterline. It must have cost a fortune and yet it looked as if no one had yet sprawled out on the sofas to watch TV on the huge TV. I worry about people sometimes. With the river just outside the window, why would you ever want to watch TV?

Just after Marlow, Cath showed us her river knowledge and made us paddle to one spot in the middle of the channel where she instructed us to look back at Cliveden House, a National Trust property. From our spot in the river, we could see the house perfectly framed by forest on the steep banks as if we were floating on a fountain in their back garden.

From Cliveden, it was just a short paddle down to Boulter's Lock and Maidenhead, the end of the trip. We hauled out the boards and deflated them in a car park on the riverbank. As the air rushed out of the valves, the magic of being on the river subsided, leaving us with nothing to do but hug each other, say goodbye and get ourselves a late lunch.

The traffic was murder in Maidenhead. As we crossed the river to get back to the campsite, we looked back down at the calm, cool water sliding gently by beneath us. We had crossed over from one world into another for the briefest period of time. We had made a journey in two days that we could have done in the car in less than an hour (traffic allowing) and we had emerged richer, with a deeper understanding of our friends, of the river and the way it moves, always marching on, but always in another time.

Plus, my arms were aching.

DO IT THE HARD WAY

The great thing about inflatable paddleboards is that you can deflate them and roll them up into a rucksack. This means they are portable. Heavy, yes, but portable enough to be carried in a van, car or on the train. And that means you have flexibility! Also, on this stretch of the Thames, the stations at Goring, Pangbourne, Purley on Thames and even Reading are just a short walk from the river. The stations at Shiplake and Henley are close by the river, too, which means there are a lot of options for distances.

Pick up boards from Paddleboard Maidenhead (www.paddleboard maidenhead.uk), then take the train from Maidenhead station to Goring station (about 20 minutes). Walk from Goring station to Goring Lock (it's about 200m/219 yards). Pump up the boards below the lock and launch from the portage steps. Paddle down the river.

Option 1: Paddle for 25 miles (40km) to Hurley campsite (allow eight or nine hours). Leave the river. Rest up for the night at the van and start again the next day for the last 8 miles (13km) to Maidenhead. Get out of the river just before Boulter's Lock and deflate the boards. Pack up and walk the boards to Paddleboard Maidenhead. Taxi back to Hurley.

Option 2: Paddle for 20 miles (32km) to Henley through Reading and Wargrave and land at Henley. There is a public landing spot just before

the Angel pub on the left bank. Let down the boards and pack up, then get a cab at the rank in Henley (92m/100 yards from the river).

Option 3: Get a taxi from the rank in Henley to Hurley Campsite. Rest up for the night at the van and start again the next day for the last 8 miles (13km) to Maidenhead. Get out of the river just before Boulter's Lock and deflate the boards. Pack up and walk the boards to Paddleboard Maidenhead. Taxi back to Hurley.

You will need:
- a British Canoeing On the Water licence. Membership covers this
- a paddleboard (inflatable)
- a wetsuit (if not confident on a SUP)
- dry clothes

CAMPING
Hurley Riverside Park, Hurley: A well-organised touring and mobile home park that's right on the river, with good river access. https://hurleyriversidepark.co.uk

DO IT THE EASY WAY

If you have never paddleboarded before, call Tara at Paddleboard Maidenhead. She will teach you the basics. Then, when you are comfortable with paddling, deflate your boards and head back to Hurley Riverside Park. Start out there and paddle back to Maidenhead. Taxi back to Hurley. www.paddleboardmaidenhead.uk

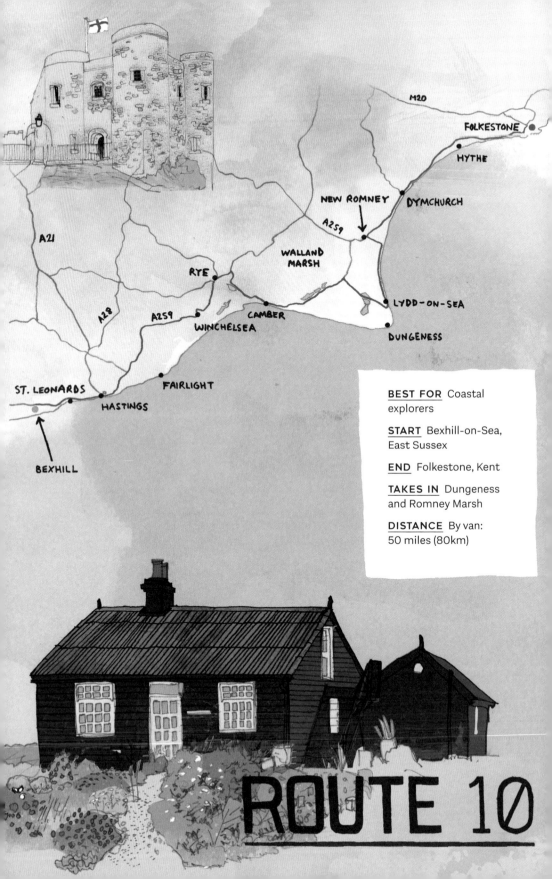

M20

FOLKESTONE

HYTHE

NEW ROMNEY

DYMCHURCH

A259

A21

WALLAND MARSH

RYE

LYDD-ON-SEA

A28

A259

CAMBER

DUNGENESS

WINCHELSEA

ST. LEONARDS

FAIRLIGHT

HASTINGS

BEXHILL

BEST FOR Coastal explorers

START Bexhill-on-Sea, East Sussex

END Folkestone, Kent

TAKES IN Dungeness and Romney Marsh

DISTANCE By van: 50 miles (80km)

ROUTE 10

DUNGENESS DESOLATION

A PILGRIMAGE TO PROSPECT COTTAGE,
28 JUNE 2021

Dungeness is famous for being a wild and lonely place, often described as desolate. It's the end of the line, figuratively and literally, with shacks built from old rolling stock by railway workers in the 1920s. Today, those shacks go for a lot more than their original cost of £10, with the price of peace soaring in recent years for those seeking solace. It remains a wilderness and a wasteland, a place of great contrast, where rusting tractors sit side by side with bright blue echiums and yellow poppies.

IT WAS TIPPING DOWN when we arrived in Bexhill-on-Sea. The rain was fat and heavy, running in rivers in the gutters at the side of the promenade, sending people in flip-flops dashing from cars to doors through inch-deep puddles. We parked just down the seafront from the De La Warr Pavilion and looked in the windows. Lights off and closed up for the night, it looked grubby and derelict and not like itself at all. That's what a wet Sunday afternoon can do for you I suppose.

We realised we'd have to reschedule our love affair with Bexhill for another, sunnier day and move on. That, disappointingly, would be a pub car park just outside St Leonards that didn't do food on Sunday evenings, but where we knew we'd have a safe overnight and a bag of crisps, at the very least. Between now and then we'd have to improvise. Most of the restaurants and bars in

Bexhill were closed, with the exception of one we had passed, which was enjoying an afternoon of rambunctious business. People were dancing barefoot in the street as we cruised by. I didn't think we were quite ready for that.

Fish and chips it was then. We both went for rock salmon, a charmingly posh name for dogfish. We parked up a little further down the front, on Galley Hill, set up the table in the van and scoffed our meal, thanking our lucky stars that we had shelter. Looking out at the wet beach, the sodden grass and the deserted seafront, we would have been excused for thinking it was a wet February Sunday in the 1980s, not June in the 2020s. Still, we were dry and the rock salmon was tasty. Fishier than cod but not as fishy as coley, if you must know.

Bexhill was the start of our journey to explore Dungeness, an area I had long wanted to visit. I first heard about it because of Derek Jarman's seaside shack and garden, but the property was only ever described as an oasis in an otherwise bleak, desert-like and desolate landscape. The nuclear power station as backdrop just added an extra layer of pathos to the place.

I liked the idea that we could go somewhere that was forgotten or neglected, but that nevertheless promised some kind of beauty. The journey would take us from Bexhill to Hastings and then over the cliffs to Fairlight and Winchelsea, Camber Sands, Rye and on to the promontory at Dungeness before bringing us to Hythe through Romney Marsh, an area of reclaimed land that, like much of the Dungeness area, is below sea level.

To say that Romney and Dungeness are uninhabited and forgotten would be to misunderstand them completely. They have been inhabited, it is believed, as far back as 2000 BC and have seen much of England's history unfold upon them. It's a story that begins with the great shingle banks at Dungeness and a touch of longshore drift creating lagoons and lakes, a perfect wetland for settlers and farmers. The Vikings, Anglo-Saxons, Romans and Normans took turns to invade the marsh and built churches and castles and used the land to make salt and rear sheep. That's it in a nutshell. If you add in the Great Storm of 1287, the Black Death and some wool smuggling on the side, it's potted, at the very least.

Despite the colourful history, the area remains isolated and insulated from the south coast sprawl that infects much of West Sussex. They have had a go, of course, and there is an almost continuous line of bungalows (with the odd Victorian villa thrown in for good measure) perched precariously below the sea defences, between the marsh and the sea, that stretches from Lydd-on-Sea as far as Hythe. On one side of the houses lies the sea, on the

other the protected marsh, much of it below sea level.

We approached Dungeness from the west, via Camber Sands (with the Squeeze song running through my head all the while) and across Walland Marsh. On our right, firing ranges, fences and old concrete, on our left, wind turbines turning slowly and sheep grazing the flat grassland. Further to the north the darker, low line of the Downs. The road weaved in and out between ditches, gravel pits and fences, always a contrast between the scars of industry to our right and the abundance of grassland to our left. As we approached Lydd, the landscape changed into more of what I had been expecting: shingle, scrub, police compounds and half-used land that seemed no longer wanted or needed. It started raining. Beyond Lydd were fields of rape and linseed interspersed with brick houses and disused compounds, menacing gates to empty lots and the occasional yellow-jacketed security guard. The road ran parallel to the railway and alongside Lydd Airport, then between two large gravel pits, now recolonised by birds.

After that, it was a sea of shingle with clumps of vegetation leading towards the sea. We turned right, crossed the railway tracks and headed west along the coast towards the point. The road ran straight towards the lighthouse, bordered by wonky telegraph poles with low-hanging lines strung between. The beach and sea were on our left now, a couple of hundred metres away. Between them and us sat a series of shipping containers, rusty tractors and the detritus that goes with fishing: old nets, fish crates, ropes and pots. Most of the dwellings, a row of well-spaced-out shacks and detached houses and bungalows, lay on the landward side of the road to our right. Many followed the same style: black wooden clapboard with bitumen roofs, a door in the centre and windows either side, but others were painted white or blue. There are a few ultra-modern properties too, a sign that things have changed. Here and there, a few abandoned cars, half-empty dumpy bags and more fishing gear. The rain didn't help.

We drove to the end of the road, passing the Britannia pub and the new lighthouse and parked up in a shingle car park next to the old lighthouse, a black-painted tower in the Trinity House style complemented by a pair of keeper's cottages and the round building that was once the base of an older light. Behind loomed the mass of the power station, a huge series of angular hulks. A sea mist had started to come in and this made the power station fade into whiteness. It was there, but not, providing a half-lost backdrop. Chain link fences separated it from us. We sat in the van and waited for the rain to stop, looking out at the shingle and the vegetation.

The sun was still obscured by mist when the rain stopped. Despite this, it created a bright white glare, reflecting furiously off the banks of sea fret rolling in. The power station was almost completely lost now, and was no more than a faint shape in the distance.

I stepped out of the van and noticed the sound of my boots as they landed in the shingle: a deeply satisfying crunch with low and high tones throughout with a sharp beginning and gentle taper as my weight shifted to my other foot. It reminded me of Chesil Beach and the Isle of Wight and places I had been before. It's a very particular sound you don't get with gravel drives (too high) or stony beaches (too deep) and is particular to the south coast, to climbing up banks to get out of the sea, walking across Brighton Beach and now being here, in Dungeness.

Once out of the van, we could hear cracks of small arms fire, presumably carried on the easterly wind from the firing range at Hythe. Above that, and coming from a source much closer to us, was the intermittent honking of the foghorn. Between the two, the consistent and persistent staccato song of skylarks.

We walked towards the sea and found a wooden (hollow-sounding) boardwalk across the shingle to the ridge of the highest tide. There, below us, beyond a few more banks of shingle, lay the sea. It scraped and scoured backwards and forwards, with a crash and whoosh as the small waves broke and then retreated across the shingle. With no horizon to see, because of the sea fret, the sea had the appearance of being finite and backing up against a white infinity cove. For all we knew, it could have ended about 18m (20 yards) offshore. Anglers cast their multipliers into the gloom, sending their lines way beyond the visible end, into the unknown.

As the mist began to dissipate and melt away, the visibility improved. The sun warmed us as we sat and watched a fisherman catch a dogfish and throw it back. When I lay on my back, I could feel the heat of the shingle against my spine.

We crunched along the shore a little further, aiming for Derek Jarman's Prospect Cottage, which lay back up the road on the landward side. We passed a few fishing boats, hauled out on the shingle. Around them lay the mess of industry. More discarded nets, fish crates, plastic barrels, floats and rope. Alongside were rusted-out bulldozers and tractors, oxidised cables and bits of tractors, left to die on the exposed beach. A sign urged us to take our litter home. I've picked up a lot of rubbish off beaches in my life and most of it has been from the fishing industry, so this seemed a little rich to me.

Lizzy, as ever, wasn't so concerned by the litter, preferring instead to focus on nature and its positives. She strode out over the shingle to look at the plants, ignoring the mess. I wandered over so she could show me what she'd found. It was a beautiful brassica, a sea kale with pale green leaves and deep purple stalks. I'm constantly amazed by nature and always when I have it pointed out to me by Lizzy. In conditions where tractors made of iron and steel rust to bits, these plants thrive. They grow in salt, in a loose and vulnerable substrate, self-seeding year by year to stabilise the beach,

no matter how fast longshore drift takes the sea away. We were lucky to catch them at their finest. The plant doing best was the echium, a lovely wild variety about 30cm (1ft) tall with bright blue flowers growing straight in a slim cone. It grew in clumps all over the shingle, between the ropes and cables and along the side of the road.

The further away from the sea we got, the more established the vegetation became, with gorse and broom, and even willow a few hundred yards in from the sea. A fine example of succession that would have ended

in established woodland were it not for the farmers sowing their crops further inland on the flats that was once marsh.

We reached Derek Jarman's house, Prospect Cottage, a jolly black shack with bright yellow windows, much like the others but somehow better kept, and surrounded by a beautiful garden. A few cars were parked up on the road and there were some people wandering around taking pictures. It felt a little strange to find people drifting around, but the property has been 'saved for the nation' after it was bought in 2020 by an art charity, which raised £3.5 million to prevent it falling into private hands.

The garden was blooming with natives and it was hard to tell where it began and the beach ended. Red and yellow horned poppies waved in the breeze, echiums stood to attention and sea kale formed edible clumps, while all the usual suspects vied for attention, including lavender, valerian, curry plant and alliums. Between them, a series of beach finds turned to sculptured treasure created shapes, columns, angles and points of interest. Different-coloured pebbles made beds. On the side of the cottage, a poem by John Donne, 'The Sun Rising', in wooden blocks caught the late afternoon light, creating long word shadows. I took a few snaps and then stopped to

look. I was overwhelmed by the beauty of the place. I loved the shack ethic and the way the garden bled into its surroundings with barely a marker. Beyond the invisible boundary I found a wild sea pea, blooming purple. What a stunning place! I could have stayed, but I didn't want to intrude. Jarman was an influence on my early life, as an earnest film student, and I didn't want to walk on such hallowed ground without some kind of permission. I wanted it to be forever what it was to Jarman: a garden unsullied by tourism and popularity. An escape. A place of calm and intense beauty in a sea of … what? Desolation? I wasn't so sure.

We walked back along the beach to another shack, a converted railway carriage-cum-art gallery, where we weaved between beach finds and outhouses to view artworks by the owner and their invited friends. On one wall, I found a message saying 'Dungeness is not Desolate'. Nearby, a string of bunting led my gaze to a view of the lighthouse with the power station beyond.

No. Dungeness might be isolated, off the beaten track, odd, otherworldly, mysterious, exciting and changeable, but it isn't desolate. Just a little forgotten sometimes.

And that's no bad thing.

Check it out on the way

DE LA WARR PAVILION, BEXHILL-ON-SEA This wonderful 1935 art deco building has been saved and restored for all of us to enjoy. Its fabulous setting and architecture gives us all hope that we can reconcile the past and the future. Art, music, comedy, food. What's not to love? www.dlwp.com

RYE AND RYE CASTLE Rye is like a film set of a perfect English olde worlde town. There is parking big enough for campers at the railway station. Great views over the river from the castle. Lovely place and setting. www.ryemuseum.co.uk

ROMNEY, HYTHE AND DYMCHURCH RAILWAY The smallest public railway in the world, this third-scale railway, complete with diddy rolling stock and steam locomotives, runs between Hythe and Dungeness. It's one of Kent's most popular attractions. www.rhdr.org.uk

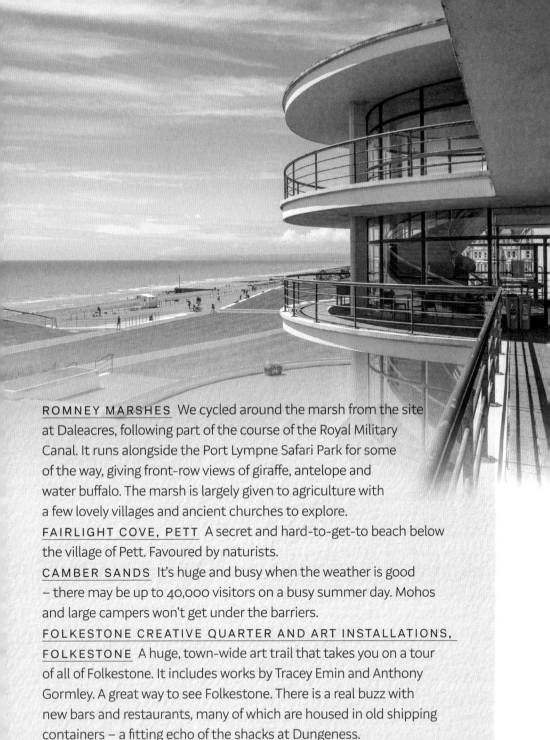

ROMNEY MARSHES We cycled around the marsh from the site at Daleacres, following part of the course of the Royal Military Canal. It runs alongside the Port Lympne Safari Park for some of the way, giving front-row views of giraffe, antelope and water buffalo. The marsh is largely given to agriculture with a few lovely villages and ancient churches to explore.

FAIRLIGHT COVE, PETT A secret and hard-to-get-to beach below the village of Pett. Favoured by naturists.

CAMBER SANDS It's huge and busy when the weather is good – there may be up to 40,000 visitors on a busy summer day. Mohos and large campers won't get under the barriers.

FOLKESTONE CREATIVE QUARTER AND ART INSTALLATIONS, FOLKESTONE A huge, town-wide art trail that takes you on a tour of all of Folkestone. It includes works by Tracey Emin and Anthony Gormley. A great way to see Folkestone. There is a real buzz with new bars and restaurants, many of which are housed in old shipping containers – a fitting echo of the shacks at Dungeness. www.creativefolkestone.org.uk

DO IT THE HARD WAY

There's no hard way to visit Dungeness, except maybe in high summer when, I am told, the cars back up into Rye trying to get to Camber Sands. So go early or late or out of season when the traffic is quiet and the visitors have yet to rise or are already in the pub. If you approach this as a journey, Dungeness is at the centre.

Getting here, if you follow the A259 from Bexhill-on-Sea, will carry you along the coast, through busy Hastings and up into the hills above Pett Level, itself an isolated wonder, before taking you along the coast to Winchelsea, Rye, Camber and then Dungeness. The contrast between the sea of caravans at Camber and Winchelsea and the open spaces beyond couldn't be greater. Afterwards, it's a seaside drive to Hythe, with options to explore Romney Marsh. Folkestone, the final stop, is busy and thriving but also worth a look, if only to wander along the pier, enjoy the music and seek out the art installations of Britain's biggest outdoor art project.

CAMPING

Daleacres Caravan Club Site, Hythe: Another standard Caravan and Motorhome Club site with good facilities at the Hythe end of Romney Marsh. www.caravanclub. co.uk/club-sites/england/south-east-england/kent/daleacres-caravan-club-site

Black Horse Farm Caravan Club Site, Densole: Handy for Folkestone, and, as usual, all the standard facilities. www.caravanclub.co.uk/club-sites/england/south-east-england/kent/black-horse-farm-caravan-club-site

Fairlight Wood Caravan Club Site, Pett: My favourite C&MC site yet. It's set in a wood and is spacious and light, with lots of vegetation to hide the white boxes. www.caravanclub.co.uk/club-sites/england/south-east-england/east-sussex/fairlight-wood-caravan-club-site

You will need:
- an OS map
- time to go during the off-season, or early or late

DO IT THE EASY WAY

The easy way to explore Dungeness would be to park in Hythe and take the train. You'll see the marshes, the bungalows and the sea and will get deposited by the old lighthouse, from which it's just a short walk to the sea and Jarman's cottage.

ROUTE 11

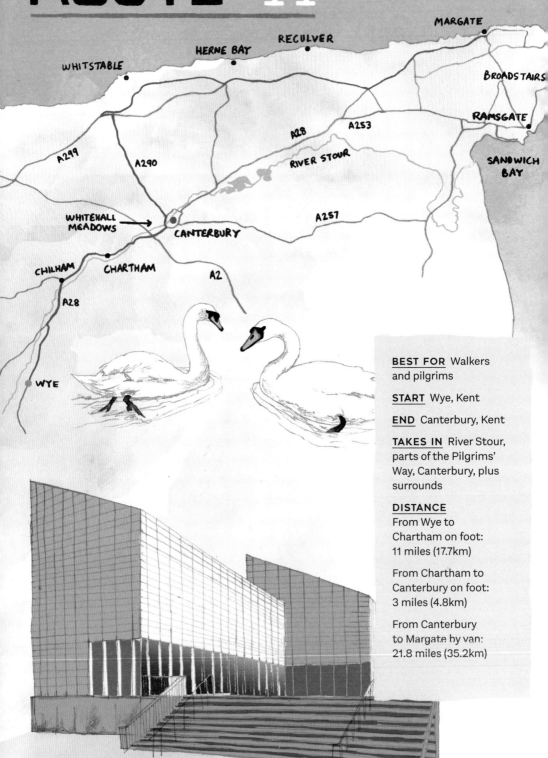

MARGATE

BROADSTAIRS

RAMSGATE

WHITSTABLE

HERNE BAY

RECULVER

SANDWICH BAY

A299

A290

A28

A253

RIVER STOUR

A257

A299

WHITEHALL MEADOWS

CANTERBURY

CHILHAM

CHARTHAM

A2

A28

WYE

BEST FOR Walkers and pilgrims

START Wye, Kent

END Canterbury, Kent

TAKES IN River Stour, parts of the Pilgrims' Way, Canterbury, plus surrounds

DISTANCE
From Wye to Chartham on foot: 11 miles (17.7km)

From Chartham to Canterbury on foot: 3 miles (4.8km)

From Canterbury to Margate by van: 21.8 miles (35.2km)

KENT'S PILGRIMS' WAY

Canterbury has been a site of pilgrimage for almost 1,000 years and was occupied for thousands of years before that. The routes in, across the North Downs, were once part of a network of corridors of movement that stayed on high ground for safety and to avoid marshy river valleys. Our particular journey was a pilgrimage to Kent to find a tiny stretch of the route and to walk into the heart of a city under our own steam. On the way, we found ancient woodlands and species-rich hedgerows that are really showing their age.

TRAVELLING WITH A BOTANIST has its advantages. Having someone to identify the plants we encounter enables me to be a better writer. Where before I might have noted a few of the basics from reading Ladybird books when I was young, I now have the benefit being able to describe landscape in much more detail because of the plants that grow there. I am also beginning to understand the complex relationships between plants and place, and this has really helped to open my eyes.

Seeking out different types of habitats give us a reason to go places, too. Over the years, Lizzy and I have taken off to see wildflower meadows in the Alps, the plants of the machair in Scotland and the orchids of the Burren in Ireland. It was no different for us going to Kent. While searching for quiet places and forgotten roads, we were also searching for signs of the diversity of plants the Downs are famous for.

One of the downsides of being the partner of a botanist is that making progress can take ages. Often on walks, I'll find myself jabbering away about something deeply inconsequential or ranting about some aspect of life's injustices when I'll realise I'm alone on the trail. When I turn around and look back, I find Lizzy crouching in the bushes taking a photo on her phone or examining some plant she's found. Occasionally, I'll be disturbed by a yelp of delight as she sees something extraordinary. It's the kind of noise that anyone else would let out if they had seen some kind of rare creature: a dolphin, otter or golden eagle perhaps. But to Lizzy, plants are rare treasures too and deserve every bit of excitement as a red squirrel or kingfisher.

We decided to spend a couple of days walking the Pilgrims' Way into Canterbury for a number of reasons. One of them, of course, was a chance to look at the plants and landscape of the North Downs. For me, it was also the opportunity to walk along an ancient pathway and into a city in the same way many have done before us. I wanted to experience a little of what many thousands have felt since the death of Thomas Becket in 1170 and what few

of us experience today. Approaching a city, for us, in the 21st century, often
means taking a motorway junction, sitting in traffic and looking for a place
to park. We've lost something vital by travelling in the same cab of the
same vehicle.

On top of that, the North Downs Way, despite following the route of one
of Britain's most ancient pathways from Farnham to Dover, is often thought
of as the lesser-walked cousin of the South Downs Way, an extremely popular
walk above the Sussex coast. After Thomas Becket's murder in Canterbury
Cathedral almost 900 years ago, the route diverted into Canterbury as it
became second only to Rome in importance to Christian pilgrims. It was
vitally important to so many, and yet today it's become more obscure:
a walk off the beaten track.

Despite my noble intentions to walk into Canterbury we still entered the
city in the wrong way, in the van, taking an age to locate the park and ride on
the New Dover Road, where we would leave the van, take the bus into the city
and then take a train straight out again along the Stour Valley to walk back in.
The park and ride has a secure, dedicated motorhome area where overnight
parking is allowed so it made perfect sense.

Being imperfect pilgrims, we also decided that progress should be gentle
on our first day, so opted not for the Pilgrims' Way but for the Stour Valley

Walk, an easy 3-mile (4.8km) stroll into the city. We got the bus (no incidents), jumped on a train to Chartham, a few stops from Canterbury East station and began to walk the Stour Valley Way, along the Stour into the city. It took us a couple of easy hours to amble along the river, past the gravel pits and nature reserves, in the damp afternoon. Lizzy spotted aspens trembling in the breeze, while the willows whispered along the banks, their branches weeping towards the water. We passed a family of swans resting on one of the banks, the fluffy cygnets yawning and stretching as we wandered by. The Whitehall Meadows Nature Reserve took us almost up to the West Gate, across the path of the old Roman road that once crossed the river just outside the city walls, where we entered the city (dodging traffic, of course) and almost immediately landed right among it in at the high street.

From there, it was just a short stroll to the cathedral, where we explored the cloisters, gawped at the magnificence of the building and the dedication of the architects and builders, and spent a few quiet moments reflecting at the light that burns for Becket. We drifted, a little culture shocked, around the city. The change from natural to built environment was quite remarkable and gave us a real taste of what it might have been like to cross the city walls and transition immediately from country to city in a few paces.

The next day, we drove out along the Stour to Chartham, parked the van and took the train a couple more stops further to Wye, the point nearest to the Pilgrims' Way we could find, for a more 'authentic' experience. Wye is the point where the original route, to Dover, meets the later route to Canterbury. We waded through fields of wheat and barley on muddy, little-used footpaths in search of the path that I hoped would offer us views of the cathedral from the Downs.

We crossed a field of almost ripe barley and found a gate at the bottom of a steep hill leading to an overgrown footpath. A faded sign on the gatepost indicated this was indeed the Pilgrims' Way. The path led us steeply up, away from the fields and on to the Downs. With the pathway almost blocked by huge stems of cow parsley, nettles and brambles, we had to tread down the tendrils to avoid being stung. I pulled up my socks as high as they could go until the path widened and we could walk easily between the tall hedgerows without fear of the nettle's sting. I walked on, while Lizzy, always the botanist, stopped to look. One might almost have called it dawdling. When I was some way ahead, no doubt muttering to myself about some worldly injustice, I heard a yelp. I stopped to turn around,

expecting, as always to see a flash of red squirrel dart up a tree or an eagle disappear with a fish over the horizon. But no. Lizzy was caressing the leaf of a tree and looking at it in wonder.

'*Viburnum lantana*,' she half shouted at me, 'I knew we'd find one up here. It loves chalk grassland. I haven't seen one of these for years.'

I wandered back to Lizzy, admired the tree, and continued walking with her as she named and counted the plants in the hedgerow. Hooper's Rule states that you can tell the age a hedgerow by counting the number of species over a 27m (30-yard) stretch, taking an average over two or more stretches. You then multiply

the number of species by 110 to get an approximate age (give or take a couple of hundred years each side).

We walked along the path, which was more like a tunnel of green shoots, and counted what we saw, finding hazel, dogwood, spindle, blackthorn, elder, dog rose, field maple, privet, *Viburnum lantana* and *Viburnum opulus*, which would give this path an approximate age of 1,100 years. I had been a little cynical that we would be walking in the footsteps of the pilgrims who had gone before us, but this was remarkable. I had never (knowingly) walked any path this well established and it was incredible to think that, actually,

Check it out on the way

TURNER CONTEMPORARY, MARGATE Put this on your pilgrimage list if you like art and great seascapes. Margate is undergoing a renaissance and it was a pleasure to see it first hand from the glass-fronted galleries of the Turner Contemporary. Great cafe. There's also a brilliant tidal pool at Walpole. https://turnercontemporary.org
RECULVER Site of a monastery and Roman fort at what was once the coast of England, with the Isle of Thanet across the water. The adjacent country park has a cafe and education centre. http://visitreculver.com
CANTERBURY CATHEDRAL, CANTERBURY Magnificent building that dates back to around 600 AD, although it was rebuilt and extended around the time of Thomas Becket (1100s). It is a Gothic masterpiece and is quite incredible, rising up in design and beauty, especially when you're inside. The cloisters are beautiful and the light that burns in the place of Becket's tomb is quite moving. All in all it's a truly wonderful, mesmerising building, whatever your feelings about the church. www.canterbury-cathedral.org
WHITSTABLE Another pilgrimage for those who like oysters. I do, but they were off the day we went. Even so, there was great seafood, an attractive harbourside and, when they're on, the best oysters in Kent. Parking may be an issue in season – it's very popular. www.whitstable.co.uk

this could well be the exact path taken by thousands of walkers before me, over the course of many centuries. I felt like I was in good company, doing something my body was meant to do instead of sitting behind a desk or at

the wheel. It felt good to be putting one foot in front of the other, climbing steadily away from the river and up into the chalk downs, and gaining 100m (328ft) of vertical height in total, to join my ancestors on a walk into a sacred city. I took a deep breath and smiled, happy to be out here, feeling good and exploring more of Britain's (slightly) forgotten underbelly.

As we walked, Lizzy provided a running commentary about the land and the species she was seeing, how the nature of the soil – chalky on the hillsides and with more soil on the hilltops – affects what grows. On the steeper slopes, we found stands of beech and oaks with hazel. We passed areas of dark yew and silvery hornbeam, delicate coppices of birch and then, as we got to the highest points, rich sweet chestnut. Below the hornbeam we found an understory of bluebells, while ferns proliferated among the birch. Under dark forests of beech, the ground was more open, starved of light beneath the luscious, green canopy of the giant trees. Over the course of a couple of miles we noted so many mini ecosystems and landscapes it was amazing. And all of it was native. I had never encountered woodland in this way before. Lizzy, who usually prefers cycling to walking, was equally enthralled, at home in her element.

We came through the beeches and found a sign showing us the point where pilgrims would get their first glimpse of Canterbury. Sadly for us, the furious growing of spring had all but obliterated the view and we could only just make out the pointed crowns of the tower of this 1,400-year-old Gothic masterpiece. It was disappointing really, because I wanted to share a little of what the pilgrims must have felt during the Middle Ages when they first set eyes on this hallowed place. Cathedrals were the biggest buildings at the time – by a massive margin – and the sight of it must have been truly awe-inspiring to those who lived in single-storey wattle and daub cottages. We stood on tiptoe and tried to imagine.

We walked through plantations of sweet chestnut and stopped at Chilham – an incredibly beautiful village of half-timbered houses and a stunning Tudor manor house. We popped in for a refresher at the local pub before walking through Old Wives Lees and more chestnut plantation, discovering a badger sett in the woods. We emerged into bright sunshine in a field of

shimmering blue linseed and then found our way, through a gap in a hedge, into a huge orchard. Every step seemed to offer something different, whether it was a view, a building, a tree or something else.

We dropped down through the orchards, threaded our way through a sea of caravans, presumably dedicated to apple pickers, through the heavily industrialised farm, back down to the Ashford Road and into open fields on the river. A weir, with a deep pool, was too much for Lizzy and she stripped off and waded in, swimming breaststroke among the reeds.

I sat on the bank and felt the warmth of the sun on my face. After 10 miles (16km) of walking my feet were a little sore and ready for fresh air. I teased them out of my boots and let them breathe. The van was just a mile away at Chartham so we were almost back to where we started. I felt I now had at least some idea of what the Pilgrims' Way was like and realised that I'd have to put in a lot more time if I wanted to see all that the North Downs Way has to offer. Logistically, we'd made it happen, too, without having to retrace our steps, which was a bonus. And the whole while we'd encountered just a couple of dog walkers, a pub landlady and a cyclist. Even here, so close to the city, we felt like we were alone bar a few sheep grazing on the meadow behind us. Just as well really, I thought, as Lizzy stepped out of the river and slipped into her clothes.

DO IT THE HARD WAY

The North Downs Way is a long-distance trail that stretches from Farnham in Surrey to Dover in Kent. It's 156 miles (251km) long and, for much of its length, follows the tops of the North Downs. The latter-day diversion to visit Canterbury leaves the Way at Wye, close to the station. Trains from Canterbury West station leave every 30 minutes or so.

You will need:
- good footwear
- weather-appropriate clothing
- a picnic lunch
- OS maps

CAMPING

New Dover Road Park and Ride, Canterbury: Canterbury council allow motorhomes and camper vans to stay overnight, which is handy if you want to leave the van and walk. The bus into town takes about 10 minutes and comes free with your overnight parking fee. It costs £8 for 12 hours. Water and grey waste emptying available. www.canterbury.co.uk/directory_record/687/new_dover_road_park_and_ride

Reculver Country Park: This is an important Roman fort on the North Kent

coast, which is available for motorhomes to stay overnight. It's only slightly sloping, but the surface is plastic and it's really hard to get a purchase on your wedges. Even so, it's a brilliant overnight spot. There's a pub next door. www.searchforsites.co.uk/marker.php?id=31398

DO IT THE EASY WAY

Take the train to Chartham from Canterbury West and walk along the Stour into the city for that country-to-city feeling. Arrive at Canterbury feeling like you've been on some kind of journey.

ROUTE

12

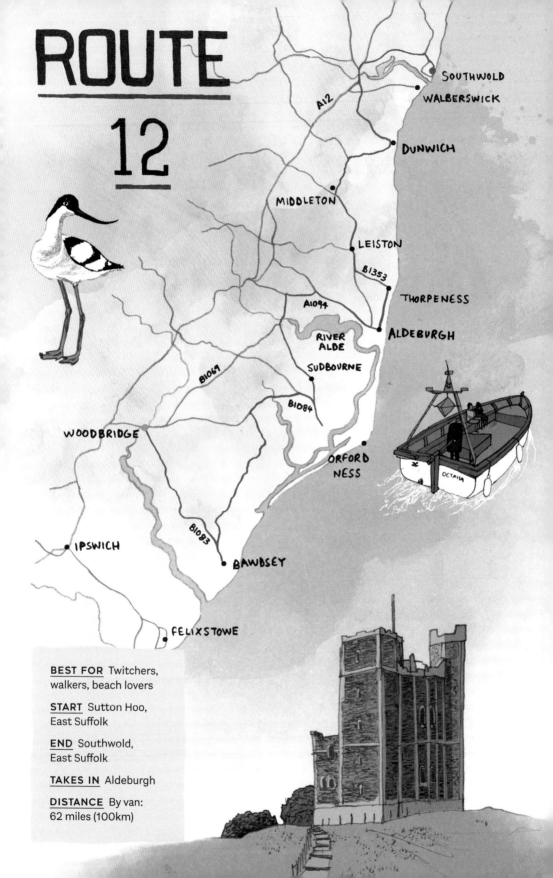

SOUTHWOLD

WALBERSWICK

A12

DUNWICH

MIDDLETON

LEISTON

B1353

THORPENESS

A1094

RIVER ALDE

ALDEBURGH

SUDBOURNE

B1069

B1084

WOODBRIDGE

ORFORD NESS

OCTAVIA

B1083

IPSWICH

BAWDSEY

FELIXSTOWE

BEST FOR Twitchers, walkers, beach lovers

START Sutton Hoo, East Suffolk

END Southwold, East Suffolk

TAKES IN Aldeburgh

DISTANCE By van: 62 miles (100km)

THE SUFFOLK COAST

LOST AND FOUND, OCTOBER 2021

Suffolk isn't really a secret, it has to be said. But it does offer slices of heaven and vast open skies between the busy, well-heeled villages and the changing shingle. The AONB between Bawdsey and Southwold has been saved from the developers and the carousels and remains unspoiled in many places. It's also very welcoming to motorhomes, with lots of campsites and places where you can overnight within moments of a swim. That's precious in itself, but worth even more when you add in sunsets over the marshes and sunrises over the sea. Spectacular.

THIS JOURNEY AROUND THE COAST of Suffolk began as an idea
to visit the ex-MOD land at Orford Ness on one of Europe's longest shingle
spits. It's a wild and remote place that has a troubling history. Used as a
testing centre for weapons, even atomic bombs, it was off limits for a long
time until the National Trust took it over in 1993 and then opened it to the
public in 1995.

For me, though, it still remains off limits. My attempts to find a way there
were thwarted almost as soon as I decided to go. The tiny ferry that takes visitors
out to Orford Ness runs daily in the summer and then at weekends until the end
of October. Tickets are booked online. I tried to secure a seat, but it was booked
up almost as soon as the tickets were released, like a Cold War Glastonbury.

I decided to go anyway, in search of the slices of silent heaven in between the
golden, rising-sun, former-fishing-villages-now-swanky-resorts of Southwold
and Aldeburgh, themselves lost and found, although these days it's hard to tell
if they are indeed found or whether they have seriously lost their way.

The coast of Suffolk is constantly changing, along with its fortunes,
creating new land while destroying the old. It's a dynamic landscape of sandy
soils, sandy cliffs and beaches, and miles and miles of ever-moving shingle. In
places, where humans have made changes, nature has seen an opportunity,

taken over and colonised. In other places, where humans have colonised, nature has made no bones about taking it back. Exploring this part of England means taking dead ends and no through roads to tiny places and coastal towns that feel as if they've been cut off forever. It's on the map but at the end of the world. Lost and found.

Our journey began at Sutton Hoo, just outside Woodbridge, to find something that was lost and is now found. The imprint of an Anglo-Saxon ship, and the burial treasures it contained, excavated from a burial mound on the site, is considered to be one of the most important archaeological finds ever made in the UK. While the ship was only ever a ghostly imprint, a steel sculpture depicting the size and shape of it sits outside the visitor centre, showing the scale of the ship. Recreations of the treasures found in the boat are nearby. The real things have long since departed for the British Museum in London. A tower, built in 2021, overlooks the site of the ship's burial, allowing visitors a better view of the burial mounds. It wobbles as you climb. Even up there, looking down on the ancient landscape, and the small mound

that kept its secret for more than 1,000 years, the essence of Sutton Hoo, and the significance of those buried here, felt tantalisingly out of reach.

I drove to the mouth of the River Deben and found a spot at which to park up for the night at Bawdsey Harbour with views of the river and Felixstowe Ferry opposite. Lizzy and I walked to the end of the shingle spit at the mouth of the river and along the steel coastal defences as far as Bawdsey Manor. Sea kales and yellow poppies were growing between the groynes and in the shingle while the defences were crumbling, rusting and broken. Twisted metal, rotting groynes and broken concrete were no match for the roaring sea and delicate poppy.

We rose at first light to watch the sun rise over the sea and light up the buildings across the river in stunning, fiery orange. It was a fleeting but dazzling show before the low clouds on the horizon blocked the light and returned the day to standard autumnal grey. We watched kite surfers as they set up and flew out to sea, travellers on the wind.

Venturing north, away from Bawdsey, took us through the Suffolk Coast AONB, an area that has been protected for more than 50 years. A stop at the wild and lonely Shingle Street revealed the location used by Danny Boyle in his Beatles film, *Yesterday*, more vast shingle flats and a Martello tower that's now a holiday let. We drove through woodland, sandy heath and farmland, around the Butley River and into Orford, a beautifully tidy village on the edge of the marshes and only a few yards from Orford Ness across the River Ore.

Walkers strode along the dykes and coastal defences and dinghy sailors blew up the river. Across the water, I could see the radio masts and strange pagoda-like structures of the former MOD facility.

We overnighted at Aldeburgh, at the south end of the town at the neck of the Ness itself, on a car park overlooking the marshes on one side and the sea on the other. Dawn brought more golden moments of dazzling sun as we walked as far as the path would take us on to the Ness, but it didn't last. As the road disappeared into the sea, the sun disappeared behind the clouds and broke the spell. We got our spark from a dip in the sea.

I loved Aldeburgh but worried about it, too. It's long been overtaken by second homes and its high street is populated with well-to-do fashion brands and art galleries. A few places still sell smoked fish but few boats, if any, work the beach any more. It's a place that reeks of wealth and privilege, all country tweeds and mumsy gilets, big cars and entitlement, set against a backdrop of beautifully preserved brick cottages and a wide shingle beach. Yet for a £4 parking charge we were able to stay next to the sea, with the added bonus of being able to run from the van to the water and back in a matter of seconds.

The Minsmere RSPB reserve is up the coast from Aldeburgh. The drive, thorough a sandy-floored forest of oak, hawthorn, birch and chestnut, takes you along the edge

Check it out on the way

SUTTON HOO, WOODBRIDGE The site of Anglo-Saxon burial mounds where the ghost ship and Britain's greatest treasures were uncovered. www.nationaltrust.org.uk/sutton-hoo

SNAPE MALTINGS A converted Victorian maltings that includes a concert hall, galleries, shops and cafes. It's artsy and wonderful, and provides retail therapy, if you need that kind of thing. www.brittenpearsarts.org/visit-us/snape-maltings

ADNAMS BREWERY TOURS, SOUTHWOLD Southwold is home to Adnams Brewery. Take a tour and sample an amazing selection of beers and wine. www.adnams.co.uk/experiences

RSPB MINSMERE, SAXMUNDHAM Family-friendly nature reserve with hides and walks for the twitchers and their amateur friends. Worth a look. www.rspb.org.uk/reserves-and-events/reserves-a-z/minsmere

ORFORD NESS, ORFORD Former secret base for evil regimes, now a nature reserve with a weird history. Book ahead or experience similar disappointment to that which I felt. www.nationaltrust.org.uk/orford-ness-national-nature-reserve

ORFORD CASTLE, ORFORD An impressive keep that's a short stroll from Orford Ness. Just turn up if they won't let you on the boat to the Ness. www.english-heritage.org.uk/visit/places/orford-castle

of the Minsmere levels and to the visitor centre above the Scrape – a wartime defence that was soon taken over by wading birds. It was quiet and peaceful, despite being half term. Even in the hides, which were busy with twitchers, a reverent silence fell over us as we scanned the water for glimpses of birds we couldn't recognise. My favourite was an avocet, a bird that was absent for more than 100 years until the Minsmere reserve was taken over by the RSPB. It's hugely symbolic of the success of Minsmere and appears on the RSPB's logo. As I sat silently in the hide trying, but failing, to get a decent photo, I wondered if it knew either that it was famous or that I was absolutely delighted to see it.

A little further up the coast lay Dunwich. Actually, I should say that it once lay a little further up the coast. Over a period of hundreds of years, Dunwich was lost to the sea in a series of storms. It was once a thriving port and city of 4,000 people and the unofficial capital of East Anglia. At its height, it had a bigger population than London. Then, in 1286, a huge storm destroyed its port and rerouted the river to the north at Southwold and in 1347 another storm swept 400 houses into the sea. All that remains today are the ruin of Greyfriars Franciscan friary and the last grave, which sits next to the cliff edge, above another vast sea of shingle and bordered to the north by wetlands and marsh.

The last swim, or stop, was at Southwold, a picturesque town on the edge of the AONB. It's a beautiful place with a high street of big names, plus a lot of indies, a fantastic pier and a lovely beach of pale yellow sand. As the sun began to set, we walked from the council-run campsite to Blackshore Quay, the collection of black-painted fishermen's huts, cafes and smokehouses on the north bank of the River Blyth. It was messy and jumbled, with the carcasses of boats lying between black sheds, and crab pots piled up on short wooden wharfs. The rutted, puddled road seemed to be much more authentic than the rows of neatly painted houses in Aldeburgh and felt, to me at least, like we'd stumbled upon a version of Suffolk that can please everybody. Fishermen and boatbuilders still work from here, sitting side by side with the cafes and the Harbour Inn. There's even a designated crabbing area for holidaying families. The black huts remain, in total contrast to the brightly painted beach huts – which could cost you more than the price of a cheap house in nearby Ipswich – on the beach 0.5 miles (0.8km) or so to the north.

Standing on the quayside, watching the sun go down over the marshes behind Walberswick, with the smell of estuarine mud and fish and chips invading our nostrils, felt like an appropriate end to the journey.

Blackshore Quay might be a tourist draw for Southwold, but it still retains a little of its integrity and soul. It's away from the town and out on a limb, connected to Walberswick by a tiny ferry and cut off by the sea, the marshes and the elements from the rest of the world. But of course, change is always around the corner in Suffolk. Who knows what it will become?

For now, though, the Suffolk Coast remains very special, with moments of off-the-beaten-track calm between the busy, well-to-do resorts, if you need it. There's also a great pint to be had from Adnams, lots of lonely beaches to walk, wildlife to spot and woods to wander in. I absolutely loved it.

DO IT THE HARD WAY

If I am honest there's no real hard way to enjoy Suffolk, if you discount the horror of having to travel along the A12 to get there. However, getting out of the van and walking will reveal the real rewards. The Sailor's Path is a 6-mile (9.6km) walk from Aldeburgh to Snape Maltings. Minsmere has miles of great walking, either around the Scrape or through the forest. And, of course, you can walk the Suffolk Coast Path or just let your feet take you. Heading out of any of the villages will bring you to wildly beautiful countryside, heathland or coast. Places like Aldeburgh, Bawdsey and Shingle Street are out on a limb anyway, with one road in and one road out, making them feel isolated and far away from any kind of civilisation.

I began my journey at Woodbridge and headed to Bawdsey, then felt my way up the coast to Southwold, often on tiny, unnamed roads. There are rivers to work around and lots of dead ends to try. And that's why I love it.

You will need:
- good maps
- binoculars for bird spotting
- walking boots
- swimming togs

CAMPING

The Village Hall, Butley: The hall offers a wonderful welcome with water and grey and black water facilities for motorhomes (donation £5) plus overnighting. Bravo and thanks! www.butleyvillagehall.co.uk

The Eel's Foot Inn, Eastbridge: This caravan site and pub with rooms near Minsmere has hook-up and camping facilities. Great pub, too. www.theeelsfootinn.co.uk

Southwold Camping and Caravan Site, Southwold: Situated in a great position near to the beach and walking distance from the town. Handy for Blackshore Quay. www.southwoldcamping.com

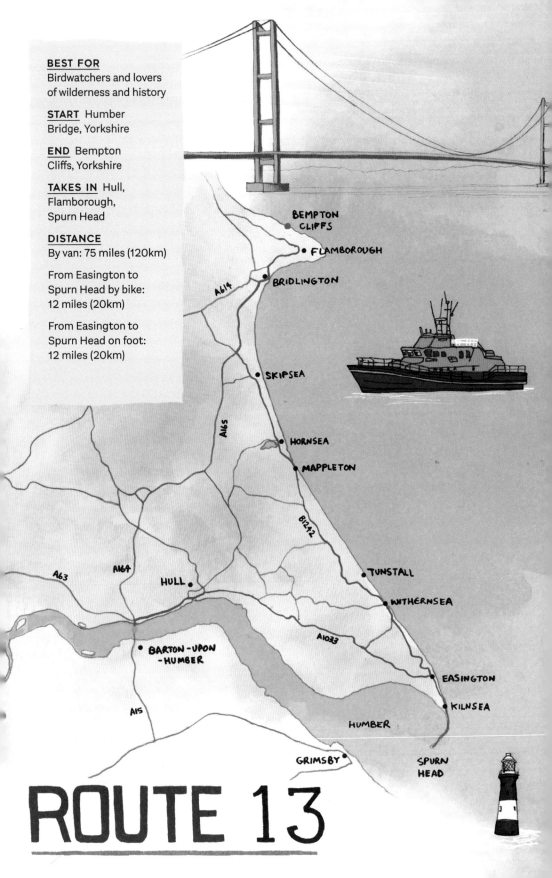

BEST FOR
Birdwatchers and lovers
of wilderness and history

START Humber
Bridge, Yorkshire

END Bempton
Cliffs, Yorkshire

TAKES IN Hull,
Flamborough,
Spurn Head

DISTANCE
By van: 75 miles (120km)

From Easington to
Spurn Head by bike:
12 miles (20km)

From Easington to
Spurn Head on foot:
12 miles (20km)

BEMPTON
CLIFFS

FLAMBOROUGH

A614

BRIDLINGTON

A165

SKIPSEA

HORNSEA

MAPPLETON

B1242

A63

A164

HULL

TUNSTALL

WITHERNSEA

BARTON-UPON
-HUMBER

A1033

A15

EASINGTON

KILNSEA

HUMBER

GRIMSBY

SPURN
HEAD

ROUTE 13

SPURN HEAD AND THE HUMBER

NATURE WILL FIND A WAY, 28 AND 29 JULY 2021

*Spurn Head is a spit of land that's always shifting.
It's off the map and hard to get to, which makes it a
perfect destination for an off the beaten track adventure.
Here, now that the humans have moved out and nature is
being allowed to win, it's possible to see how everything
changes and evolves – and the results are amazing.*

'**WHEN I TOLD MY FRIENDS** I was coming to Hull for my holiday,'
Terry said, 'they laughed. But here I am. And I've got this.'

Terry gestured, with a heavily tattooed arm, towards the empty riverside
parking spot he had all to himself and laughed. His van, an old Ford transit
motorhome in 1970s livery with an old ply interior, was shabby and worn
but clearly still worked well enough to take him places. We found out that it
had taken him to Gibraltar and around the NC500 in the last year. A cabbie

from London with no work after 2020's first lockdown, Terry bought the van and took off, travelling to Scotland in time for the solstice at John o'Groats and then heading to Europe when things got worse. He was happy to tell us the places to go to stay away from the crowds and we shared some of ours. He had clearly done well to find this place, a quiet parking spot at the end of a lane leading nowhere other than the salt marsh on the Humber Estuary.

Terry had found this spot by accident and had stayed the night without any hassle. The police had come around and waved hello at him, clearly not bothered by his presence. The view out of Terry's van was of the Humber Estuary, with Spurn Head to his left and Hull to his right, just visible on the horizon as a block of angular shapes. Right out front was a grass-topped dyke of boulders leading down to the mud flats where curlew, plover and shanks were poking about for titbits in the silt. Between the land and the marsh were patches of samphire and purple sea lavender. Sea purslane and bright green cord grass grew in clumps on stands between the rivulets.

Terry was heading the same way as us, up the coast to Northumberland, so we wished him well and said that we'd see him again. He settled back into his seat with a book and we cycled off, back to our campsite and the van.

The following day, Terry had gone. We cycled past his spot, on to the spit and out along the road that used to run the whole length of Spurn Point.

Where the roadway collapsed into the beach, we took to the hard sand and cycled across the 300m (328-yard) stretch of beach separating Spurn from the mainland on higher tides. It was here in 2013 that the spit was breached during a storm.

The tide was just pulling back from the soft sand at the high tide mark, and it was still early, so we were the first ones out. A brisk westerly wind chopped up the water on the landward side, while the seaward side was flat and calm, small waves breaking on the sand.

We pushed our bikes through the deep, soft sand and remounted once we found the old concrete road beneath the drifts. We cycled down to the very end, past the RNLI base and old lighthouses, next to the coastguard station and the old military parade ground, the land that was once the pub

and all the other fragments of man's occupation. A narrow path led us towards the point, past the gun emplacements and the searchlight bases that were here during WWII. At that time, the land beyond the emplacements was flattened so that the sight lines were clear, but today nature has taken control again. We were confronted by dense bush consisting of sea buckthorn, dog rose, elder, marram grass and bracken. Far from being flat, the dunes had built up to several

metres tall, making the path undulating, twisting and overgrown, with the final rise giving way to a view of the Humber, a deserted beach and a sun-bleached bench someone had made from driftwood. Lizzy and I sat on the bench and talked, looking out to sea, tracking the fast-moving clouds and watching the birds.

I wanted to visit Spurn Head because it's one of those places that's off the map. Well, actually it's one of those places that doesn't quite fit on to the map. On the Ordnance Survey Explorer map number 262, Spurn Head sits in a box in the corner because it doesn't fit on the whole map, and presumably, to put it elsewhere might be to lose it altogether. But Spurn Head is like that. It's an adjunct, an epiglottis-shaped appendix formed by longshore drift and the wind and tides. It's a shapeshifter, a will-o'-the-wisp of land that won't be the same tomorrow as it was yesterday.

Over Spurn's history, it's been many things. A home for fishermen. A permanent base for the Humber lifeboatmen and their families. A military base. A Napoleonic battery. Today, though, it's a place for nature. Yorkshire Wildlife Trust bought Spurn in 1959 and have since managed it, alongside the RNLI, who house their only full-time crew there. They have allowed it to rewild while also restoring its former lighthouse. The decay has continued though, and the breach of the sea wall in 2013 saw the road access to the head washed away. Today, on high spring tides, the point becomes an island.

Spurn is within a few miles of Hull, but it couldn't be further away in lots of ways. The land around it is flat, much of it, like Sunk Island, reclaimed by drains and ditches. It's an area of big fields, big skies, agriculture and red-brick houses. It feels like *Dad's Army* country, a place where red phone boxes might hide spivs with Spam in their trench coats. Easington, our base for the visit, is like a classic English village, with church and terraced Victorian and Edwardian houses, a couple of pubs and a square filled with huge sycamores. On the outskirts, neat bungalows with tidy lawns and names like 'Dunroamin' give clues to who comes here.

We had arrived on a sunny day and decided to spend the afternoon exploring the area. A short stop on the seafront in Withernsea and a cup of tea and map gave us a destination for the afternoon: we'd search for the

Check it out on the way

HUMBER BRIDGE COUNTRY PARK, HESSLE Gives you great views of the Humber Bridge from right beneath it.

WITHERNSEA LIGHTHOUSE, WITHERNSEA It's right in the town and looks like a proper lighthouse that you can actually go up. If affords wonderful views of this busy little seaside town. https://withernsealighthouse.co.uk

RSPB BEMPTON CLIFFS, BEMPTON In summer, puffins arrive and make their nests here among the gannets, guillemots and kittiwakes. You might even catch a glimpse of the albatross. www.rspb.org.uk/reserves-and-events/reserves-a-z/bempton-cliffs

FLAMBOROUGH HEAD A popular place to watch seabirds or get some chips. There's a lighthouse, too. I wasn't keen as it was busy, but the beach at Selwicks Bay is absolutely spectacular, with caves and a stack. www.trinityhouse.co.uk/lighthouse-visitor-centres/ flamborough-lighthouse-visitor-centre

submerged forest marked offshore from Tunstall, a tiny village a short drive to the north.

We followed the tiny lane to the village, past a huge holiday camp and on to a road leading to the sea. We ignored the 'road closed' sign and carried on past a couple of men tinkering with a quad bike. They looked up at us as we went by. We followed the road to the point where it was coned off and parked on a grass verge. The road passed a couple of houses and then stopped, dropping off abruptly into an abyss above the beach, tarmac killed dead by coastal erosion. Beyond the road lay the beach, about 30m (100ft) down the crumbling cliff. We stood on the edge and scoured the beach for evidence of the forest. The tide, while low, wasn't as low as it goes, so we gave up the search and turned for the van.

A family, comprised of mum and dad, two teenagers and a young boy of about six, walked towards us. The young boy held a bucket in one hand and a spade in the other. He skipped excitedly towards the beach and then stopped abruptly when he realised the beach was further than he thought. The rest of the family caught up and stood in a line at the edge, looking down. Mum held the picnic, dad held towels. The teenagers held more buckets. They looked bemused, upset, a little frustrated.

They had done what we had done and assumed that the beach would be at the end of the road. Why wouldn't you assume that if you didn't know this coast and how it changes so quickly? I wonder how long it had been since the road fell. Was it weeks? Months? Years? Living in the houses

on the edge must be frightening, I thought, especially in the winter when storms and high tides undercut the cliff.

Like Spurn Head, the cliffs were a reminder that the world is ever changing and that nature will find a way. We can't fight it or control it, we just have to look after it and roll with it. Leave it alone to do its thing and it will find a way. I loved the wildness of Spurn and the fact that it's a place where you can get lost in a landscape that's recovering from our presence. You can see how succession is taking place with marram grass being taken over by brush and small trees. The next stage, if it's allowed by the wind and tides, would be forest.

We bumped into a Twitter friend who lives nearby and who moved to Spurn to be closer to his beloved birds and to enjoy the peace and quiet that living next to a national wildlife reserve can bring. I can see his point. Here, off the map and away from the ravages of man and progress, it would be easy to think nature was winning.

Later, when we headed up the coast to the RSPB reserve at Bempton Cliffs, we were able to report that we'd seen the albatross on the cliffs that had been sighted a few times among the gannets. Blown off course from his usual oceanic home in the South Atlantic, this rare bird was more living proof that nature will find a way, if only we can let it.

DO IT THE HARD WAY

Spurn Head is relatively easy to get to, but it does require a bit of widdling about in flat farmland. Starting out at the Humber Bridge will give you a good start point and take you along the banks of the river towards Spurn, with options to stop on the marshes between.

Walking from the car park at the Wildlife Trust Centre to the tip of the point will take a few hours – it's a 6-mile (9.7km) round trip – but it's worth it for the silence and solitude. The drive up the coast to Bempton is easy, too, and will get you to some relatively quiet spots along the B1242 (as well as Flamborough, which is very busy!).

You will need:
- a decent pair of walking boots
- wet weather gear
- binoculars (or a telescope or telephoto lens)

CAMPING

Sandalwood Certified Location,
Easington: A really friendly site on
the outskirts of Easington. From
here, it's a 10-mile (16km) round trip
cycle to Spurn. www.caravanclub.
co.uk/certificated-locations/
england/east-riding-of-yorkshire/
easington/sandalwood

DO IT THE EASY WAY

Drive out from the Humber Bridge and down to Spurn. You'll have to leave
the van at the Wildlife Trust Centre car park and walk or cycle. Alternatively,
you could always just head to the bird hide and watch the swallows, swans
and seabirds from there.

ROUTE 14

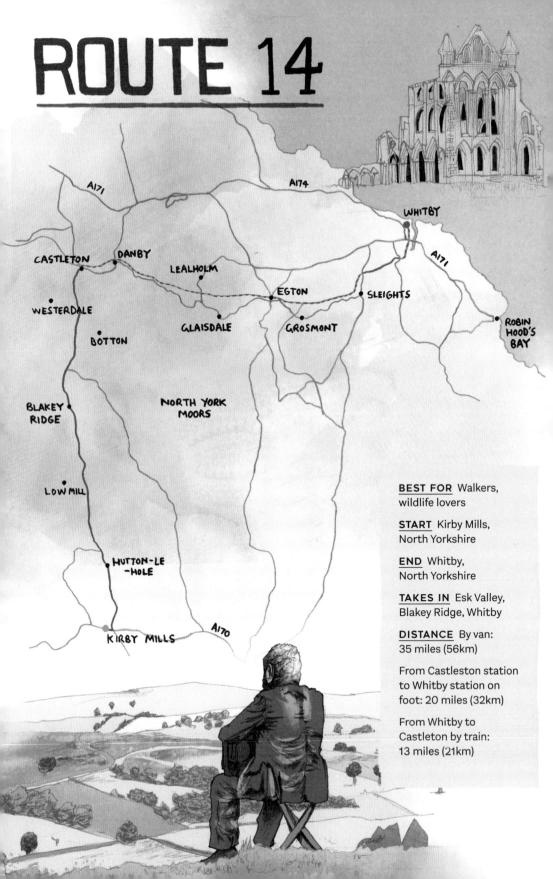

A171

A174

WHITBY

A171

CASTLETON

DANBY

LEALHOLM

EGTON

SLEIGHTS

WESTERDALE

GLAISDALE

GROSMONT

ROBIN HOOD'S BAY

BOTTON

NORTH YORK MOORS

BLAKEY RIDGE

LOW MILL

HUTTON-LE -HOLE

KIRBY MILLS

A170

BEST FOR Walkers, wildlife lovers

START Kirby Mills, North Yorkshire

END Whitby, North Yorkshire

TAKES IN Esk Valley, Blakey Ridge, Whitby

DISTANCE By van: 35 miles (56km)

From Castleston station to Whitby station on foot: 20 miles (32km)

From Whitby to Castleton by train: 13 miles (21km)

THE NORTH YORK MOORS

THE ESK VALLEY TO WHITBY, 1 AND 2 AUGUST 2021

The Esk Valley is one of the prettiest valleys in the North York Moors. With high moorland, pasture, farmland, steep ravines and heavenly villages, it offers the very best of Yorkshire. Exploring the Esk Valley isn't easy by vehicle, but on foot it provides an ever-changing landscape to saunter through – and an easy way back to the campsite in the form of a fabulous railway.

THE DRIVE OVER Blakey Ridge was spectacular. The road rose quickly out of the pretty (and popular) village of Hutton-le-Hole and on to the heather-clad tops. Despite the rain, the vivid purple glowed in contrast to the green beside it. The wet tarmac snaked out in front of us like a river of silver. We stopped to take pictures.

Despite its relatively short length, the route that goes over Blakey Ridge to Castleton is one of those roads that offers oohs and ahhs all along its length. It's desolate and beautiful, with steep drops either side and fantastic views of the surrounding dales. The Lion Inn, at 404m (1,325ft) above sea level, is the highest point, making the road one of the loftiest in the North York Moors.

All too quickly the drive was over and we dropped into Castleton – at 270m (886ft) – to find the station that we'd use as our start and finish point for the day's walking. The idea was that we'd walk the Esk Valley – supposedly one of the most beautiful in the North Yorkshire Moors – into Whitby from here and then catch the train back to the van. Simple. We had about seven

hours until the last train back so we figured we could cover the 20 miles (32km) comfortably in that time.

The station car park was small, with room enough for about ten cars, and was guarded by a closed gate, presumably to prevent livestock getting on to the tracks. We loaded up our lunch, double-checked the train times for the return journey, pulled on our boots and set off.

The waymarked path from the station led us up and away from the river, behind a farm and a row of stone-built cottages on a little path punctuated by gates and drystone walls. On one side, rising steeply, was open moorland. On the other, behind a stone wall, were the cottages, beyond which lay fields. Castleton faced us across the river, the sandstone houses sitting on a ridge between us and the high moorland of Blakey Ridge.

The final gate led us into a forest of silver birch. The elegant white trunks grew straight out of the deep understory of bracken and grasses, holding up the canopy of delicate, weeping branches, the small, light-green leaves seeming to drip off them. It was dense and bright at the same time, as if this wood could hide terrors and delights. I found it magical to be in such a striking forest so quickly on our hike and hoped that the rest of it would live up to this. I thought of a painting of a weeping silver birch that hangs in my mother's house that my grandfather painted in oils in the 1920s. Being among such beautiful trees made me appreciate the skill with which he captured its essence. I wonder now, thinking about it, whether this birch forest was somewhere that could be described as 'thin', where the real world collides with the otherworld, the fabric between them fragile and easy to slip behind. We walked on.

The path progressed, crossing fields and the railway at Danby and then again soon after, heading steeply up to Beacon Hill. We voted unanimously to stay in the valley bottom and walked along a beautiful, quiet road with grass growing down the middle into Lealholm, one of Yorkshire's prettiest villages with a bridge, great tearoom and a pub with a green, reached, from some parts of the village, via stepping stones over the river.

The path continued, along the river, over bridges and through fields and woods to Glaisdale, where we encountered the Beggar's Bridge and then climbed high on to the sides of a steep gorge. Here, in East Arncliffe Wood, we found the first flagstones of the Packman's Trod, a series of sandstone slabs laid in a pathway up the hillside like a carpet. They were well worn enough to be almost U-shaped, surely a sign that they had been here for centuries. The Trod led us to Egton Bridge and two sets of stepping stones across the river. We stopped for lunch, figuring we'd made it about halfway. Here, we joined a bridleway behind Egton Manor that had more human traffic on its

mile-and-a-bit section than we'd seen all morning.

The quiet resumed soon enough as we rose up into the fields and trees again above the valley. We crossed pastures and walked through more woods, following the Trod often. In a field somewhere near Newbiggin Hall, I had to stop and give my feet some tenderness and care. A tiny grain of something was bothering my left foot and it was getting worse. I felt like the princess with the pea, feeling every aberration in my boot, but I had to deal with it. Off came my socks and out came my pocketknife. I clipped my toenails and rubbed my feet, waved my socks in the air and picked out the balls of woollen fluff that had gathered on their soles. It didn't help, of course, but it did give me a breather for a few minutes. Lizzy and I don't saunter or amble. We usually crack on at a good pace, especially when it comes to walking on roads or featureless bridleways, unless there's something to look at, in which case we're the worst kind of dawdlers, gazing at plants, swooning over birds of prey or taking pictures of glorious views. This walk, comparatively, had been slowed up by the views and the plants, the Trod and the river. It was all lovely and a real pleasure to walk through such interesting

countryside on such an ancient pathway.

We took a wrong turn at Sleights, the last stretch before Whitby, missing a chunk of the trail and instead walking along the B1410 from Sleights into Ruswarp. By the time we realised the mistake we were too far down the road to contemplate retracing our steps and decided to continue to where we could pick up the trail again. It probably saved us a couple of hundred metres, for which we were very grateful. We followed the path across a meadow, up a steep incline and down a set of steps into the Scarborough Cinder Track, an old railway that runs along the coast. We climbed out of the old railway cutting and on to the playing fields of Whitby Sixth Form centre. This brought us out on to the A171, the main road through Whitby. By following a narrow path beside the road we found our way under the road bridge that spans the river and down a steep path into a housing estate behind Whitby's harbour.

From there, all we had to do was trudge along the quayside and down to the beach. You'd have thought that it would have been easy, but it wasn't, simply due to the number of people and pushchairs we had to navigate.

It was a form of culture shock. To see so many people after being alone for most of the day was difficult to cope with. I bear no grudge against those enjoying a day out at the seaside, crabbing, eating chips or candyfloss, drinking outside busy pubs or playing on arcade games. On some days it would be right up my street, but not today. I did my best to sidestep, overtake and dance around the ambling masses, but my feet were so sore it was all I could do to hobble. Lizzy was the same, frustrated at having to slow our pace and comply with the rest of the holidaying mob.

It wasn't what people were doing, it was the number of people doing it. The quayside was lined with people crabbing, their lines almost entangled as they sunk to the depths and the pavements were thronged with strollers and amblers. A slice of humanity gathered to have fun in one of Yorkshire's most popular destinations.

Eventually, we made our way down the slipway beside the west pier and on to the sand. We dropped our bags on the dry sand and unlaced our boots. I walked into the sea. The cold water rushed between my toes, sloshed around my ankles and sploshed up my legs. I stood on one spot for a few moments, savouring the coolness and the relief. Lizzy walked in deeper and stood still too, letting the waves splash her shorts, not really caring about anything other than soothing her feet.

We ordered haddock and chips to take away at a chippie overlooking the west pier and walked slowly back to the station with it in our hands. It seemed cruel to have to wait and not scoff the lot straight away, but we didn't have a huge amount of time before the train and to miss it would mean trying to get a taxi back to Castleton. There didn't seem much chance

Check it out on the way

BEGGAR'S BRIDGE, GLAISDALE Built in 1619 by Tom Ferris, a wealthy merchant who became sheriff of Hull in 1614 and mayor in 1620, this beautiful packhorse bridge has a great legend attached to it. Ferris was the son of a poor Egton farmer and loved Agnes Richardson, daughter of a squire across the River Esk in Glaisdale. Ferris was rejected by the squire as a suitable husband for his daughter because he was 'a beggar'. He resolved to go to sea to seek his fortune, but was prevented from saying farewell to Agnes by flooding. After making his fortune in the Caribbean, Ferris returned to marry Agnes and built the bridge to help future lovers.

THE MOORS NATIONAL PARK CENTRE, WHITBY The HQ of the National Park is set on the banks of the Esk near Danby. Lots of activities are on offer, including climbing, trails, walks and a gallery. www.northyorkmoors.org.uk/visiting/see-and-do/the-moors-national-park-centre

NORTH YORKSHIRE MOORS RAILWAY This heritage railway is the longest in the UK and one of the most significant, running trains between Glaisdale and Pickering and occasionally to Whitby, too. The railway also controls stations on the line and has recreated different periods of railway history at each. www.nymr.co.uk

THE LION INN, BLAKEY RIDGE An atmospheric pub that dates back to the 16th century and sits high on the moors on Blakey Ridge. https://lionblakey.co.uk

of that, judging by the number of people milling about.

The fish was still hot when we parked our tired arses in a sunny spot on a creamy coloured stone wall outside the station. As I tucked in, I thought about the day we'd had. It wasn't over yet, of course, but the walk had been long and tough in places. We'd done about 20 miles (32km) in total, a distance I haven't walked in a very long time. I felt very proud of myself, and even more proud that we'd managed to have a day to ourselves before getting to Whitby. We'd walked in the footsteps of pilgrims, packmen and sinners before us and loved (almost) every moment of quiet. The moments when we had been interrupted by other people felt like an intrusion, a breaking of the spell.

As we whistled back along the Esk Valley Railway on the train we listened to the conversations of the other passengers. A group of four well-oiled women in their glad rags talked about the day they'd had, laughing raucously, slugging down small bottles of pinot grigio.

We pulled into Egton Bridge station and I looked out of the window. Below us, I saw a small village pub with tables outside and a look about it that said 'come inside'. I love country pubs and this one seemed like a good one: it was stone built with a slate roof, and a small grassy garden surrounded by lush flowerbeds and black-painted railings. A traditional, hand-painted pub sign swung gently from a tall post next to the road, while a warm glow from the lights within spoke to me, my tired limbs and my need for comfort. I felt sure I'd find it at the bottom of a glass. I said to Lizzy that I would do anything to be in there right now, supping a cold pint.

An hour later, having failed to find a campsite or a Brit Stop, we parked up in the deserted station car park at Egton Bridge and strolled over to the Postgate Inn, ordering two pints of creamy amber ale that we took outside to the garden and sloshed down almost in one.

DO IT THE HARD WAY

The Esk Valley Walk is a 37-mile (60km) trail that takes in the source of the River Esk and ends in Whitby, going from high moorland to the sea in one long waymarked route. It's a brilliant walk, in a beautiful, quiet valley, with a few lovely pubs along the way. For sections of this walk, you'll see no one else, which is why I have included it in this book. The railway means the walk is linear, which makes it easier and could even allow you to walk sections at a time, although the trains are very infrequent.

Leave the van at Castleton station (go through the gate and park in the small car park) and head out up into the section that covers Blakey Ridge and goes up into the moor to the source of the Esk and the Lion Inn. Alternatively, from Castleton, head down the valley and walk the last 15 miles (24km) to Whitby. Expect it to take four or five hours at least. At Whitby, jump on the train back to Castleton. It takes around 35 minutes and will take you back up the valley.

You will need:
- walking boots
- lunch
- OS maps
- weather-appropriate clothing

CAMPING

There aren't many campsites in the Castleton area, but there are plenty in Whitby if you wanted to take the train first and then walk back to your van.

Wild Slack Farm, Lealholm: This is a lovely, peaceful site with lots of farm animals nearby and basic but good facilities. It's a steep walk to the village pub. https://wildslackfarm.co.uk

DO IT THE EASY WAY

It is possible to drive the whole route, more or less, but the roads can be steep and difficult and weave about, going up and down the dale frequently. You could also divide up the route into stations and walk those sections you want to. There are car parks at Danby, Lealholm, Egton Bridge and Grosmont stations. If you were to pick just one section, I would recommend walking from Lealholm to Egton Bridge or from Castleton to Lealholm.

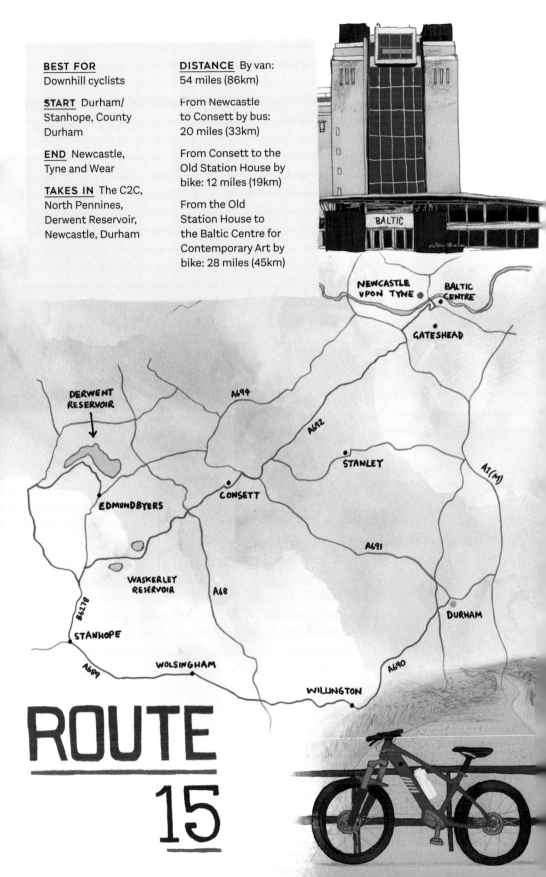

BEST FOR
Downhill cyclists

START Durham/
Stanhope, County
Durham

END Newcastle,
Tyne and Wear

TAKES IN The C2C,
North Pennines,
Derwent Reservoir,
Newcastle, Durham

DISTANCE By van:
54 miles (86km)

From Newcastle
to Consett by bus:
20 miles (33km)

From Consett to the
Old Station House by
bike: 12 miles (19km)

From the Old
Station House to
the Baltic Centre for
Contemporary Art by
bike: 28 miles (45km)

BALTIC

NEWCASTLE
UPON TYNE

BALTIC
CENTRE

GATESHEAD

A694

A692

STANLEY

A1(M)

DERWENT
RESERVOIR

EDMUNDBYERS

CONSETT

A691

WASKERLEY
RESERVOIR

A68

DURHAM

B6278

STANHOPE

A689

WOLSINGHAM

WILLINGTON

A690

ROUTE

15

15

STANHOPE TO NEWCASTLE

ENGLAND'S LONGEST FREEWHEEL,
7 AND 8 AUGUST 2021

The Coast to Coast (C2C) cycle goes from Workington in Cumbria to Sunderland on the east coast. The last third, which starts a little to the north of Stanhope, follows old railway tracks into Newcastle. From a height of 450m (1,476ft) above sea level at the Old Station House, the route drops to sea level in a little under 30 miles (48km), making most of the route downhill.

I FIRST FOUND OUT ABOUT this journey when I was researching trips for a motorhome magazine series that I called 'Great British Adventures'. In those articles, I billed it as 'England's Longest Freewheel'. Quite a promise, if you consider the first leg is 29 miles (47km). Strictly speaking, it wasn't a freewheel, simply because it has some short uphill sections and places

where you do actually have to pedal, but, on the whole, it's a nice easy gradient and for much of it, you could freewheel it you wanted (possibly).

Even if I didn't believe it, I certainly sold it to my kids as 'more than 20 miles where you don't have to pedal. And the wind's always behind you!' They found out the truth very quickly as we set off on a sunny but freezing morning in late April when they were aged about ten and eleven, if that. They haven't let me forget it.

Despite the grumbling and whining I loved it, which I why I sold the trip to Lizzy using the same lie so I could do it again for this book. She'd heard about the previous trip and remained sceptical, but I assured her that it would be worth it for the spectacular ending in Newcastle at the Baltic Centre for Contemporary Art cafe. That was enough of a bonus to swing it as being 'a good idea' and we set off early from our campsite in Durham to get 'on the mountain' early. It was a beautiful day, the wind was favourable (from the south-west) and I was really looking forward to it. On top of that, we had our

e-bikes with us rather than the bog-standard bikes so I was confident it'd be a good day. I expected a little 'purist' grumbling for having e-bikes in the first place when normal bikes would be just as good, if not better, from the lady who has cycled up and over just about everything, but I knew, when it came to it, that she'd be grateful for not having to put up with my grumbling on any uphill sections.

We drove out of Durham on the A689 to Stanhope and then followed the steep and narrow B6278 out of town and up to the Old Station House, a cafe and pit stop that marks the last section of the C2C. The car park was empty, apart from a family who were unloading bikes

and reassembling them. A few people cruised past from Allenheads, but apart from that we were alone on the sunny moor.

After a slight setback in the form of a broken valve on Lizzy's front tyre (tip: carry spare inner tubes), we set off downhill across the moor. With the wind at our backs and smooth gravel under our wheels we moved at a good pace and kept it up as much as we could as we cruised downhill. Without

any dramatic peaks or hills to break up the horizon, the sky was huge and seemingly endless: pale blue with fluffy clouds making a light and weightless ceiling. To the north and west, we could see across the moor towards Hexham. Behind us, the hulk of the heather-clad moor pushed us further down the hill. The reservoirs of Waskerley and Smiddy Shaw reflected blue back at us as we passed. We entered Waskerly wildlife reserve and left the high moor, taking a sharp turn north and cycling through low cuttings before crossing our first viaduct at Hownsgill, a deep, forested valley.

Shortly after, we arrived at the point where we had a decision to make: head into Newcastle or Sunderland. Here, a huge red smelting pot sits on rails at the side of the path, a testament to local history and heavy industry. Consett, the nearest town, was an Industrial Revolution boom town, and was home to Consett Steelworks until it closed in 1980 when the government of the day, under Thatcher, reworked their plans for the steel industry. The town went into steep decline and, despite the steelworks being in profit on the day it closed, it became the UK's unemployment black spot.

We pedalled on, into Consett and around the ring road that now sits on the site of the former steelworks. Here, we found a Tesco and an Asda, side by side, along with outlet stores, out-of-town superstores and new builds. It was all bright and shiny – some might say better – but it's sad to think that we have reverted to type and become a nation of shopkeepers and social climbers, aspiring to values that depend on selfishness and greed. The dignity of those who proudly made the steels for the Blackpool Tower has been stripped away and replaced with McJobs in out-of-town shopping centres, the contents of which were more than likely made in China.

We passed a few streets of back-to-back terraced houses, which sparked a debate about classic, brick-built terraces. I find them warm and homely – much more so than the chocolate-box cottage we romanticise over as a nation – and have always loved living in terraces. For me, they exude community and a kind of wealth that isn't about money or new cars, possessions or flash holidays. I liked being there, in an older part of town, enjoying the pull of gravity as it led us into a Victorian park and out of town along a wooded and steep-sided embankment.

This is where the old railway joined up with the Derwent valley. It brought us to the Derwent Walk Country Park, a fabulous stretch of the route that followed the weaving and changing course of the river, always heading downhill. For the first time, we met people here other than fellow cyclists and got into a conversation while stopping for lunch. 'Hard to believe this was once hell,' a man said as he leaned over a railing to talk to us. We were sitting beside a weir, below a bridge. 'Right here. This was Derwenthaugh Coke Works, part of Europe's biggest steelworks. Beautiful now though, isn't it?' We had to agree. The park was an oasis of calm and serenity. From where we sat, we could see that the river was clean and clear. Behind us was a meadow and, across the river from us, a dense copse.

The park was busy with walkers but, as we left and headed closer to the heart of Newcastle, we saw fewer people on the path. It followed the Derwent to the Tyne along deserted footways beneath roads and alongside factories, through Gateshead and past the Metro Centre (deathly quiet outside) until it reached the coal staiths at the mouth of the River Team. Here, we felt like we were entering modern Tyneside. People jogged, pushed prams, drank coffee in cafes, sat on benches, walked and talked. It was a far cry from the moor but no

Check it out on the way

BEAMISH OPEN AIR MUSEUM, BEAMISH Near to the southern spur of the C2C (direction Sunderland) is Beamish, a world-famous open-air museum of life in the north-east. www.beamish.org.uk

BALTIC CENTRE FOR CONTEMPORARY ARTS, GATESHEAD On the Gateshead side of the Tyne lies Baltic Wharf, an old flour mill that is now an impressive contemporary arts venue. A great place to rest and unwind after a cycle. https://baltic.art

STANHOPE OPEN AIR POOL, STANHOPE One of only a handful of heated open air swimming pools. Owned and run by the community. https://stanhopehosting.co.uk/pool

less enjoyable. The pace slowed and we arrived at Newcastle's bridges; seven of them all close together, each one carrying trains, cars or, in the case of the Millennium Bridge, just people. It was buzzing in the August sunshine. We sat outside a bar opposite the Baltic Centre for Contemporary Art and enjoyed coffee while people watching and checking times for our return lift to Consett.

It was all going great – we found the bus station and the correct stand –

until our bus turned up. It should have been a cycle bus, one of a fleet of buses that operate on some lines in the Newcastle area that will carry bikes, but it wasn't. Covid, once again, had played havoc with the timetable and there wasn't one available. The bus company, Go North East, offers a Bike Bus Guarantee that promises to get you to your destination if their buses can't take you. Seeing as the driver hadn't heard about this, I called their operator, waited for quite a while, then got told they would locate a bike taxi for us. We waited. Before long, a bus turned up that was going to Consett. It wasn't our bus, but was a bike bus, but shouldn't have been. We hopped on, strapped the bikes in the allotted space and paid our fares. Forty minutes later, we disembarked at Consett bus station. For there, we had 12 miles (19km) to cycle back to the Old Station House, most of which was uphill, deserted and exciting.

When we reached the Old Station House, we continued over the moor in the van to explore Derwent Reservoir. The B6278 led us over the wild moor, up to a height of 476m (1,562ft) above sea level and then down into the lush Derwent valley again. We drove around the reservoir and camped at Millshield Picnic Area, a Northumbrian Water approved overnight stop with toilets and recycling almost at the water's edge. We were the only ones there, waking in the morning to another sunny, clear day and a light dew on the grass outside the van.

From there, it was an easy and pleasant run on the A694 into Newcastle via Shotley Bridge and Rowlands Gill to pick up the A1 north.

DO IT THE HARD WAY

We started at Durham, drove to Stanhope, cycled into Newcastle and back, and then drove back into Newcastle. It made a really satisfying loop and the cycle enabled us to savour the city as well as feel the wildness and open skies of the moors in one day. It also feels like a real achievement if you aren't used to cycling distances.

The C2C goes from Workington in the Lakes and finishes at Tynemouth. The last 29-mile (47km) section – from Stanhope to Newcastle – is almost all downhill and 99 per cent of it is off road. It's not steep, which means you can easily manage cycling uphill if you didn't want to do it one way.

Leave the van at the free car park at the Old Station House (they do great hot chocolate) and head east to Newcastle via Consett. Once in Newcastle, you can cycle back or pick up the X70 or X71 bike buses from Newcastle's Eldon Square, which will take you as far as Consett. Thereafter, you have to cycle back from Consett to the van. It's about 12 miles (19km) but all off road on easy-gradient cinder track.

You will need:
- a mountain bike, a gravel bike or an e-bike
- a packed lunch and water
- waterproofs

CAMPING

Durham Grange Caravan and Motorhome Club Site, Durham: A standard
C&MC Club Site but in a difficult position by the side of the A1(M), which
makes it a good stopover, but not so good if you want to explore Durham.
The cycle into town was difficult and not signed. That said, the city is
beautiful. www.caravanclub.co.uk/club-sites/england/north-east-england/
county-durham/durham-grange-caravan-club-site
Millshield Picnic Area, Derwent Water: A Dark Sky stop and overnight
with toilet facilities. Costs £10 for 24 hours. Lovely location.
www.searchforsites.co.uk/marker.php?id=28404
Derwent View Camping, Derwent Water: A small campsite next door
to a cafe and glamping site, right on the water. Book ahead.
www.derwentviewglamping.com

DO IT THE EASY WAY

There are a number of car parks along the C2C where you can park up and
ride out into the wilderness, either way. The moors are spectacular. Riding
from Consett into Newcastle and then taking the bus out again will take you
to the Derwent Park and through some beautiful countryside before arriving
in Newcastle. The X70/X71 buses will bring you back again.

ROUTE 16

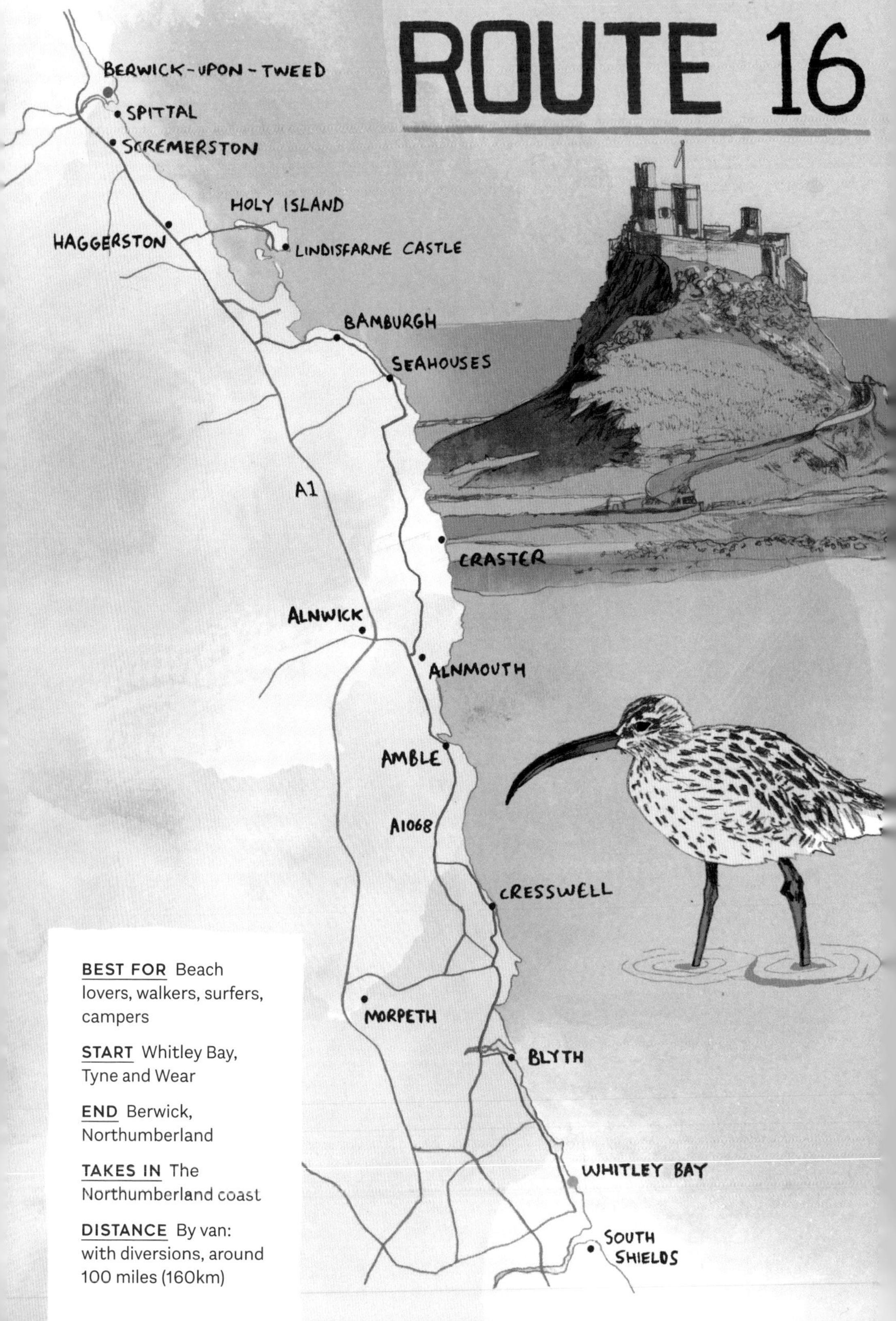

BERWICK-UPON-TWEED

SPITTAL

SCREMERSTON

HOLY ISLAND

HAGGERSTON

LINDISFARNE CASTLE

BAMBURGH

SEAHOUSES

A1

CRASTER

ALNWICK

ALNMOUTH

AMBLE

A1068

CRESSWELL

MORPETH

BLYTH

WHITLEY BAY

SOUTH SHIELDS

BEST FOR Beach lovers, walkers, surfers, campers

START Whitley Bay, Tyne and Wear

END Berwick, Northumberland

TAKES IN The Northumberland coast

DISTANCE By van: with diversions, around 100 miles (160km)

THE NORTHUMBERLAND COAST

DISCOVERING SECRET BEACHES, AUGUST 2021

The Northumberland coast is many things. On its day, it's as good as anywhere, with incredible beaches, fabulous castles and beguiling towns and villages. Yet somehow, despite having a reasonably healthy tourism industry, it gets overlooked by mainstream holidaymakers, who prefer the more clement resorts to the south. Not to worry. That's in our favour. You can still find peace and quiet here, even in high summer.

I HAVE WRITTEN about the Northumberland coast before. In *Take The Slow Road: England and Wales*, I drove up the coast in winter, visiting every beach and getting out of the van momentarily to take pictures or stroll on the sands between snow and hail storms. It was easy to dawdle and find vast, empty beaches. They stretched off into the distance, footprint-less and clean, as we stepped out of the van, the biting wind and drifting, stinging sands sending us back after a few moments. We got up early to see drifts of snow on beach huts and lonely dog walkers, and, of course, no one else. It was

stunningly beautiful, but cold and mostly, when it came to campsites and attractions, closed.

How would it be in the height of summer, I wondered. Would we still be able to find empty beaches in August? When we crawled through Seahouses on a warm August day to find the streets thronging with families in full holiday mode scoffing chips, trailing rock pooling nets and yapping dogs I started to doubt the wisdom of doing it all again. And when we sat in a queue to get into Bamburgh, passing cars parked on the verges on Links Road only to find the car park full, campsites packed and camper vans parked up anywhere they could, I more or less gave up. This was post-lockdown Britain in the summer Spain was banned. We'd have to work a bit harder to find solitude. My Facebook feed was full of horror stories of home, Cornwall, straining under the pressure of the 'summer of the staycation'. Why should it be any different in Northumberland?

But then we got to Berwick. We found the lovely beach at Spittal, by accident, trying to find the Caravan and Motorhome Club Site. Seeing a sign for the promenade, we followed it in the hope that we might be distracted by some surf. We discovered a quiet beach backed by beautiful, elegant stone houses with big gardens and terraces of neat cottages, all within a stone's throw of the beach. Some had gardens that backed on to the promenade. Bounded by the railway and cliffs, Spittal is a dead end kept quiet by a lack of through traffic. If you're there, you're there for a reason (unless you are lost, like us). I fell in love with it straight away and listed it in my 'I could live here' memory bank. Wide streets, a quiet beach and the sea. What's not to love? There were probably no more than 20 people on the sand and 20 more walking along the promenade. It definitely showed promise, though I was still a little undecided about looking for solitude in Northumberland.

A few days later, after we had completed our kayak down the Tweed, I got chatting with Jim, at a caravan site in Chainbridge, about places he'd been. He gave me the clue I was looking for.

But first I needed to follow a clue of my own. In 2010, I had sat on the step of my old Type 2 camper van, whipping up mayonnaise to go with a lobster I had 'caught' while 'helping' on a fishing boat from Holy Island. As I sat on the step by the sliding door I ruminated on all things 'camper van' for the TV cameras that were making *One Man and his Campervan* for BBC2, a series I presented.

As I'd looked out of the van from this simple, small park-up spot I'd been able to see the coastline and the beach below me and wondered what it

would be like to come back here and surf, sometime, anytime, when the cameras weren't being shoved in my face every day and the pressure of cooking for the camera was a thing of the past.

I wasn't sure which beach it was or how I had got there, but I knew it was north of Lindisfarne and had an idea it was near Cocklawburn Beach. We headed off to find it, to see if it was as idyllic as I remembered. Cocklawburn Beach lies on a no through road just south of Berwick, beyond the tiny village of Scremerston, across the mainline railway. There are a couple of small car parks above the beach. I felt sure one of them would be my spot.

Driving along the road that skirts the coast I knew we were in the right place. As we pulled up to the lay-by at the head of the beach I was absolutely positive. A car pulled out, leaving us the prime position on the little headland. We pulled in and I opened the slider. This was it! Almost exactly where I had parked 11 years earlier. I never thought I would come back here! Despite the wind and the light drizzle, it was still just as beautiful. A series of small bays stretched out to the north and south. In front of us, despite the strong onshore wind, a reef was creating some half surfable waves. I got changed into my wetsuit quickly – I wasn't going to miss this chance to do what I had dreamed of – and paddled out into the beautiful clear water. Behind me on the beach, a woman in a bikini played with her four young children in the water, while the wind frothed up the waves and the light drizzle fell. A few other people walked the sands, while a family sat in their motorhome watching.

Talking to Jim at the Chainbridge campsite changed my mind about including a route in this book about the Northumberland coast. I had come here expecting what I had found before but had been disappointed at the honeypots, Bamburgh and Seahouses. I should have known it would take a little sideways thinking to see Northumberland at its best, without the baying hordes, in summer, and it was Jim who showed me the way.

I said I was keen to go to Holy Island, having not been there for more than ten years, but was afraid it would be too busy. He told me that he had driven over the tidal causeway on an evening when the tide had been full all day, which meant no one was able to cross, so, by the time the tide had dropped enough, most people were queuing on the causeway to get home. Jim waited and then drove over to the island late in the afternoon, on the dropping tide, having it almost to himself. I liked the idea of this. It felt like a neat workaround I could cope with. Yes, you can still visit busy tourist attractions and feel like you are off the beaten track, but you just need to time it right. Of course!

I checked the tide tables. In a couple of days' time the high tide would be receding at about 18.30, meaning that those 'stuck' on the island for the day would be able to get off and we'd be able to get on for the evening. Sure enough, when we turned up to wait on the mainland for the tide to draw back enough to cross the causeway on to Holy Island, there was a queue of

cars waiting for the last fingers of the tide to recede so they could return to the mainland. Just one small patch of it was still covered. When it had dropped enough for the first cautious motorists to cross, they edged through the water and drove away, their cars dripping with seawater.

We walked up the causeway to watch the cars go by, take pictures and wait until the queue had gone. The causeway crosses a channel in the mudflats and then the mudflats themselves, which are about 1 mile (1.6km) across. Just in the first 27m (30 yards) of being on the salt marsh we saw samphire and orache, eelgrass and salt-marsh grass. Clouds of busy ringed plovers and sandpipers darted about, flying low and fast with furious beats. A juvenile curlew waded close by, oblivious.

We made it on to the island at about 6.30 p.m. The huge car park was deserted bar a dozen or so cars, and the streets were quiet. Most people seemed to be in the three village pubs, which meant there wasn't a table to be had. No problem, we thought, we'll enjoy the island while they eat. We walked to the ruined priory and then on to the promontory above it. The beach below it was deserted so we walked along the pebbled shore and picked up sea glass and litter, looking

Check it out on the way

CRASTER Kippers! Also, park here for a coastal walk to Dunstanburgh Castle. It can be a bit tricky with parking so get there early. www.visitcraster.org.uk

AMBLE Great fishing town with a nice seafront, lots of seafood shacks and a quirky harbour village. www.ambleharbourvillage.co.uk

WARKWORTH CASTLE, WARKWORTH Stunning castle on a bend in the river. www.english-heritage.org.uk/visit/places/warkworth-castle-and-hermitage

ALNMOUTH The 'Tobermory of Northumberland' is a pretty seaside village on a beautiful estuary.

BAMBURGH CASTLE, BAMBURGH Another of Northumberland's stunning castles. www.bamburghcastle.com

across to Bamburgh and the mainland. Lindisfarne Castle, once a fort, then a Lutyens-designed holiday home, now a National Trust property, to our left, was ever present. We encountered few people, other than a group of vloggers, one of who declared 'Instagram Darling' (I am not kidding) as she changed her jacket for a photo.

As we drove away, the evening light was spectacular, illuminating the castle and the refuge hut on the causeway with cool orange light. It really was the best time to visit.

We drove further south the following day, back through Seahouses and Beadnell, avoiding the shanty town of statics, to a tiny road leading us to a small car park at the southern end of Beadnell Bay. Lizzy took off her shoes to walk through the dunes to the beach. It was a warm day, with thin wispy cloud and little wind. When we emerged from the marram grass we looked out at a low-tide beach with maybe three of four people on it. Most of them were walking. Lizzy guided me off to the south to show me her favourite beach, which we reached via the coast path. It led us around a low headland of rocks with flat areas of reef, marked on the map as Snook.

We walked through the dunes, across the cool, still-damp sand, pushing our way through the tall grasses and came to a small arc of sandy beach with a rocky reef in the middle and points on either side. There was no one on the

beach. A couple walked along the coast path. It was perfect. We walked to the waterline.

Without talking to Lizzy, I started to undress, piling my clothes and camera on top of my boots, on a rock I felt sure wouldn't be inundated by the small swell. I hadn't got any swimming trunks or a towel with me so skinny dipping was the only option, if I wanted to swim. I waited until the couple were out of sight, then took off my undies and waded into the sea. Lizzy followed.

The beach was gently shelving so it took us a while to get deep enough to dive in and swim. With no one to watch us, we swam a little and then ran up the beach to put our clothes on again.

If ever there were a standard for finding a beach that's off the beaten track it is the ability to go skinny dipping. If you can take off your clothes and run into the sea without fear of recrimination or arrest then you've scored. Some people don't mind onlookers and thrive on shock, but I don't. I love to skinny dip, but I don't want to do it in company, thank you. This beach was perfect for it.

I realised then that I had been wrong about the Northumberland coast. It's got its hotspots and favourite places, but even then it can be worked around. It's cooler than Cornwall or Devon and the sea is most definitely for the hardy, but it's absolutely stunning. There are spots where you can find a place to call your own or rip off your clothes, if you feel the need. Along the way, we found a few of these places. Little bays with no one on them. A drop down to a sandy beach without footprints. Places of delicious calm and eye-opening beauty. Golden sands and golden opportunities.

We camped by the side of the beach at Druridge Bay, another glorious sweep of sand between Amble and Cresswell, with just a short walk between the tiny car park and the sea. At dawn, we wandered out of the van in our swimming costumes and swam again, in the orange glow of the sunrise, on the high tide. As always, the thrill of cold water on my skin made me feel alive for hours after. It's something that I can't explain, that is to do with happy hormones and chemicals. Something about the cold water, and our body's reaction to it, triggers feelings of ecstasy, similar to those experienced during sport. It's a feeling of well-being, of being and doing that's far away from chips and seagulls, ice creams and guest houses, TV and amusement arcades. It's the thing about nature, about being alone in the world, if only for a moment. Of being me, simply and honestly. And I love it.

We left Northumberland at Blyth, taking the A1 towards home, still glowing with the morning's swim and the solitude we'd found in Northumberland, even in the middle of August in the middle of the busiest summer for British holidays in living memory. I felt we'd found it: a place for quiet, sandwiched between Blyth and Berwick. A coastline of dunes and sand, rock and sea, offshore islands and nature, neglected by many, loved by us. I vowed to return again.

DO IT THE HARD WAY

There is no hard way to explore the Northumberland coast. You just have to point the van to the middle of the UK. Start at Whitley Bay and head north if you're coming from the south. Start at Berwick-upon-Tweed if you are coming from the north. Hug the coast as much as you can. A very good map will be useful as you may need to go down some tiny lanes to find the prime spots. Many of the best, out-of-the-way places are down roads that lead only to the sea.

Along the way, you'll switch between harbour towns (Amble), stunning castles and estuaries (Alnwick, Bamburgh, Alnmouth, Dunstanburgh), lovely fishing villages (Craster), huge open beaches (Beadnell, Druridge Bay, Bamburgh) and tiny coves (Football Hole). There is variety, too, with offshore islands offering trips to see wildlife (the Farne Islands and Coquet Island), a Holy Island (Lindisfarne) and a lighthouse (St Mary's Island).

Some walk the coast or even cycle, but exploring by van is just as good. Take a picnic and enjoy the view.

You will need:
- OS maps
- a swimming cossie (or not!)
- binoculars

CAMPING

Budle Farm Campsite, Bamburgh:
A gem of a place adjacent to
Bamburgh and right on Budle Bay.
No website – just turn up and text
the owner on 07707 299430.

Beadnell Bay Camping and Caravan Club Site, Beadnell: This is a huge site on the dune slacks behind Beadnell Bay. Right on the coast but big enough for hundreds of campers. www.campingandcaravanningclub.co.uk/campsites/uk/northumberland/chathill/beadnell-bay-camping-and-caravanning-club-site

Old Hartley Caravan and Motorhome Club Site, Whitley Bay: Situated on the coast above St Mary's Island, this site has some of the best views. A great start point for your adventures in Northumberland. www.caravanclub.co.uk/club-sites/england/north-east-england/tyne--wear/old-hartley-caravan-club-site

Berwick Seaview Caravan Club Site, Spittal: A brilliantly situated site overlooking the sea at Berwick. Nice wardens and good facilities, as usual. One of the best C&MC sites we've been to. www.caravanclub.co.uk/club-sites/england/north-east-england/northumberland/berwick-seaview-caravan-club-site/

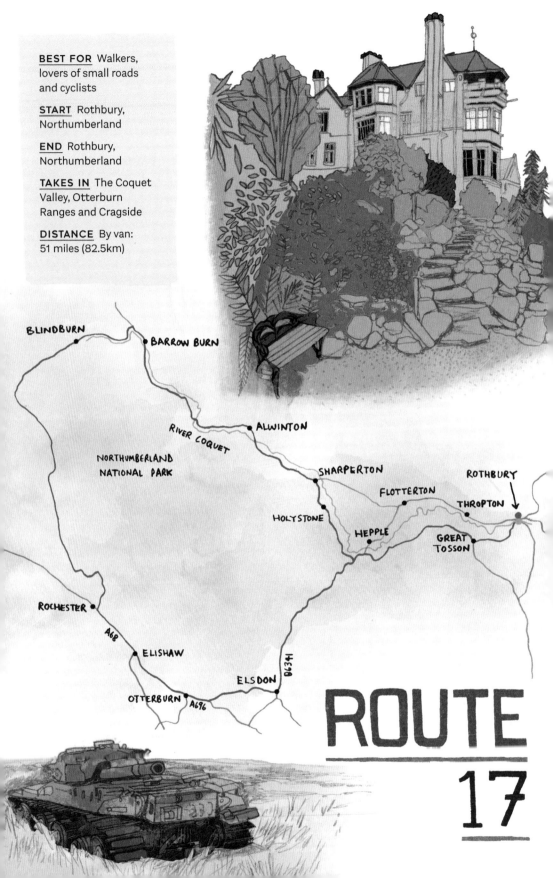

BEST FOR Walkers, lovers of small roads and cyclists

START Rothbury, Northumberland

END Rothbury, Northumberland

TAKES IN The Coquet Valley, Otterburn Ranges and Cragside

DISTANCE By van: 51 miles (82.5km)

BLINDBURN

BARROW BURN

RIVER COQUET

ALWINTON

NORTHUMBERLAND NATIONAL PARK

SHARPERTON

ROTHBURY

FLOTTERTON

THROPTON

HOLYSTONE

HEPPLE

GREAT TOSSON

ROCHESTER

A68

ELISHAW

B6341

ELSDON

OTTERBURN

A696

ROUTE

17

17

THE OTTERBURN RANGES

INTO THE GREAT NOTHING, AUGUST 2021

In a county that's generally unpopulated, empty and wild, the Otterburn Ranges must surely take the prize for being the most remote and difficult-to-access part of it. That's some accolade. Owned by the MoD and off limits to all when the firing ranges are in use, it really is a beautiful and remote area that's bordered on one side by Scotland, with the Cheviots to the north and the vast emptiness of Kielder Forest to the west.

AT ALWINTON, we weaved our way through the narrow village, past the Rose and Thistle pub, waved at the bikers having a pint outside, and drove straight on. A sign at the side of the road indicated that this was a no through road, but only after 12 miles (19km). At this point, the Coquet Valley was wide and flat, with hills either side and pasture in the middle that was bisected by

the river, to our left. It soon began to close in on us as the single track headed higher on to the moors and the river cut deeper into the valley. We drove over cattle grids, and further on, over undulating ridges and around sharp bends, past gorges with the river, now the Upper Coquet, running fast and deep below us. We passed a farm and a few houses, crossed a bridge and ran alongside a meadow. The progress was slow.

We drove alongside drystone walls with fields and meadows behind and open moorland above. The further we got, the more extreme the landscape became, the steeper the valley sides and the faster the river. Each mile took us deeper into the wilderness. At points along the way, we came across MoD notices and gates, the places where the red flag flies on days when the army practises shooting. All the gates remained open so we pressed on, even though we felt that the road could come to an abrupt end at any time. We drove on for all of the 12 miles (19km), until the river was just a stream. We passed a postman and a pulled over for a plumber who was rushing to get somewhere, but other than that it was just hundreds of begrudging sheep – some of which wandered out of our path lazily, as we slowed to avoid them, as if we didn't belong up here with them – the odd crane, lots of grey wagtails

and a few birds of prey cruising overhead. Dotted around the fields were sheepfolds, circular drystone pens for sheep to shelter in during bad weather. Some appeared well used, others filled with nettles and bracken. In other places, we saw unidentified mounds or shapes in the valley bottom.

We reached a car park that was marked on the OS map as the end of the road. This was the 12-mile (19km) limit. Here, we wandered over the moor in a drizzle to find the low mounds of a Roman camp in the rough grass at the end of a track. At the top of the hill lay Scotland, and a signpost indicating the path of the Pennine Way, a long-distance footpath. We looked across the valley at the earthworks on the opposite hillside. Even in times of more clement weather, a posting here must have been brutal.

Despite it being marked on the map as the end of the road, it

seemed this was just a stop. The tarmac continued up the steep hillside opposite and disappeared over the ridge. We stopped for lunch and to let the drizzle abate a little before carrying on. At the top of the hill, the scenery changed. From being in a tiny valley with a tiny river, we climbed out of it and on to the tops, confronted by massive views and undulating moorland, with hills in the far distance. It was huge, with a dark and heavy sky sitting over us like a blanket. The colours – muted purples, greens and browns – filled the lens of my camera.

Colour perspective made the distant hills become ever greyer the nearer to the horizon they were. Punctuated by white blobs of sheep, the hills dipped into creeks and gorges that we couldn't see. To our left, there was a swift and sudden movement as a stag, scared by our presence, leapt over bracken and grasses to get away from us. He disappeared into one of the hidden valleys. The last we saw of him was his white tail as he sprang away.

We were on the Roman road now, and as we descended slowly it lay in

front of us, shining like a silver ribbon. Either side was lush green grass and heather, with the odd sheep wandering across the road in front of us. On the left, we saw an abandoned tank and destroyed military vehicles that were, we assume, used for target practice during firing. The camouflage hid them well and we imagined how hard it must be for the squaddies to have to fight in such a huge, open landscape.

We continued to descend, passing a couple of farms, finally arriving, after another 8 miles (13km), rather abruptly, at the A68. It seemed a little too sudden to be confronted with traffic and 'civilisation' so quickly. We drove on, back towards Rothbury on the B6341, itself a fabulous drive, if a bit easier than the rough single track we'd just done 20 miles (32km) on.

We pulled into Cragside to look around the house and garden. I wanted to see it because of its champion trees (the largest known trees of a particular species), but also because it was ultra-modern in its day. The place was busy with people, a complete contrast to where we'd just been, and there was a queue for the car park. The house was quite stunning, but the garden moved me more. It was easy to get annoyed with riches, the huge marble fireplace, the opulent rooms and the art collecting, but harder to be cross with nature, no matter how fabricated it is. Having been designed and planted by Lady Armstrong, wife of the 'great' inventor, arms manufacturer and industrialist in the 1840s, the trees were huge, standing tall and almost dwarfing the house itself. I found it hard to imagine the landscape as it had been before the house was built and the gardens created. It was a simple fishing lodge on a crag above a river, presumably much like the landscape we'd just been in. Today, it was very different from the moor. It was so managed and yet still felt so wild and free, a testament to the wisdom of Lady Armstrong and the strong arms of those who worked for her.

I felt, however, that the countryside had somehow been betrayed and I didn't know which was better or more meaningful – the moor or the garden. The Victorians believed in romanticism and creating perfect landscapes were a part of that. It was ultra-modern to believe in Arcadian landscapes evoking simpler, better times, even more so to be able to create them. But I wondered which was the truth. Was the empty moor, with its thousands of acres of grazed, harsh, low scrub, pockets of trees and gorges any more real or genuine than this stunning garden with its huge pines, sculpted paths and beautiful iron bridge?

One of them was absolutely empty, the other thronged with milling hordes, so it wasn't hard to see where the attraction lay. Mind you, the Otterburn Ranges doesn't have a gift shop and oat milk lattes.

And that's why it's fabulous.

DO IT THE HARD WAY

The Otterburn Ranges cover an area of almost 100 square miles (250 square km) in the Cheviot Hills and take up around a quarter of the Northumberland National Park. They are very sparsely populated, with only a few farms in the area. Some of the Ranges enjoy open access, while other parts – the majority – have permitted access only when the MoD isn't firing and only on footpaths and bridleways.

Getting to the ranges is relatively easy. The B6341 from Alnwick passes Cragside and Rothbury before heading to Thropton and you can then turn onto Greenside Bank and

You will need:
- OS maps
- a pair of comfortable shoes

Check it out on the way

CRAGSIDE, ROTHBURY

An incredible house, full of the latest Victorian wizardry and with a garden full of champion trees. As the original smart home, Cragside was created out of virtually nothing and was the first home to use hydraulics and hydroelectricity. The garden was planted and created and contains remarkable trees. There is a fantastic 6-mile (9.7km) carriage drive that makes an easy cycle, with a great downhill at the end. www. nationaltrust.org.uk/cragside follow the road to reach Alwinton. At Alwinton, there is a sign that says the road is a no through road, but ignore this. Continue onwards to Blindburn, unless there are red flags flying, in which case you may not be able to.

After Blindburn, the road passes close to the Scottish border and the Roman camp of Chew Green, then it heads uphill steeply, following the rough course of the Roman road, Dere Street, and reaches a height of around 500m (1,640ft) above sea level. The road then goes downhill in a straight line (more or less) to Rochester and the A68. Follow the A696 to pick up the B6341, which will take you back to Rothbury.

Check the firing dates and times here: www.gov.uk/government/publications/otterburn-firing-times

CAMPING

Clennell Hall Riverside Holiday Park, Alwinton: It's a hotel and static park as well as a campsite. Set in lovely countryside close to Alwinton. www.clennellhall.co.uk

ROUTE 18

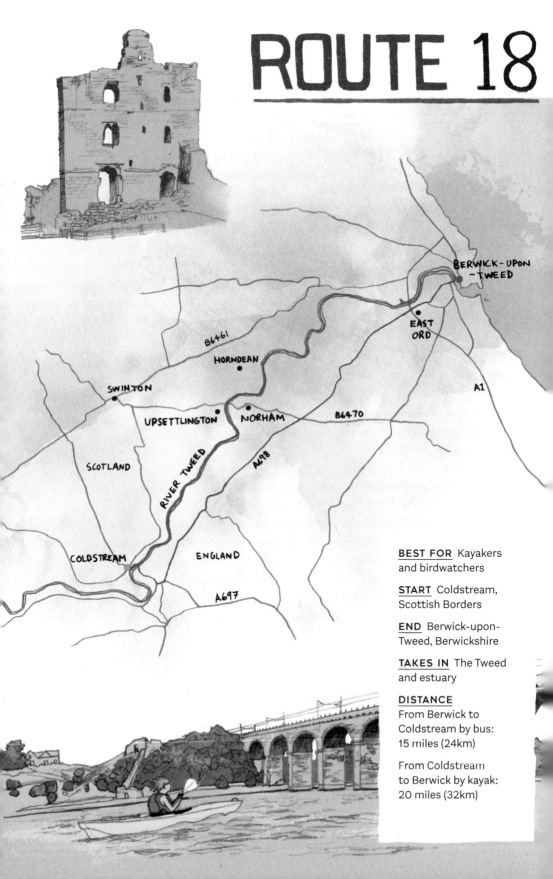

BERWICK-UPON-TWEED

EAST ORD

B6461

HORNDEAN

SWINTON

UPSETTLINGTON

NORHAM

B6470

A1

SCOTLAND

RIVER TWEED

A698

COLDSTREAM

ENGLAND

A697

BEST FOR Kayakers and birdwatchers

START Coldstream, Scottish Borders

END Berwick-upon-Tweed, Berwickshire

TAKES IN The Tweed and estuary

DISTANCE
From Berwick to Coldstream by bus:
15 miles (24km)

From Coldstream to Berwick by kayak:
20 miles (32km)

THE TWEED VALLEY

KAYAKING THE BORDERLANDS,
7 AND 8 AUGUST 2021

The Tweed marks the boundary between Scotland and England for the last 20 miles (32km) of its length. It's famous for salmon fishing and for seabirds. This easy journey by kayak along the border will bring you to Berwick-upon-Tweed past castles and crags, through woods and under historic bridges. And the only people you'll see along the way are the fly fishermen.

THE PHONE RANG when we were about halfway back to Berwick-upon-Tweed. We'd already dropped off the kayaks and all our paddling kit under the bridge at Coldstream and were heading to a parking spot under the new road bridge over the Tweed. The next part of the plan involved getting on a bus to take us back to the kayaks and then making our way down the river – 20 miles (32km) or so – to the van. Simple.

The phone call didn't change anything, but it did change my focus a little. It was a researcher from *The Jeremy Vine* show on Radio 2 asking if I would appear to talk about caravans and why I liked them. The 'opposing' caller would be Mike Parry, a broadcaster who had recently been in the news spouting some interesting opinions on caravans.

I agreed, on the basis that it might be good for 'publicity' for my books, and agreed a time to be available on the phone. It was too good an opportunity to pass up, I thought, so I hoped that I would have some kind of signal on the river in a few hours' time. I'll admit I was looking forward to it.

In the meantime, we had an adventure to get on with. The Tweed is a river that isn't often kayaked, and certainly not in the way that somewhere like the Wye is. There are few operators locally who hire kayaks, and they were busy, so we brought our own. For me, this was a sign that we were about to see the Tweed in a way that few people do, and that meant we'd be getting off the beaten track in true style.

We chose Coldstream as a starting point because it's easy to get to the river and launch there and the bus (the 67 to Kelso) goes past. The driver even stopped for us right on the bridge so we could save ourselves a walk from the bus stop in town. The bridge is a great start point. You can avoid the weir by launching below it, which means you don't have to tackle any obstacles for a few miles.

We kitted up, slid off the bank and started paddling, looking for the fastest and deepest water to take us quickly. A fisherman and his ghillie were casting into the stream a few hundred metres below us and stopped to let us past. We waved at them as we went by and they wished us luck on the river, asking how far we were going. 'All the way to Berwick,' we replied. Or so we hoped.

The going was good and the river, although low, was forgiving and easy. The occasional rapid would give us a whoosh and a bit of a boost, but for the most part it was easy and flat water. The skill was finding where the faster water was flowing to avoid slogging it out for the whole 20 miles (32km). We paddled over a couple of low weirs, which weren't much of problem, and through some really nice fast and narrow sections. As we paddled, we saw plenty of birdlife, from red kites above us to the iridescent blue of a darting kingfisher, dippers, grey wagtails and even what we thought might have been a peregrine falcon. Every so often, we met fly fishermen in waders or in oar-powered punts, who waved us past and joked that there were no fish. They all said more or less the same thing: 'Send the salmon up to us!'

At 12.55 p.m. we rounded a bend and came across a beach of shingle. The wind started to pick up so, when my phone rang, I used my splash deck to shelter from it, putting it over my head. I must have looked a bit strange to the fishermen nearby. Lizzy sat down and tucked into her lunch, while I waited to be put through to the studio. When Jeremy Vine introduced me I explained where I was and how lovely it was and that it was my van that had brought us on this adventure. That was about all I had a chance to say, with the exception of a few snippets.

Mike Parry launched into a scathing and rather ignorant and baseless attack on caravans, no doubt based solely on some terrible trauma from his past. I listened – and didn't interrupt – out of politeness, but he just wouldn't shut up. I couldn't believe some of the things he was saying. I just had to snigger. He wanted to ban caravans from the roads so he wouldn't have to sit behind them on the A14 on the way to his holiday home. I suggested he should drive at night instead. When he said that camping was all about eating baked beans, I invited him for tea. He said that caravans were about

being far away from civilisation. I didn't have the chance to tell him that I'd camped in the middle of Paris, San Sebastián, Bilbao, Berlin, Copenhagen, York and Tallinn.

It was rather humiliating, if I am honest, and I was cross for allowing myself to be taken for a ride by the show. I felt dirty. They wanted an argument, but I wasn't prepared to give it to them. I couldn't understand how someone could be so obnoxious about somebody else's hobby because it inconvenienced him a little bit. I hung up and got back to the river, but not before taking a moment to check Twitter. I noticed I wasn't alone in thinking people were dumbfounded by his ignorance and bigoted, narrow-minded views. A cheap Michael Winner, someone commented.

A pair of fishermen were casting their lines into the deep part of the river. Beyond that, standing on an outcrop, I could see the ruins of Norham Castle above the trees. The wind rustled the willows on the bank and the clouds rushed past above. I was glad I was here. It was a blessing to be on the river rather than on some awful road in East Anglia (the A14 is among the worst

Check it out on the way

THE GRANARY GALLERY, BERWICK-UPON-TWEED This is a cafe and art space that's free and a nice place to hang out. They also have rooms for YHA members. www.maltingsberwick.co.uk

NORHAM CASTLE, NORHAM A ruin, but a nice one, situated on a crag overlooking the Tweed. It was once of huge importance and saw a whole lot of action with the Scots. www.english-heritage.org.uk/visit/places/norham-castle

BERWICK-UPON-TWEED, THE CITY WALLS AND RAMPARTS Berwick has an interesting history, some lovely arty shops, a great waste-free shop and some cool eateries. Book ahead for Audela or Atelier or you'll end up in the beautiful chaos that is Limoncello Restaurant. After dinner, walk the ramparts. www.english-heritage.org.uk/visit/places/berwick-upon-tweed-castle-and-ramparts

roads I have ever driven on) so I had my lunch, sat back in my kayak and headed off down the river again.

Norham was about the halfway mark and felt like a watershed. We were over the worst. Or so we thought. The wind had started to come up, which meant we had to criss-cross the meandering river looking for the best shelter beneath trees and outcrops. At Union Bridge, a few miles downstream from Norham, we reached the upper reaches of the tidal river. The river made a right turn, heading east and straight into the wind for a long stretch. We paddled into the southern shore and stayed close to the bank, paddles scraping the bottom as we tried to avoid the gusts. In the middle of the river the chop was breaking into white water as the wind fought against the flow and the outgoing tide. Thanks goodness, I thought, that the bus times had coincided with high tide. It would have been awful to paddle against the incoming tide as well as the wind. As it was, the tide pulled us ever

closer to the sea, even though progress was tough and slow.

I was tired by now and really feeling the effort my arms were making. My shoulders and neck ached and I thought about what it meant to 'press on' when you are tired. We had no choice, of course, other than to continue. To stop now would mean pulling our kayaks on to the mudflats and walking back to Berwick across the fields. There would be no way to retrieve them easily as there were no roads. While it was painful, we just had to continue. It gave me a real sense of pride in completing the journey, when I eventually did, because I knew that moment was tough going. It reminded me of the times I have urged my children to carry on cycling or walking when we had come too far to go back, but the end seemed so far away they felt they couldn't keep going. I felt sorry for them and what I had put them through on occasions. But they were better for it, I told myself, as I put in another stroke and my shoulders screamed at me to stop. It was time to apply my own teachings to myself. The harder the wind blew, the more I told myself to take it one stroke at a time and to just keep paddling.

In the distance, I could see a bridge through the trees, which gave me a little boost, but it took an age to get there – it was about 2 miles (3.2km) – and when we did I realised it was the bridge to the A1. This meant we still had another 2 miles (3.2km) to the rail bridge and the finish. The river helped a little at this point as it took a left turn towards the north for a while,

giving us precious shelter from the easterly wind. We stuck to the southern bank and paddled past a gathering of about 20 herons as well as oystercatchers, lapwings, egrets, turnstones and sandpipers. We were able to get really close to them as we were in kayaks but still not close enough to get photos with my small waterproof camera. Further downstream, we encountered whooper swans among a gang of mute swans cruising the river

without a ruffled feather between them, while we struggled against the wind constantly.

We paddled into the middle of the river to pass under the road bridge and to get photographs of us doing so. It wasn't easy as the wind kept whipping my boat sideways so I couldn't get the right angle and Lizzy couldn't hear me above the wind. Eventually, I gave up trying to get the perfect shot and paddled into the bank, where the van was waiting.

The kettle went on before our kit came off and we changed into warm, dry clothes. It didn't take long before we were sitting with our drinks on the step on the van – our favourite place to sit – and looked back at the river. All in all, we agreed, it had been a good day. The only people we'd seen were jolly fishermen. The only person I'd spoken to – other than Lizzy – was professional loudmouth Mike Parry.

Oh well. You can't have everything.

DO IT THE HARD WAY

The area around Berwick is lovely and actually quite benign, despite the Cheviot Hills brooding darkly to the south. The area is fantastic – and very under-visited compared with other places – so it's perfect for getting away from it all. The coast is lovely, too, so perhaps combine this trip with a drive around the Cheviots (Route 17) and a trip down the coast.

Anyway. There is an ingress point just below the weir beneath the Coldstream Bridge. Here, you can park up in a lay-by and portage your boats down to the river. It's an easy in. Thereafter, you can paddle to Berwick. It'll take a few hours (probably around five) and will take you past the Union Chain Bridge Bus and Norham Castle. There are a couple of small weirs to watch for, but they are easily paddleable. If you are dropping the boats and then leaving the van in Berwick there is a free parking space beneath the new road bridge. This is very handy for reloading boats, and just up the road from the bus stop for the number 67, which will take you to Coldstream to recover the boats.

Make sure you time your paddle with the bus but also with the outgoing tide so you won't have to paddle against it on the incoming. Depart Coldstream around two hours before high tide.

You will need:
- a kayak and paddles
- a mobile phone (in a waterproof case)
- a buoyancy device
- food and drink

CAMPING

Berwick Caravan and Motorhome Club Site, Berwick-upon-Tweed: A brilliantly situated site overlooking the sea at Berwick. Nice wardens and good facilities as usual. One of the best C&MC sites we've been to. www.caravanclub.co.uk/club-sites/england/north-east-england/

northumberland/berwick-seaview-caravan-club-site
Chainbridge Caravan Site, Horncliffe: An adults-only site that's neat and well kept with fantastic facilities, including underfloor heating in the showers! www.chainbridgecaravansite.co.uk

DO IT THE EASY WAY

As the Tweed is tidal you can do an up and back with the tide. This means putting in a couple of hours before high tide at Berwick, paddling with the tide upstream (the limit of the tide is just above Chainbridge) and then paddling back to Berwick with the outgoing tide.

For local kayak hire and tuition, try http://active4seasons.co.uk or www.driftwoodadventure.org

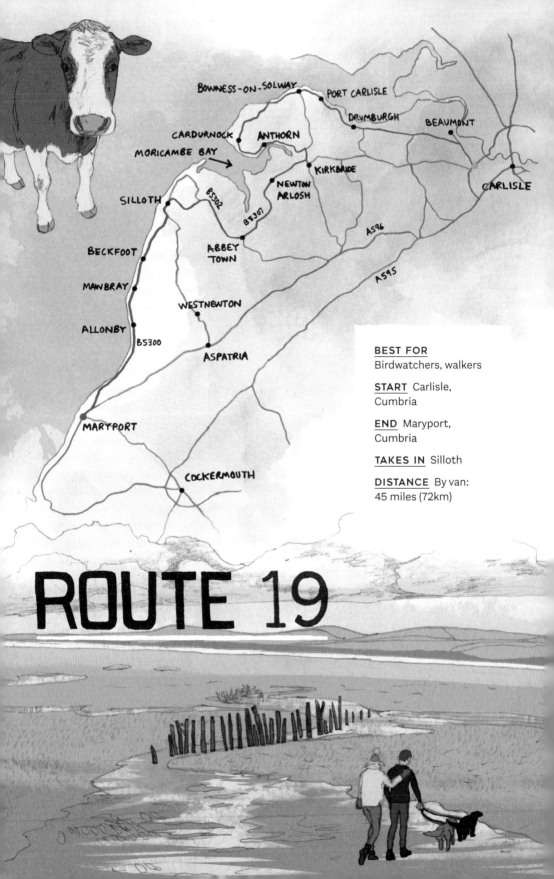

BOWNESS-ON-SOLWAY   PORT CARLISLE

DRUMBURGH

BEAUMONT

CARDURNOCK   ANTHORN

MORICAMBE BAY

KIRKBRIDE

CARLISLE

NEWTON
ARLOSH

SILLOTH

BS302

BS307

A596

ABBEY
TOWN

A595

BECKFOOT

MAWBRAY

WESTNEWTON

ALLONBY

BS300

ASPATRIA

MARYPORT

COCKERMOUTH

BEST FOR
Birdwatchers, walkers

START Carlisle,
Cumbria

END Maryport,
Cumbria

TAKES IN Silloth

DISTANCE By van:
45 miles (72km)

ROUTE 19

19

THE SOLWAY FIRTH

ISOLATION ON THE SOLWAY FIRTH, OCTOBER 2021

As the area with one of the least popular OS maps for England, the Solway Firth is a surprise. But then it's also a tease, because much of what was once here is now gone. But don't miss it on your way to the Lakes. It's atmospheric and ethereal, wild and remote. And, because it's estuarine, the tide brings constant change. There are tantalising glimpses of the Roman past all along the route.

THERE ARE 403 ORDNANCE SURVEY Explorer maps in total, covering the land mass of Great Britain. Some are more popular than others, with Yr Wyddfa (Snowdon) being the most popular. Having seen photos of the queues of people waiting to summit the mountain in 2020 it definitely wasn't on my list of places to explore for this book. However, the idea that there could be a chart based on sales figures piqued my interest. Sure enough, I found an article from the OS archives naming their least popular maps. They even produced a chart for maps of England. Perhaps unsurprisingly the majority of the top ten least-selling were in Lincolnshire. But one that caught my attention was the entry for number six. This was the Solway Firth, the area of England that faces off against Galloway across the huge estuary.

When I looked at the map itself I noticed that the area included Bowness-on-Solway, the point that marks the western end of Hadrian's Wall. How could it have been so overlooked? And why should it be so unpopular?

I set off to find out.

It's true that Hadrian's Wall's best bits are east of Carlisle where it is still possible to admire the actual wall, whereas in the Solway Firth things have become a little less easy to see. The course of the wall is plotted on maps but little remains. Some of it, I understand, was taken to make buildings and churches, while the fort at the very end point remains unexcavated in Bowness.

I didn't let that put me off. I headed out of Carlisle on a very mizzly day. The rain was the sort that settles in for the day and soaks you thoroughly in minutes, even though the drops are fine. The Irish would call it 'soft'. It didn't make for good exploring. I headed along the coast towards Port Carlisle and followed the dead straight road along the estuary that follows the course of Vallum, the huge ditch that traces the route of the wall. Running just below

Check it out on the way

SENHOUSE ROMAN MUSEUM, MARYPORT A museum with artefacts collected by the Senhouse family from the 1570s onwards, and housed in the former battery. www.senhousemuseum.co.uk
THE LAKE DISTRICT COAST AQUARIUM, MARYPORT
Situated on the extensive quayside in Maryport. Great for kids. www.maryportaquarium.co.uk
SOLWAY WETLANDS CENTRE, BOWNESS-ON-SOLWAY
First point of call for those looking for information about the AONB's work and the wildlife to be seen here. www.solwaywetlands.org.uk

the high spring tide mark, it occasionally gets flooded. I loved this road. On one side was the ditch and embankment, on the other the salt marsh and then the estuary. Beyond that, Scotland.

As I drove towards Kirkbride, my stop for the night, along the coast I sensed the nature of the place. It felt like a real frontier, with the Galloway hills mysteriously dark on the horizon. This was the northernmost corner of the Roman Empire and beyond lay the crazy Picts, lawlessness and chaos. Some of the houses reminded me of crofter cottages with fat, squat walls and a window either side of the door. Other houses were grander, made from brick and with columns outside. I passed Anthorn Radio Station on the perimeter road. As the antennas pierced the gloom, I was reminded of the old wartime emplacements in Westward Ho!. They too sat at the edge on a forgotten piece of land. The fields were flat all around.

I passed a difficult night in the van outside the Inn at the Bush in Kirkbride, thanks to a noisy bunch of drunken revellers who shouted, banged and made merry while I tried to sleep inside.

I woke at first light. I opened the sliding door and looked out at the still-dark dawn. Birds were singing and there was heavy dew on the windscreen. The skies, thankfully, were clear. I parked up and set off to find a spot for breakfast at the side of the estuary from where I could walk.

I love being up before anyone else because it feels like you get a chance to look at the world like many before have looked at it. Dawn light is timeless and telling. Its softness reveals the depth of everything and yet somehow hides the shape. Early mornings, for me, reveal the truth and all those secrets that only the early risers can share.

That day's early shift didn't disappoint. The fields were covered in a heavy mist that was burning off slowly, revealing dew-laden cobwebs in the hedgerows. The fields were glinting with dampness and there was barely a breath of wind as I parked up just before Bowness and slid open the door. With the kettle on, I sat back to enjoy the view. A few fellow early risers were walking their dogs out on the flats beyond the clumps of samphire and sedge. The sun was about to rise above the bank behind me until a bank of mist a couple of hundred of feet high rolled down the river like a weather system. It moved slowly, a thick wall of rolling white enveloping everything in this flat, soulless light. The dog walkers disappeared into it.

I walked into the fog, along the permissive path between the houses and the river to the village, in search of the Roman fort that was once here. But of course, as with this coast, it's all been lost to the village, with the exception of a few earthworks and the knowledge that, allegedly, some stones were used to build the church. Like the Vallum, which might actually be the raised

embankment of a disused railway, on the tidal road between Burgh by
Sands and Drumburgh, it was tantalising, like I was looking for a ghost.
The fog made it feel all the more mysterious and intangible.

As the sun burned the mist away, the Solway Firth was revealed to me.
Across the water, as ever, Scotland lay, ready to pounce. I liked it being there,
solid and unbending in total contrast to the mud flats and salt marshes of
this side. The creeks and rivers were filling up again as the tide was rising.
It was ever changing hands between the land and the sea, just as it had
between the Romans, Celts and Normans.

I continued on into the morning, retracing my steps back to Kirkbride
and then on to Silloth, where I walked along the huge sea wall. I felt like
I could have been in a quiet Victorian resort anywhere, except that it was

out on a limb, in the middle of nowhere, at the edge of the coast, caught out by the disappearing railway – a victim of Beeching's vicious cuts – like a tourist stranded on a sand bank by the rising tide. I liked Silloth a lot. It retains its grandeur and the Victorian brick-built terraces, cobbled streets and genteel air and yet it's completely isolated. Fabulous.

DO IT THE HARD WAY

Bowness-on-Solway is the start of the Hadrian's Wall walk, an 84-mile (135km)-long walk from Bowness to Wallsend near Newcastle. Alternatively, you can pick up the walk at any point between Carlisle and Bowness. The section from Burgh by Sands to Bowness follows the coast closely and is largely flat.

Driving this area is easy as it's flat and the roads are often straight. Set out from Carlisle on the B5307, then follow signs for Kirkandrews-on-Eden. This is the road that follows the course of the Wall and will take you to Bowness. From there, take the road out along the estuary towards Cardurnock and the radio station. Next, head into Kirkbride, then follow the B5307 and B5302 to Silloth. The B5300 will take you along the coast to Maryport.

You will need:
- maps
- walking boots

CAMPING

Inn on the Bush, Kirkbride: This is a stopover for camper vans with an Elsan point and water. https://innatthebush.co.uk

ROUTE 20

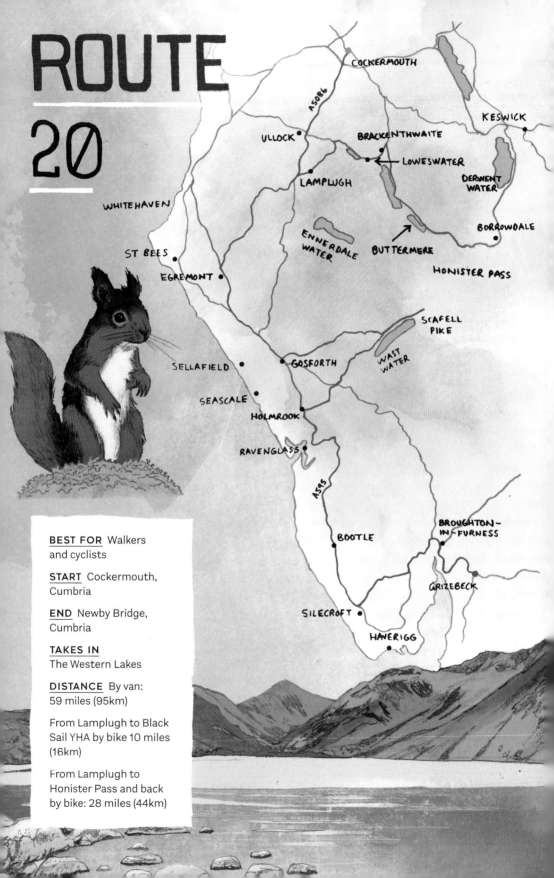

BEST FOR Walkers
and cyclists

START Cockermouth,
Cumbria

END Newby Bridge,
Cumbria

TAKES IN
The Western Lakes

DISTANCE By van:
59 miles (95km)

From Lamplugh to Black
Sail YHA by bike 10 miles
(16km)

From Lamplugh to
Honister Pass and back
by bike: 28 miles (44km)

Map labels

COCKERMOUTH

KESWICK

A5086

BRACKENTHWAITE

LOWESWATER

ULLOCK

DERWENT
WATER

LAMPLUGH

WHITEHAVEN

BORROWDALE

ENNERDALE
WATER

BUTTERMERE

HONISTER PASS

ST BEES

EGREMONT

SCAFELL
PIKE

SELLAFIELD

GOSFORTH

WAST
WATER

SEASCALE

HOLMROOK

RAVENGLASS

A595

BROUGHTON-
IN-FURNESS

BOOTLE

GRIZEBECK

SILECROFT

HAVERIGG

THE WESTERN LAKES

JOURNEYS ON THE QUIETER SIDE, OCTOBER 2021

While the whole of the Lake District is popular, busyness is relative. That's why I headed for the Western Lakes, for some epic cycles and easy walks in the most stunning landscapes. Away from the roads and the hotspots, it's easy to get lost in the lakes. All you have to do is pull on your boots or saddle up and take off.

I HEADED FOR the Lake District because I felt I had unfinished business there. In *Take the Slow Road* I travelled through the area in January, when it was quiet and there were few people about. It was bliss. This is hardly surprising when you consider that the majority of the area's annual 12 million visitors (compared with 42,000 residents) descend in the high season.

The Lake District is popular, of that there is little doubt. And, in 2021, it was always going to be difficult to find that slice of serenity I am always searching for. I couldn't deny anyone the chance to escape their Covid-19 confines, but I definitely didn't want to contribute to the problems in areas that were under severe pressure.

That's how I came to spend a few days in the Western Lakes at the beginning of October. I waited until the tourist season was just about over and then made it my mission to visit the lakes on the western side of the two big

passes, Honister and Hardknott. The climbs make them just that little bit more difficult to reach than the main centres as the drive-around is a fair old hike from the M6.

I arrived on a cold day, driving from Cockermouth on the curvy and twisty A5086, the road that runs below the mountains and above the coastal plain, offering views of both. On the right, the Irish Sea and on the left, the fells looming over the verdant valleys in between. I took a left turn at Lamplugh and found the Caravan and Motorhome Club site, where I pitched up. I chose the site because it's about halfway between Ennerdale and Loweswater and has Cogra Moss, one of the Western Lakes' smaller reservoirs, just behind it.

Eager to recce the area, I got on my bike and cycled out of the site and up to Felldyke before climbing to the pass between Kelton Fell and Keltonfell Top. From there, I got my first real Lakeland view, of Ennerdale and Ennerdale Water, the steep craggy hulk of Bowness Knott and Crag Fell. Behind them, Ennerdale Fell sat like a hulk, all rocky outcrops and browning bracken. To my right, open fields spread out into Ennerdale, punctuated by lines of tree-filled hedgerows and drystone walls. I stopped to take photos at a gate where sheep grazed below me. In the hedgerow, I noticed the deep red hues of red rowan berries hanging on to the branches while the brisk, cool breeze took the leaves with ease. The road dipped sharply down towards the lake, taking a couple of hairpins before dropping into the valley bottom. My eyes watered as I flew down the hill.

Ennerdale is the only lake in the Lake District that doesn't have a road running alongside it, so it was quiet. A couple of cars were parked up in the forestry car park and a few people were walking. I followed the forestry road down to the water's edge and cycled the length of the lake and then followed the river a few miles into the forestry leading up to Black Sail Youth Hostel and Black Sail Pass. I passed a few walkers, but most of the time I was alone, lost in the scenery,

feeling elated that I was here, in such magnificent surroundings.

The next day, instead of walking around Ennerdale as I had planned, I set my self a challenge to cycle to Buttermere and to take a look at Honister Pass. The ride would take me out of Lamplugh, through some beautiful avenues of ancient beech trees (to rival the dark hedges, I might add), down the brilliantly named Fangs Brow and down the steep hill to Loweswater and then on to Crummock Water and, eventually, Buttermere. I noticed my first 'caution red squirrels' sign as I rode into the wooded northern shore of Loweswater, which gave me a further mission. I hoped the whirring motor of my e-bike wouldn't put them off too much. I scanned the trees as I cruised past, but, as always with red squirrels, if you go looking for them you rarely see them. They sort of creep up on you and give a flash when you've dropped your guard.

The road along the side of Crummock Water is lovely. It follows the water's edge closely and then makes an almost alpine-style traverse around Hause Point, guarded by a low wall of sharp slate. The views are wonderful. True to form, just as I was riding up towards the pub at Buttermere a red squirrel scampered across the road. It was red with a dark black tail and dashed

across the tarmac, changing direction suddenly when it saw me. It dived into a hedge and up a tree before I could even think about getting my camera out. I stopped and watched it disappear.

At Buttermere, I stopped at the small shingle beach before Peggy's Bridge where, a couple of years earlier, in January, Lizzy and I had swum. It was bitterly cold but a lot of fun. Now, here alone, I wanted to get the chance to linger and take in the views on the way up to Honister Pass. I also wanted to see if I could cycle up it. The pass has been a tourist favourite since the Victorians included it in day trips from Keswick. The other side of the pass is the Elysian valley Borrowdale, which leads on to Derwent water.

The first views of the road that snakes up to the pass almost put me off. I'm no cyclist – in the sense of those who relish hill climbs – but I love cycling so this would always be a mental challenge for me. I have been brought up to seek out the path of least resistance, to find the cheat or the workaround, so going at something for the sake of it just isn't in my DNA. I'd sooner avoid the hill if I could. But I had set myself a challenge. I was here, on my own and I wanted to prove that I could do it and that I didn't need anyone else to cajole me into it.

The road snaked away up the valley, a ribbon of single-track, slate-grey tarmac weaving between boulders and alongside the beck. I could see a couple of places where I knew it would be steep – it is 25% in some places – and it made my heart flutter. All those aches and pains – the chest and back pain – suddenly seemed to be amplified. They were the voices telling me to quit, to give up and to take the easy way out by turning around and freewheeling back to Buttermere. I talked myself into it: you can do this. I blew out hard, dropping down the gears to tackle the steeper sections.

I am glad to say I made it to the top, which is an achievement for me, even on an e-bike. And it didn't matter that I was on my own. In fact, I was glad I was. As I freewheeled down, with the brakes jammed on hard and tears streaming from my eyes, I thought how nice it was that I had no regrets to ponder over that evening in the van. I stopped to take photos and looked around. What an amazing place! The scree-covered fells rose up above me steeply, grey with patches of browning bracken in between. In the bottom of the valley, the beck chuckled and rushed towards the lake between banks of soggy grass and peaty bog. A few cars passed, bikes too, and the sun dipped just behind Bell Crags.

That afternoon, I walked to Cogra Moss, a reservoir behind Lamplugh

Check it out on the way

MUNCASTER CASTLE, RAVENGLASS A haunted castle, home of the Fool of Muncaster and to some fine gardens. One of the Lake's finest houses, dating back to the 13th and 14th centuries. www.muncaster.co.uk

RAVENGLASS STEAM RAILWAY, RAVENGLASS 7 miles (11.3km) of steam railway that will take you to Eskdale and back. Lovely lovely!!! www.ravenglass-railway.co.uk

HONISTER SLATE MINE, HONISTER Mine tours as well as a via ferrata and all kinds of other terrifying trips for people who like heights. Screw that! www.honister.com

and took a shortcut through a bouncy bog of marsh grass, myrtle, reeds and mosses down by the water's edge. The only other people there were fly fishermen, casting in search of rainbow trout. It was quiet, if a little wet underfoot. I walked across a rickety wooden walkway made up of a couple of rotting planks to an island in the middle of the lake.

Wastwater, the starting point for Scafell Pike, was as beautiful as I remembered it from years ago. The road followed the shoreline almost all the way up the lake, ending at Wasdale Head. It seemed, though, that someone had got there before me. All along the side of the lake, at pull-ins and passing places, I found signs warning of 'no camping' and 'no parking on the verges', and even an electronic sign warning that fines will be issued to people blocking the clearway, an indication that the place had faced pressure in the summer. It was quiet now, with the exception of a dozen or so cars parked up along the lake, but I can only imagine what it must have been like in high summer. This demonstrates that going out of season can help to spread the load and take pressure off, even here, in the quieter dales of the lakes. I'm glad I did. I parked (legally) and took some photos. If I turned my back on the road I could just about make it look like I was lost in the wilderness. Almost.

DO IT THE HARD WAY

Driving in the Western Lakes is easy. You just have to remember to be polite, to give way and to reverse if need be. How hard can it be? The road that skirts the Western Lakes and joins them up is really easy and can be busy with trucks and traffic, but it still passes through some lovely countryside.

The A5086 heads out of Cockermouth towards the south and skirts the hills, passing close by Lamplugh and eventually joining up with the A595 just outside Egremont. From here, the A595 takes you to Calder Bridge and Gosforth, where you turn off towards Wasdale via Lane Side. This will bring you out halfway along Wastwater. Turn left to take the road alongside the lake up to Wasdale Head and for the car park to Scafell Pike if you are climbing.

Getting back to the main road means following the lakeshore and following signs for Santon Bridge. Eskdale – another stunning valley – can be reached from here. After Santon Bridge, the A595 takes you further south to Ravenglass, a lovely village by the sea, and Muncaster Castle. It skirts the hills all the way to Grizebeck, where you pick up the A5095 for the drive to Newby Bridge and the link to the M6.

ON YER BIKE:

Cycling from the Caravan Club Site in Lamplugh is easy, but there are some serious hills in and out because it sits on a ridge between Ennerdale and Loweswater. Both ways are steep and long, but with an e-bike you'll find it relatively easy. If you're the kind of cyclist who likes hills then you'll love it.

You will need:
- a bike if you like cycling
- walking boots and waterproofs

CAMPING

Dockray Meadow Caravan Club Site, Lamplugh: Perfectly placed but without a shower block, this is a great site from which to explore the Western Lakes. www.caravanclub.co.uk/club-sites/england/lake-district/cumbria/dockray-meadow-caravan-club-site

NT Wasdale Campsite, Wasdale Head: This National Trust-run campsite at Wasdale Head is situated in a great location. Book online. The Trust also run a campsite at Eskdale in an equally impressive site below Hardknott Pass. www.nationaltrust.org.uk/holidays/wasdale-campsite-lake-district

The Old Post Office Campsite, Santon Bridge: A beautifully situated campsite at the heart of this pretty village. www.theoldpostofficecampsite.co.uk

DO IT THE EASY WAY

Drive to Honister Pass and down into Borrowdale and Keswick for a fantastic day out and amazing views.

HIGH BENTHAM

HORNBY

WRAY

CLAUGHTON

A683

CATON

LOWGILL

LANCASTER

SALTER

BOTTON HEAD

QUERNMORE

STOCKS RES

ABBEYSTEAD

FOREST OF BOWLAND

SLAIDBURN

MARSHAW

NEWTON

DUNSOP BRIDGE

M6

WHITEWELL

WADDINGTON

CLITHEROE

<u>BEST FOR</u> Walkers, cyclists, foodies

<u>START</u> Clitheroe, Lancashire

<u>END</u> Slaidburn, Lancashire

<u>TAKES IN</u> The Trough of Bowland, The Cross of Greet

<u>DISTANCE</u> By van: 51 miles (82km)

From Dunsop Bridge to Brennand Farm by bike: 7 miles (11.3km)

From Brennand Farm to Whitendale Hanging Stones on foot: 4 miles (6.4km)

ROUTE 21

THE FOREST OF BOWLAND

FINDING THE CENTRE GROUND,
12 NOVEMBER 2021

Somewhere, in the middle of Great Britain, hidden in plain sight, is a diminutive Area of Outstanding Natural Beauty. It's not as popular as its neighbours The Lakes and North Yorkshire Moors and is often overlooked. But no matter. Within its 500 square miles (800 square km) lie some of the finest walking, cycling, fishing, stargazing and eating in England. And a lonely moor that's right at the heart of Britain.

MY ARRIVAL IN THE FOREST of Bowland wasn't exactly as I had planned it. The idea was to come to this often-overlooked AONB, sandwiched between the North York Moors and The Lakes, and take advantage of its lack of light pollution to bathe in starlight and perhaps even to take a night ride out into open countryside.

The Forest of Bowland is a designated Dark Sky Park because of its remoteness, even though it isn't that remote, really. It's bordered to the west by the M6 and to the east by the hulk of the Yorkshire Three Peaks, and to the south by Preston, Blackburn and Burnley. Yet it remains largely untouched and undiscovered by mass tourism, which is due, in part, to the fact that much of it is in private ownership and has been for centuries. As a forest, it was once a hunting ground for the gentry, and to some extent it is now, if you like shooting innocent birds.

In latter days, though, the Forest of Bowland has slipped under the radar somewhat. It's got a lively food scene, and plenty come to walk or ride here, but tourist numbers are still far below the number you'd expect elsewhere.

The forecast for my visit wasn't all that I had hoped for, but I went anyway, eager to have a mooch about. I had heard a lot about it and wanted to see it – and the stars above – for myself. Sadly, it wasn't to be. As I drove out of Clitheroe on the B6478 and left the sodium lights behind me, I felt the weight of the darkness. With no moon, no stars, a cover of cloud and a persistent mizzle, it was inky, sloe-berry black and driving was difficult. Every time

I flipped on the full beams on my headlights I faced a wall of drizzle. Almost as soon as I left the town the road rose out of the valley and kept rising, sending me upwards into the impenetrable darkness. By the time I had reached the top of the pass I was totally disorientated. I trundled over a cattle grid and began to descend into the trees of the Hodder Valley in search of a place to park up for the night.

The next morning, as I looked out of the van windows to the damp, dreary autumnal morning, I more or less gave up on the idea of stargazing. A quick flick through the weather sites proved me right: there would be cloud cover for the next two nights. I sat with a cup of tea and looked at my maps before picking up the phone.

Mark, a fellow writer who lives in Clitheroe, the gateway to Bowland, a little to the south, is someone

I have got to know through the Caravan and Motorhome Club over the last few years. He's a nature lover and outdoorsman and a fount of knowledge. As we chatted and Mark explained to me a little about his homeland, I explained my now-abandoned plans and that I was looking for a new mission. He mentioned that the geographical centre of Great Britain lies on desolate moorland a little to the north of Dunsop Bridge. I almost let it pass, but something about it drew me: I would go there. Mark said, 'It's brilliant because, at the heart of Great Britain, there is absolutely nothing.'

I set off to find Dunsop Bridge. The black-and-white fingerposts took me out of Slaidburn, through Newton and on to Dunsop along a glorious road that would, eventually, take me to the Trough of Bowland, a beautiful pass between Dunsop and Lancaster. I drove slowly to take it all in: a landscape that's well managed but beautiful, like Oxfordshire on steroids. The River Hodder meandered in the valley bottom and farmhouses and cottages of creamy stone peppered the slopes. Mature trees, now in their autumnal

plume, marked the boundaries, standing tall above stocky stone walls.

I unloaded my bike, pulled on waterproofs and set off along the bridleway that heads up the Dunsop River. I passed Puddleducks Tea Room and a row of cottages with window frames and doors painted in sober estate colours, crossed a small wooden bridge and went up a tarmacked bridleway towards the head of the valley. The river, peaty brown and gurgling over gritstone

boulders, ran alongside. I checked the map a few times before finding myself at Brennand Farm, a small collection of stone cottages and barns below the dark and steep Whin Fell. Here, the bridleway took a turn to the right and headed out in the wrong direction. The path I wanted, despite being a gravel track, was marked as a footpath and sported a dashing 'no cycling' sign.

Without a lock to leave the bike I opted to follow the bridleway up and away from the valley. At the top of the hill, the gravel ran out and I found myself cycling over rough, boggy ground that felt like a carpet floating on a lake. I pushed the bike over a brook and then used some wobbly stepping stones to get through a gate in a huge puddle. I carried on over another brook and then, when my front wheel sank up to its forks in dark, dank peat, decided to call it a day. I turned around and followed another path, which led to a wooden boardwalk over another brook. As I hit the boardwalk, my front wheel skidded out from underneath me and I went flying, ending up under my bike, on my back. I got up quickly and checked I was in one piece: I was just a little bruised. I walked the bike back to the gravel track, cycled back to the van and spent a rather safer rest of the day there, driving through the spectacular Trough of Bowland and down the pass at the Cross of Greet. Amazing. Don't miss it.

I was determined not to be outwitted by my own ineptitude, however, so I returned the next day after a night out in Clitheroe with Mark. It was cooler but sunny, with wispy cloud giving way a little. I was happy to be out in the

Check it out on the way

HOLMES MILL, CLITHEROE A former cotton mill that's now a brewery, shop, cinema and offices. Great vibe and decent food. Hundreds of local ales. On Wednesdays, there's half-price beer! www.holmesmill.co.uk

GISBURN FOREST MTB, GISBURN Some of England's best MTB trails are here, and some serious stuff, too. www.forestryengland.uk/gisburn-forest-and-stocks/cycling-and-mountain-biking-trails-gisburn

DARK SKY PARKS, BOWLAND Great stargazing is to be had here, due to the area's remote nature and lack of light pollution. Some of the best places (of five designated Dark Sky Discovery Sites) are Slaidburn, Gisburn Forest Park and Dunsop Bridge. www.forestofbowland.com/star-gazing

THE CROSS OF GREET, LYTHE FELL This is a stone at the top of the pass that connects Slaidburn with High Bentham. It's a spectacular road with some great sections as you descend from the apex. Well worth a ride.

hills again and loved the idea that I could be the most central person in the whole of the British Isles, even if it would be just for a moment. It felt extreme, as if I were going to the most southerly point. And the fact that it was here, above a tiny valley in an overlooked part of England, made it all the more alluring.

I locked the bike to a fence at the farm and set out on foot up the steep path on to Brennand Fell, gaining around 200m (656ft) of vertical height in little over a kilometre. I stopped every so often to look behind me at the view down the valley. I noticed waterfalls in a gorge below. The more I rose, the more the landscape changed from being a benign valley to that kind of rough and ready open-access scrub that's indicative of grouse moorland. I reached the end of the path and set off across the moor, following a set of wooden posts, which marked the way. The tracks of a quad guided me between the boggiest bits.

I walked out on to the peat, my feet squelching and slipping as I skipped lightly over spongy carpets of sphagnum moss, jumped from tussock to tussock of marsh grass and strode over islands of died-back heather. Every so often I'd hear the call of a grouse – so familiar to me from the opening bars of Stornoway's song 'Lost Youth' – and would turn to see a flash of red disappear away from me.

I walked for about half an hour until I reached an outcrop of rocks like a mini-tor of gritstone, overlooking a low, dish-like valley. The posts pointed me around its rim to another outcrop on the far side. Another ten minutes of bog dodging, often moving quickly to avoid sinking, brought me to a fence and a kissing gate. On the other side were the Whitendale Hanging Stones, the nearest landmarks to Great Britain's geographical centre. I stopped at the biggest of the stones, removed my pack and looked around. The rocks were the only feature in a landscape that was nothing more than undulating bog. The light, from a low autumn sun, illuminated clouds in the valleys in the distance, behind which there were more peaty lumps. The light breeze, coming from the west, brought a low hum from the M6 now that I was up a little higher. The rocks were weather worn, ridged and rounded. They were no more than 1.8m (6ft) tall but felt bigger, as if the diminutive cousins of a mighty tor on Dartmoor. The gravity was present, just not the size.

I loved being there, at the middle of things, in the centre of a wild landscape, under a weak blue sky, on the cusp of winter. It felt fitting to be here, in a year when I'd been seeking out England and Wales' sleepiest corners, right slap-bang in the centre, where there was, as Mark had predicted, nothing much at all. I took photos and headed back across the bog.

As I trudged across the fell to the track, I walked past a few places where rain had created deep cuts. Here there were sand, pebbles of quartz that had been washed out of the stone, and banks of exposed peat. I pocketed a couple of the quartz pebbles and a wisp of bright white wool. I walked on,

happily chatting to myself, talking myself down off the fell. I thought about the peat's power as a means to sequester carbon. This set me off on a spirited appraisal of the merits of grouse moors. I considered their benefits and disadvantages. They have been a part of our upland countryside for so long that we consider them to be normal. But really, they aren't. Really, they are nothing more than deserts, where the conditions are designed to be good for shooting birds and not much else.

I liked being up among the clouds and the lonely tors, but I found it hard to truly love the vast and desolate landscapes of these uplands. They can be beautiful in their own way, I told myself, but I knew I was more drawn to the gorges and waterfalls in the valley below me. There, birches were growing tall among grasses and boulders, while the river cascaded down the ravine in a series of drops and falls.

It would be a place to return to in the summer, with a picnic, partner and swimming togs. But for now, I was happy to have been at the heart of things, in the middle of nowhere, on this cool, clear November day. I walked down the steep track, a little breathless, back to my bike, staring out at the valley below. The farmer was rounding up his sheep on the hillside opposite. I could hear his whistles and the bleating of the sheep as the sheepdogs gathered them up.

The wind blew my hair away from my face and the sun lit up the puddles in the track like silver.

It wasn't half bad.

DO IT THE HARD WAY

Getting to the centre of the British Isles is not as tough as you might think, although the walk up to Brennand Fell rises sharply. Park at Dunsop Bridge and walk or cycle up to Brennand Farm along the bridleway. It's a beautiful walk along the banks of the Dunsop River and will take you past plantations and beneath Whin Fell and Ouster Rake. Once you have passed through Brennand Farm you'll come to a junction. Follow the track that goes straight on, up the hill steeply. Leave the bike here. Follow the track up the hill and on to the moor. Carry on until you see a couple of shooting huts. A short track to the right has a post signed 'Whitendale Hanging Stones'. Follow the posts across the bog (a quad track will lead you).

You'll pass Brennand Hanging Stones and see the small gritstone shapes on the hill behind. This is the centre of Great Britain.

Be careful in inclement weather as it's a featureless landscape and I imagine it would be easy to get lost.

You will need:
- decent walking boots
- weather-appropriate clothing
- picnic or snacks
- a mobile phone

CAMPING

Clitheroe Camping and Caravanning Club Site, Clitheroe: Situated on the banks of the River Ribble and within easy reach of Clitheroe and the outlying villages. www.campingandcaravanningclub.co.uk/campsites/uk/lancashire/clitheroe/clitheroe-camping-and-caravanning-club-site

Caravan and Motorhome Club CLs: Out of season, there are limited options for camping, but a number of CLs stay open. I stayed at Halsteads Farm, Clitheroe – a working farm with friendly owners and basic but good facilities. www.caravanclub.co.uk/certificated-locations/england/lancashire/clitheroe/halsteads-farm

DO IT THE EASY WAY

Rent an e-bike from Ribble Valley E-Bikes and cycle up the valley, and maybe even up to the Trough. Easy. There's parking nearby at Dunsop Bridge. www.ribblevalley-e-bikes.co.uk

WALES

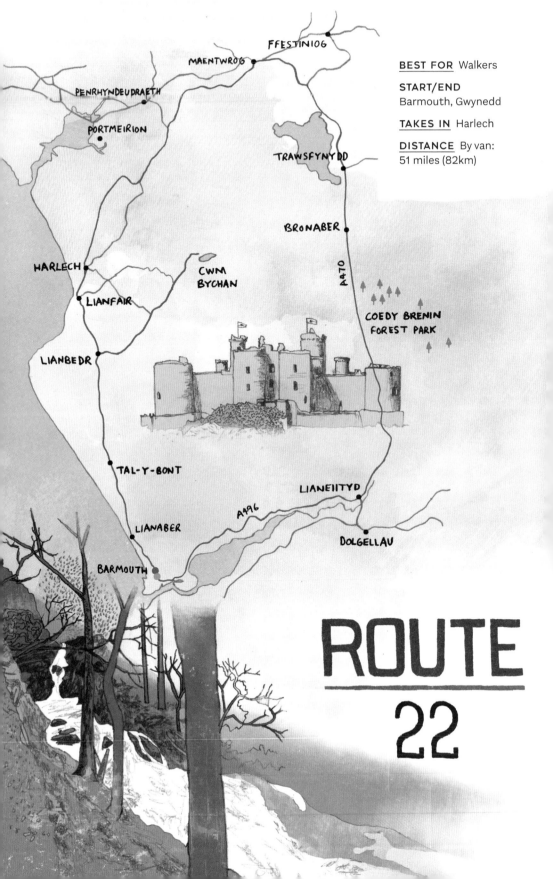

FFESTINIOG

MAENTWROG

PENRHYNDEUDRAETH

PORTMEIRION

TRAWSFYNYDD

BRONABER

HARLECH

CWM BYCHAN

LIANFAIR

A470

COED Y BRENIN FOREST PARK

LIANBEDR

TAL-Y-BONT

LIANELITYD

A496

LIANABER

DOLGELLAU

BARMOUTH

BEST FOR Walkers

START/END
Barmouth, Gwynedd

TAKES IN Harlech

DISTANCE By van:
51 miles (82km)

ROUTE

22

CWM BYCHAN AND THE ROMAN STEPS

This mystical, narrow, difficult-to-navigate valley is part of a fabulous drive in the quieter parts of Snowdonia at the head of which there is a beautiful lake and wild walking on the West Wales coast. There's camping, too, if you have a small enough van. Don't forget to pay the farmer.

THE RAIN WAS POURING down in big, fat, ripe, autumnal drops. I sat in the car park of the Co-op supermarket in Barmouth waiting for a break that never came so dashed for it anyway, getting very wet in the process. I needed supplies and this was the closest I would get to a shop without running for hundreds of soggy metres in the deeply puddled streets.

Even so, I filled the fridge and set off up the coast road to Llanbedr, wipers flapping madly to counter the ever-lashing rain. The coast road (A496) runs along the narrow strip of land between the sea and the mountains here, sharing the space with the railway. The views, from what I remember, are wonderful across the Irish Sea to the Llŷn Peninsula.

I had all but given up hope of walking up to the Roman Steps, an ancient drover's way that passes close to Rhinog Fawr, a peak of 720m (2,362ft), but decided I would head up to Cwm Bychan anyway, in case there was a break in the weather.

It was still torrential when I got to Llanbedr, the tiny village inland from Shell Island, the UK's largest campsite. I took a right up Afon Artro, the river that empties into the Irish Sea a mile or so to the west, just below Llandanwg. It was a small road that passed houses and the local school before heading off up the valley as a decent road with white lines down the middle and sharp slate walls either side. The houses, squat and cross looking, were made of stone with slate roofs and tidy gardens.

At the junction for the Rhaeadr Nantcol Waterfalls I carried on towards the lake as the road narrowed down to a single track with fierce slate running along the riverbank. The water was in absolute spate, rushing and crashing over the rocks in a peaty brown torrent. The further I went, the narrower the road became and the soggier the weather. I was now in a narrow valley of Celtic rainforest with steep sides and lots of mature oaks dripping with

epiphytes, mosses and ferns. In fact, everything was dripping. Plangent drops landed on my windscreen and rivulets gushed across the road, desperate to meet up with the bigger river that was still rushing away beside me. The slate boundary wall began to calm down a little, thanks to a thick, shapeless covering of moss.

I pressed on, wondering how far I needed to go. There were precious few passing places and nowhere I could turn around easily. My wing mirrors began to brush the overhanging branches at the sides of the road. The forest gave way to fields on my left, bordered by more slate walls and with a few sheltering sheep behind them. I entered more forest, heading upwards all the time. I stopped at a ruined bridge to try to take a few photos. I dashed out of the van and snapped a couple before the camera got too wet. Within moments, though, the lens had drops on it so I retreated to the van and wiped it.

I pressed on and the road narrowed even more, overshadowed by gnarled oaks and stands of birch and overhung in places by huge mossy boulders. The landscape was magical, otherworldy even, and I felt as if I was driving through somewhere very special indeed. One of those places that's described as 'thin' perhaps, where different worlds meet and the veil between them is most attenuated. The more I continued, the more I felt the power of the valley, despite having to concentrate hard on not taking the sides of the van out on the slates and boulders.

The valley widened and I came to a gate next to a dead tree and a thundering low set of falls. The gate was closed but unlocked. Realising that there was no way I could turn around and that it was a long, long way to reverse, I opened it and drove through. It took me into a different landscape altogether from the woods: one of boulders and bracken, stubby grass and bilberries, bog myrtle and scrub. The valley was wide but ringed with mountains on three sides. I drove on, hoping to find a turning point or a farmyard. I hoped the farmer wouldn't mind. The road took a sharp right and headed upwards around a huge boulder, more like a carpet now than a road, following the contours of the boggy and rocky terrain. I rounded a bend and came to the lake. With little wind, the lake was calm but pockmarked with raindrops, each one creating a bullseye of ripples. I stopped the van to look.

Behind the lake, the mountains were dripping with cascades of white water, disappearing into the clouds. To my left was a wall of scree and just a few feet below, the lake.

The road was only about 1.8m (6ft) wide and ran along side the north side of the lake for its entire length. I followed it and into another wood of short gnarled and twisted oaks, supporting ferns and mosses on their boughs and in their crevices. Beneath the trees, a boulder field was covered in moss and led down to the water's edge. I realised then that this place is and was truly spectacular, a rarefied landscape that, when I got out to take photos, reeked of the earth and moss and reminded me of Wistman's Wood on Dartmoor. A true gem of a place.

I continued on to reach a grassy area beside the river at the head of the lake where a sign asked for payment for parking. I dashed off a few shots and sat for a moment in the van, taking it all in. I got out of the van and ran over to the honesty box. The Roman Steps could wait, I thought to myself, as I left a fiver for the farmer and dashed back to the van. This was enough in itself. And I hadn't seen a soul since Llanbedr.

Check it out on the way

RHAEADOR NANTCOL WATERFALLS, LLANBEDR Waterfalls on private land near Llanbedr. www.nantcolwaterfalls.co.uk

COED Y BRENIN VISITOR CENTRE, DOLGEFEILIAU The UK's first dedicated mountain biking centre and base for walking and accessible trails in the forest. Visitor centre, bike shop and cafe. www.naturalresources.wales/days-out/places-to-visit/north-west-wales/coed-y-brenin-visitor-centre

HARLECH CASTLE, HARLECH Sitting on a rocky crag and commanding views over the dunes and river below, this is a truly impressive castle and inspiration for the song! www.cadw.gov.wales/visit/places-to-visit/harlech-castle

DO IT THE HARD WAY

The road to Cwm Bychan is narrow and difficult and not recommended for people who don't like to reverse or who drive wide or long vans or motorhomes. That said, it would make a brilliant cycle ride to the lake, and then a hike to the Roman Steps. There is lots of camping in the area, so leave the van and get on your bike or walk to the Roman Steps and the Rhinogs, a range of mountains between Trawsfynydd and Llanbedr. It's rugged and isolated and a much less-visited part of Snowdonia than further to the north.

The drive has lots of highlights, including sections that follow the coast between Barmouth and Harlech, Harlech, the Afon Mawddach estuary and the Afon Dwyryd estuary, as well as the open section going past Lake Trawsfynydd. The beach at Barmouth is special, with golden sands and a fabulous holiday atmosphere.

You will need:
- walking gear and waterproofs
- a small van (no motorhomes)

CAMPING:

Dinas Caravan Park and Camping, Cwm Bychan: There is camping in the field at the head of the road, but there are no facilities. Pay in the honesty box. Also a nice quiet site on the way up to the lake. www.hideaway-in-the-hills.com

Cae Adda, Trawsfynydd: A tiny site on the shores of Llŷn Trawsfynydd. www.caeadda.com

Coed-Y-Llwyn Caravan Club Site, Gellilydan: A lovely Caravan Club site near Trawsfynnyd. www.caravanclub.co.uk/club-sites/wales/gwynedd/coed-y-llwyn-caravan-club-site

DO IT THE EASY WAY

If you don't want to make the difficult drive up to Cwm Bychan then it is still possible to drive the circuit, which will take you through some truly dramatic scenery, to Barmouth, with options to cross the river to Fairbourne and other places to get out and walk/ride.

You will need:
- bikes to make the most of the trails at Coed y Brenin
- walking boots and waterproofs

FRON-GOGH

A494

BALA

LIANDDERFEL

LLYN TEGID

B4403

LIANUWCHLLYN

A470

DOLGEIIAU

A470

DINAS - MAWDDWY

CADAIR
IDRIS

A487

DOVEY
FOREST

MALLWYD

A458

MINFFORDD

CORRIS

ALTERNATIVE
TECHNOLOGY
CENTRE

A489

MACHYNLLETH

A487

DYLIFE

B4518

GLYWEDOG
RESR

A470

LIANIDLOES

BEST FOR Drivers
and walkers

START Llanidloes,
Powys

END Bala, Gwynedd

TAKES IN The best
driving in Wales

DISTANCE By van:
55 miles (89km)

ROUTE 23

THE PASS OF THE CROSS

THE BEST SHORTCUTS IN WALES, SEPTEMBER 2021

This is a simple drive, with some incredible highs, in West Wales. It takes in the best shortcut you've ever driven as well as the Pass of the Cross – an ancient pass at the head of the Dyfi Valley that's Wales' second highest road. It's not for big mohos, but the little guys will love it. Views? Incredible.

I WAS RUNNING OUT OF LIGHT, so decided to stop just out of Llanidloes, by Llyn Clywedog, at a remote parking spot overlooking the water. From the van I could see, hundreds of feet below me, the wind whipping up white horses on the black, peaty water. It was buffeting the van, making it rock in fits and starts, as if a tetchy nursemaid were absentmindedly trying to rock me off to sleep. It was raining, too, which didn't help the noise inside the van. It lashed on to the skylights and the windows, streaming in rivers down the windscreen and dripping off the window rubbers.

I didn't want to continue because I didn't want to miss the rest of the drive. It's one of my favourite shortcuts and is to be savoured for every view it throws up. This one, of the lake, is the first of many that I would get to enjoy in the morning as it took me over the mountains and into Machynlleth, rather incongruously, through the local golf course and then through a back street before landing in the wide high street.

The morning proved equally wet. Dodging downpours, I took my time to take photos, waiting out the worst of it before dashing out to capture the view. As the clouds raced across the sky and brief patches of sunlight danced across the green fields below me I snapped away, hoping the images would turn out as good as the view looked to the naked eye.

The A487 towards Dolgellau wasn't new to me, or particularly remote, even though it took me through some incredible landscapes. It snaked past the Centre for Alternative Technology, through the thickly wooded slopes of Afon Dulas and then dropped me, with a sharp right and brilliant reveal, in the Fawnog Valley, a perennial favourite that heads straight up Bwlch Llyn Bach, with Cadair Idris looming to the left and a steep crag to the right. As mountain roads go, it's beautiful and has wonderful views looking back towards the coast across Llyn Mwyngil. Spectacular, but not exactly off the beaten track.

At the top of the pass I took a right at Cross Foxes Inn and on to the A470. Again, it's not exactly a quiet road as it's the main road between Dolgellau and Welshpool, but it took me through magnificent Snowdonia scenery, especially when I crested the pass at Bwlch Oerddrws and cruised into the Cerist Valley between peaks of more than 600m (1,969ft). The valley was lush and green, but above me the mountains were brown with dying bracken, spotted with yellow gorse and the last of the heather, and of course the rock, lichen splattered and somber, looking down at me.

The road curved and careered down the valley until I came to Dinas Mawddwy. Here, a left turn would take me to the ultimate prize on this trip: the Pass of the Cross. I will admit I was a bit apprehensive about driving this 'difficult and dangerous' road, but having survived the Alps and Pyrenees in recent years, I ploughed on anyway. The road took me through the village and out the other side on the northern slopes of the steep-sided Dyfi Valley. Through the trees and over the jagged slate walls I could see the pasture below and the river snaking its way. I passed farms and homes until I reached

the plantation at Pennant and the road took a sharp right hairpin steeply upwards and away from the river into a steep valley.

From there, the road became narrower, down to a single track with few passing places, and headed upwards, at a rate of around 20–25%, into the bracken-covered slopes. I dropped down to first gear to take it slowly and steadily as the nose of the van headed upwards. I daren't stop so I chugged on until I reached a fork in the road where the cross lay. I got out of the van and whooped that I had made it up the worst part, which

is silly but it did feel like an achievement. I was shaking slightly I noticed. I took photos and then continued up to the apex of the pass, parking up and looking down now towards Bala. The sun lit up the valley and I could see farms and houses way beneath me. A few sheep bleated around me and the wind hissed through the grasses.

The descent was just as good, if not more critical, as the road was narrower, less well kept and with fewer passing places. Clinging to the southern side of the Afon Twrch Valley, it passed through a small plantation with a sharp turn, but otherwise the road was open for the first mile or so, with the hillside dropping away steeply in places. Once back in the trees and fields, I cruised into Bala Lake, taking the southern shore and following the Bala Lake Railway. I camped at the site outside Bala, with a pitch overlooking the mountains I had just crossed.

As the light faded and the dark hulk of the mountain receded into the misty rain, I thought how lucky I was to get the window to scale the pass under a deep-blue sky. For the next three days, it would rain almost relentlessly, scuppering any plans for views, elevations or even a decent walk.

Check it out on the way

CENTRE FOR ALTERNATIVE TECHNOLOGY (CAT), PANTPERTHOG
I loved going here to read all about the kinds of technology that will
save our sorry arses. It was wet and quiet and enlightening. I saw a
nuthatch in the woods. www.cat.org.uk/

BALA LAKE RAILWAY, BALA 4.5 miles (7.2km) of steam-pulled
cuteness along the shores of Wales' largest natural lake? Peep peep.
www.bala-lake-railway.co.uk/

MACHYNLLETH A lovely food and antiques town that's been
home to the alternative set for a while, now gentrifying beautifully.
www.machynlleth.net

DO IT THE HARD WAY

This is not a tough journey by any means. But it does go over the Welsh mountains and will take you to some remote areas where there is little infrastructure and where the weather could become an issue in winter (and even in the summer!). The Pass of the Cross isn't really suitable for anything bigger than around 6m (19.7ft) or for anyone who isn't prepared to reverse on a single track of around 25% in gradient. Little vans will love it.

The Pass of the Cross was used by Austin and Standard Triumph – as well as motorcycle manufacturers – for testing their cars and bikes during hill climbing. It's also been used in The Milk Race as one of Britain's toughest climbs. So, on fine days, expect cyclists.

From Llanidloes, take the B4518 to Llyn Clywedog. After the lake, take the second left, an unnamed and fantastic mountain road, which is signposted to Machynlleth. From Machynlleth, take the stunning A487 up the Bwlch Llyn Bach pass towards Dolgellau and then, at the Cross Foxes Inn, turn right on to the A470. Turn left into Dinas Mawddwy and then follow the road up to Bwlch y Groes, the steep Pass of the Cross, over the pass (stay left and don't go right to Llyn Vyrnwy) and down on to the B4403. Turn right here and follow the road along the southern bank of Llyn Tegid (Lake Bala) to meet the B4391 and Bala.

You will need:
- maps
- emergency rations: sweets, bananas

CAMPING
Gwersyll Pen y Bont Touring Park, Bala: A most excellent campsite at the foot of Bala Lake, with pitches right on the water. www.balalakecamping.co.uk

Red Kite Touring Park, Llanidloes: Adults-only site near Llanidloes and Llyn Clywedog. www.redkitetouringpark.co.uk

DO IT THE EASY WAY

If your van is too big to get over the passes it's still worth the drive from Llanidloes to Bala, cutting out the Pass of the Cross by taking the A470 north from Dolgellau and then following the fabulous but wide A4212 to Bala. It'll take you past Llyn Celyn and the Coed y Brenin Visitor Centre.

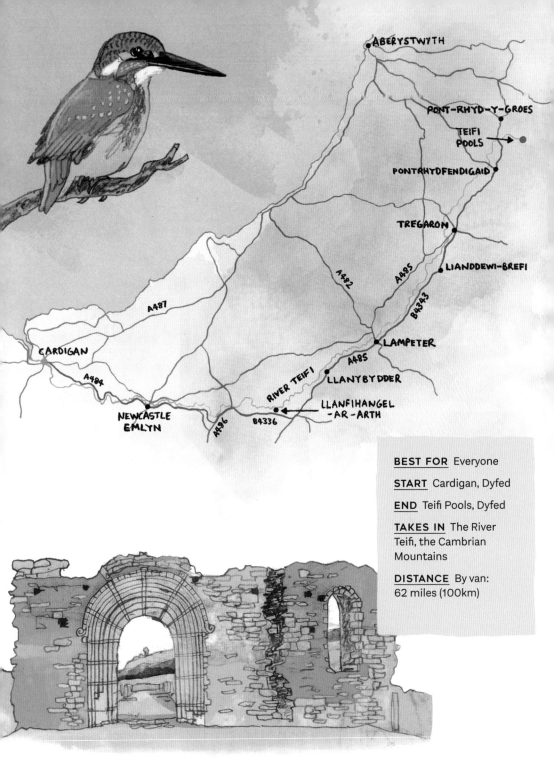

ABERYSTWYTH

PONT-RHYD-Y-GROES

TEIFI
POOLS →

PONTRHYDFENDIGAID

TREGARON

A485

LLANDDEWI-BREFI

A482

B4343

A487

LAMPETER

CARDIGAN

A485

RIVER TEIFI

LLANYBYDDER

A484

LLANFIHANGEL
-AR-ARTH ←

NEWCASTLE
EMLYN

A486

B4336

BEST FOR Everyone

START Cardigan, Dyfed

END Teifi Pools, Dyfed

TAKES IN The River
Teifi, the Cambrian
Mountains

DISTANCE By van:
62 miles (100km)

ROUTE 24

THE TEIFI

FISHING - AND FAILING - IN THE WILDERNESS, SEPTEMBER 2021

*The River Teifi is one of Wales' longest rivers.
Its source, at the Teifi Pools in the Cambrian Mountains,
sits at an altitude of 455m (1,493ft) above sea level. The pools
and the mountains themselves are one of a few truly remote
wilderness areas in southern Britain. There are few roads
here and fewer people. Fish, it seems, are a rarity too, with
fly fishing on the Pools reputed to be some of the most
remote – and difficult – anywhere.*

THERE IS A SMALL outdoor clothing company based in Cardigan that used to embroider a map of the Teifi on the back pocket of their jeans. I still have a pair. They also used to produce a beautifully shot lookbook every year, containing rich and vibrant images of their 'lives' on the Teifi – at the beach and in the mountains, fishing, camping, cycling and canoeing. It appeared to be the perfect lifestyle and the Teifi Valley a perfect place in which to live.

It was at once a wilderness and yet brimming with the kind of culture I could relate to. I wanted to go.

My friend Andy wanted to go fishing.

It was almost dark and raining heavily when we got to Cardigan to buy food. I parked outside the Spar and went in looking for inspiration. Andy, along for the trout, bought stuff for breakfast and announced that he couldn't be bothered to do any cooking or for me to do any cooking so we were going to find a chippy. I wasn't going to argue.

At the chip shop, we asked the owner where might be nice to eat the chips overlooking the sea. He gave us directions that took us down a tiny lane where the undergrowth brushed both sides of the van. It brought us to a beach of slate on the edge of the muddy estuary. We parked above the high tide line and opened the sliding door to a full face of estuarine noises and smells. Geese flew in formation above and the salty, muddy smell of the river invaded our nostrils. The fish and chips, dashed with vinegar and a liberal dusting of salt, tasted of holidays by the sea and weekends away. Truly wonderful.

It was still raining in the morning. Cardigan looked very drab as we drove through it. With deserted streets and running gutters, it wasn't showing us its best side. It was a similar story for the rest of the places we passed. The slate roofs and grimly pebbledashed walls of thick, squat stone cottages never look great through the windscreen when it's lashing down with rain. The road took us up and down some steep hills on the north side of the Teifi Valley, giving us glimpses of the river we'd be fishing later that day.

We parked outside the barbershop in Lampeter and knocked on the door. Allan, our contact at the Llandysul Angling Association, welcomed us into his chaotic hairdressers-cum-fishing tackle shop with a warm smile and a look like a golfer on his day off. We filled out the forms we needed to fish the club's water for the day and had a brief chat about fishing and the river. It was a world away from our experience on the Test: a little more down to earth, full of wry Welsh humour, and an awful lot cheaper. Also, without the help of a guide to show us the ropes, it was altogether more daunting.

With directions to the parking and a brief tip on which flies to put on, we set off for the river, finding ourselves in a water meadow in a huge bend in the river that was populated by sheep, a horse and a few cows. Woodpeckers knocked on a tree on the riverbank and buzzards buzzed the skies above us. A few fish rose, sending ripples in the still pools. We started to fish.

I find fishing to be a lot of things. It's boring but also very exciting. It's peaceful but can also be violent. It's all things at once. Today, though,

I found it to be cathartic but also infuriating. When things were going well I felt at one with the river as the line cast itself out over the water. Everything felt easy. But when the cast failed and the line plopped on to the water in a heap or a fly got caught up in the tough, dried-up stalk of an umbellifer, I found it to be deeply frustrating. I felt desperately deficient in skill or knowledge and it showed in the lack of anything resembling a bite. At times I felt like crying.

However, I loved the wildness of the river and the countryside. I liked being alone here with a friend, quietly walking the banks in search of something to cast at. Once again, fishing had brought me to somewhere really special. I didn't mind the rain or the lack of fish. It was the experience that counted.

The rain eased about an hour into the day. Andy's second-hand waders had sprung a leak and were now 'water boots' and I was starting to get more than a little despondent. We moved up the river to a spot that 'looked promising'. Why it did I have no clue, but it had a clear bank, which meant I could cast without too much interference from the vegetation. As I prepared my fly, a fish rose on the opposite bank and took something from the surface of the water. I cast and immediately got hooked up on some cow parsley. I untangled and tried to cast again. This time my fly landed in the exact spot where the fish had risen. It took the fly and disappeared with it below the

surface. I struck, too late, and the fly flew out of the water minus the fish. I was determined to keep trying and worked hard to cast accurately and cleanly. I knew from fishing on the Test that perseverance can work. I cast again, and repeated the process: cast, retrieve line from vegetation, untangle line, cast, fish takes it, strike, no fish.

My phone rang in my pocket. It was Andy, from up the bank, to tell me he'd caught a couple of small wild brown trout. I gathered up my gear and wandered up to him. He hooked another from a small, fast-flowing section as I arrived. He put it back and feeling sorry for me, passed me his rod to have a go myself.

Almost immediately I caught a tiny trout that was no bigger than the palm of my hand. It felt like cheating but it still counted as a catch. Relief.

The rain, steadily increasing in intensity, began to fall heavily so we called it a day, packed up and walked back to the van.

The next morning, I woke early to find an orange glow behind the blinds. Looking out, I could see the sun had risen and had found a clear path to light up the van in a clear strip between the hill and the bottom of the clouds. It was lighting up the chapel and the hillside opposite, too, making them glow orange. I got dressed, but by the time I was out of the van the cloud had lowered and the sun had risen. I walked towards the toilet block and saw three choughs pecking at the ground near the van. I stopped, turned and sprinted back to the van to fetch my camera. Choughs, very rare in Cornwall, are a common sight here. Even so, I was delighted.

Cardigan looked gorgeous in the bright sunshine: a little bit hippy, a little bit traditional, very Welsh and full of cafes and smiling visitors. I wanted to stay and have a coffee, but we had to be back on the river, this time at the Welsh Wildlife Centre for a Canadian canoe trip along the Cilgerran Gorge. With the sun low in the sky, the river looked so inviting and mysterious as we walked down  the former towpath to the river's edge. The water was still, like glass, moving slowly, carrying a few dead leaves down towards the sea. Steam rose from the surface where the sun warmed it. Backlit trees cast deep shadows over the water, making it appear black and unfathomable, while above, the sunbeams, backlighting the leaves, danced as the trees moved gently. We walked past abandoned slate quarries, now reclaimed by mossy and sinuous oaks and dank undergrowth growing on top of, and despite, the spoil heaped high along the banks. As a post-industrial landscape, it's fared well.

The steep sides of the gorge were densely wooded and fallen trees made ghostly shapes on and in the water. We paddled upstream with our guide and three other boats of visitors for a mile or so, below the trees and into dazzling light on the wider sections. I caught a fleeting glimpse of a kingfisher and sat in silence as I passed a patient dipper watching me from a branch just above the water. We scoured the banks for otters. Aside from our quiet chat, a little birdsong and the splosh of paddles into the water, the gorge was silent. We could have been anywhere, and yet a few miles downstream was Cardigan. I stopped paddling and sat, mesmerised by the peace and the silence. It felt as if any sudden movement or loud noise would break the spell and the gorge would melt away. The trip reached its zenith on a shingle bank below Cilgerran Castle, where we turned around and paddled quietly back to the start.

The drive to the Teifi Pools took us along the lush green valley, through

Check it out on the way

STRATA FLORIDA, YSTRAD FFLUR A ruined abbey at the head of the Teifi that is described as 'Wales' Westminster Abbey'. www.stratafloridatrust.org
THE WELSH WILDLIFE CENTRE, CILGERRAN Stunning new building in a nature reserve with nature trails, play equipment and a great cafe. If you're lucky, you might spot kingfishers. www.welshwildlife.org/visitor-centres/the-welsh-wildlife centre

Newcastle Emlyn, Llandysul, Cwmann and Llanddewi-Brefi, the village made famous by *Little Britain*, and then on to Ffair-Rhos. Our campsite, just opposite the handy Teifi Inn, gave us incredible views of the mountains to the east and the valley to the south.

We woke early, despite a night in the pub, to find a thick mist above and below us in the valley. The road to the Teifi Pools rose steeply from the village, passing a few houses and farms until it reached a shuddering cattle grid and narrowed to a single track with a few passing places. It wound around the lumpy mountains, over and around outcrops and into the misty, mysterious early morning light. We took a right for the first of the pools, Llyn Teifi, heading very steeply down to the lakeside after using our privilege as permit holders to drive through the gate that's closed to other traffic. As we drove around the rough track on the west side of the pool the sun began to burn away at the mist, creating a bright but heavy atmosphere. We parked by the dam and put the kettle on, watching the water for signs of fish.

As the mist burned off, leaving us with a deep-blue sky peppered with fluffy white clouds, I could see, for the first time, where we were. The mountains, undulating like dunes, surrounded us, with the water below us. Looking across the dam we could see the field systems of the valley floor miles to the south-west, a deeper shade of green than the light, late-summer greens of the sedges on the mountainside. Sheep dotted the landscape and stood on outcrops of rocks, bleating at each other across the reservoir.

Patches of darker bilberries and just-past-its-prime heather, along with marsh grasses, created blobs of darker greens and brown on the hillsides.

I drank my tea on the lakeside, watching the water and the landscape. I am used to driving through such places but rarely stop – really stop – and take the time to immerse myself. While the wagtails darted across the rocks by the water's edge and the sheep bleated, I drank it all in. There was barely a breeze from the south and the air was fresh and clean, smelling slightly of moss and sheep dung. Clouds of midges hung in the air, the odd one or two landing on me. The mossy ground under my feet felt spongy and forgiving, bar the odd sharp rock, and the sun felt warm on my face.

I walked back to the van, set up my rod, chose and tied a fly and made my way down to the lakeside.

I cast into the black, still water. Ever optimistic.

DO IT THE HARD WAY

The Teifi is a famous trout, salmon and sea trout river and the Teifi Pools are 'some of the most challenging wilderness fishing to be had anywhere'. So that will excuse you when you come home without any fish.

Even if you don't want to fish, the Teifi is a fabulous river to explore by canoe or even on foot or by bike. Starting at Cardigan, take the A484 through Newcastle Emlyn, then follow the A486 to Pont-Tyweli where you can pick up the B4336 to the A485 towards Cwmann. Follow the B4343 at Cwmann all the way to Ffair-Rhos. Turn right at the Teifi Inn for the pools.

You will need:

- canoes for trips on the Teifi: www.heritagecanoes.squarespace.com
- permits for fishing the Teifi Pools: www.tregaronangling.com
- permits for fishing the Teifi around Lampeter: www.teififishing.com

ADD AN EXTRA DRIVE

It is possible to cross the Cambrian Mountains to extend the drive and finish at the Elan Valley. From Ffair-Rhos, continue on the B4343 to Pont-rhyd-y-groes and then follow the B4574 until you get to the turn-off for the mountain road towards Rhayader. This will take you up the  Ystwyth Valley and through a high pass, eventually bringing you to a junction at the Craig Goch Reservoir at the head of the Elan Valley. Turn right here and follow the road past the reservoir and on to the beautiful Elan Valley. It's popular and has some really nice sections with great views.

CAMPING:

Ty Gwyn Caravan and Camping Park, Mwnt: Amazing location at Mwnt on the coast outside Cardigan. Very close to the beach. www.facebook.com/TyGwynCaravanAndCampingPark

Penrhiw Campsite, Penrhiw: A lovely small site overlooking the Teifi Valley at Ffair-Rhos. Closest site to the Teifi Pools. penrhiw-campsite.business.site

Tyllwyd Campsite, Cwmystwyth: Brilliant location on the road to Elan. www.welshaccommodation.co.uk

DO IT THE EASY WAY

Cardigan to the Elan Valley is an epic drive through wild Wales, with or without canoeing or fishing (see above).

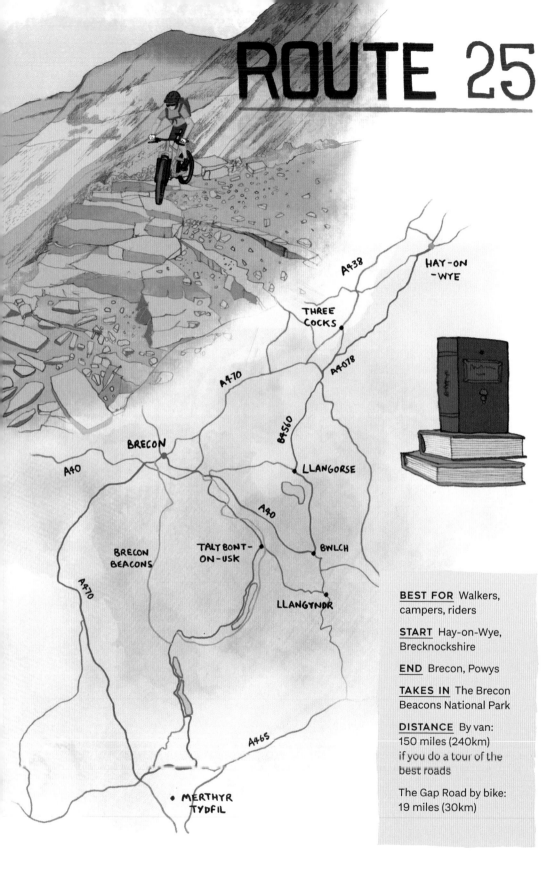

ROUTE 25

HAY-ON-WYE

A438

THREE COCKS

A4078

A470

B4560

BRECON

A40

LLANGORSE

A40

TALYBONT-ON-USK

BWLCH

BRECON BEACONS

A470

LLANGYNIDR

A465

MERTHYR TYDFIL

BEST FOR Walkers, campers, riders

START Hay-on-Wye, Brecknockshire

END Brecon, Powys

TAKES IN The Brecon Beacons National Park

DISTANCE By van: 150 miles (240km) if you do a tour of the best roads

The Gap Road by bike: 19 miles (30km)

THE BRECON BEACONS

The Brecon Beacons are magnificent. They back on to South Wales Valleys and finish in spectacular style to the north with a steep escarpment and range of peaks that include Hay Bluff, Pen y Fan and The Black Mountain. It's a very special place that's well loved by the locals in Wales' nearby cities of Cardiff and Swansea as well as those who come here to walk, cycle or just find a little bit of peace.

I STARTED THIS JOURNEY with a rough plan. I had an idea of what I wanted to do, a place to stay on the first night and then a campsite booked for two nights after that. I hated being so organised, but felt the need, especially since it was August, the busiest summer on record for UK holidays and all my feeds were panicking about England and Wales being oversubscribed, groaning under the pressure and not being able to cope with the amount of domestic tourism.

I wanted to take a look at the Brecon Beacons for this book because, while it's close to Swansea, Cardiff and the Valleys, it's the least visited of Wales' three national parks. This is despite it being more than twice the size of the Pembrokeshire Coast National Park. It has vast areas of common land, four mountain ranges (Brecon Beacons, Fforest Fwar, Black Mountains and the Black Mountain) and lots of open space. I felt sure I'd find a little solitude and wilderness somewhere.

I've always camped in Wales in the most glorious, tiny sites, in incredible locations. So it did seem to be a personal let-down to end up on a club site for a couple of nights, simply because I was nervous about finding somewhere to stay. I was travelling alone on this trip and I wanted to be reassured that I would have somewhere to empty the toilet, grab a shower and plug into the electric.

My first overnight stop, the Oxford Road car park in Hay-on-Wye, eluded me for some time. I had planned to drive over the Gospel Pass, Wales' highest road, as a start point for the journey. I got as far as Llanthony before I was turned back by signs saying the road was closed (I read later that it was shut due to a landslide). This was a blow as Hay-on-Wye is the other side of the pass. I turned around and traced my way back down the absolutely beautiful Vale of Ewyas. In the fields by the river, below the road, I spotted tents and caravans and imagined carefree times under canvas in a secret valley with long walks to the pub and afternoons in the beer garden.

Sadly, it wasn't to be. Instead, I drove along the Grwyne Fawr valley, on some incredibly narrow but beautiful roads, just to the north of the Sugar Loaf Mountain, which brought me out on to the A40 at Crickhowell. From there, it was easy to get to Hay. I drove as far as I could up towards Gospel Pass and Hay Bluff to enjoy the last of the day's views towards Hay and mid-Wales.

That night, while aimlessly googling in the van, I read about the 'Gap Road', a pass between Cribyn and Pen y Fan, south Wales' highest peak, to the west, and Fan y Bîg to the east. While it's part of the Horseshoe Walk, an incredibly popular walking trail that takes in the peaks, I read about a section of a mountain bike route that is described as a 'classic Welsh trail'. It was also described as 'tough but worth it for the views and the downhill after a long climb'. It sounded like a challenge! I decided to investigate it in the morning, my head filled with precipitous drops and cycling along knife edges.

I didn't sleep well.

In my rough plan for the Brecons I had sketched out a number of roads
I wanted to drive, as well as a couple of points I wanted to see. Among these
were the waterfalls of so-called 'Waterfall Country' to the south of the
national park and the '*Top Gear* road', the A4069 that runs north to south,
joining Llandovery with Brynamman. I decided to spend a day looking around,
with the aim of doing 'the waterfall walk' of about four hours. I drove the
B4560 from Talgarth to Bwlch and then took the unnamed road by the side
of the Talybont Reservoir to Blaen y Glyn Uchaf and then down into Pant. This
brought me to the 'Heads of the Valleys' road, the A465, and on to the A4059,
where I hoped to get into Waterfall Country at the car park at Cwm Porth.

It wasn't to be. Waterfall Country was full up! When I arrived just after
lunch, the car park was already at capacity, which rather made me feel like
I didn't want to go there anyway. Even if I could have got into the car park,
I realised later that perhaps it's time to give these places a wide berth. The
popularity of Waterfall Country, according to the National Park Authority, is
causing erosion. As I left, more cars were streaming down the tiny lane off
the A4059.

The drive back to Brecon was tremendous, on the A4059 and then the
A470, passing Beacons Reservoir and squeezing through the pass between
Fan Fawr and Pen y Fan. I stopped at the National Park Centre, just off the
A470, and chatted to one of the wardens about the Gap bike ride. We pored

Check it out on the way

THE A4069 This is one of Wales' finest roads. By alpine standards it's not particularly hairy or steep, but it does have some really good moments. Locally, it's known as the '*Top Gear* road' as some of the episodes were filmed there. It's got a switchback, a climb, some curvy corners and a lot of amazing views. Drive it either way and savour the moments. It'll be over before you know it.

HAY-ON-WYE A lovely town with lots of independent shops, markets and, of course, bookshops. A truly indy town, along with the wonderful Crickhowell. www.hay-on-wye.co.uk

MONMOUTHSHIRE & BRECON CANAL You can walk or cycle this lovely stretch of canal between Brecon and Newport. It passes through Crickhowell, Abergavenny and Pontypool. https://canalrivertrust.org.uk/enjoy-the-waterways/canal-and-river-network/monmouthshire-and-brecon-canal

THE NATIONAL PARK The Brecon Beacons are a honeypot for walking, cycling and camping. They're also a Dark Sky Park because of the lack of light pollution. If you want to get away, get away here. www.breconbeacons.org

BIKEPARK WALES, MERTHYR TYDFIL For singletrack heaven, book a day out here. It's incredible and has something for all grades of riders, from a 3.1-mile (5km) green for beginners to elite-level features and runs. www.bikeparkwales.com

over a map and he showed me the route, saying 'It's quite a difficult route' to me gently, as if trying me out. I guess he knew I was nervous.

I rose early and fussed over my kit, spare inner tubes, lunch and camera gear. I locked up the van and rode out of the site, over the busy A40 and then on to the towpath of the beautiful Monmouthshire and Brecon (Mon and Brec) Canal, an engineering marvel dating from 1799 that used to carry iron ore and coal from the mountains into Newport. The towpath is well used by cyclists and walkers and is a real joy to cycle. I cycled under its diminutive and shapely bridges, over its fabulous aqueduct across the Usk and along the banks lined with riotous purple betony to Talybont-on-Usk. Following the road up to the Talybont Reservoir brought me to the dam. I crossed over it and started up the forestry track beside the reservoir.

I rode my e-bike in eco mode in an effort to ensure I had enough power to get up to and over the Gap. The last thing I needed was for the battery to

die halfway. While the power is good, e-bikes are amazing, but once the juice goes they're a horrible thing to ride: they're heavy and the motor provides a huge amount of resistance, making it much, much more difficult to ride than a normal mountain bike. That said, I cruised up the track, alone, keeping my legs going and breaking out in an economy mode-based sweat.

As I rode up the hill – it was 5 miles (8km) of steady climbing – I had time to think. My anxiety about the ride came over me in waves of negative thoughts. I fretted about how I would feel if I got to a point where the path was too steep. I was on edge about not being able to turn back or not being able to go on. I was scared about the paths being too narrow or too steep. I was anxious about the weather changing. I worried about falling off the mountain.

I seriously needed to get a grip. I talked myself up and down during the long uphill, simply because of the unknown. But mostly because I worried

about how I would feel when I got there. My concerns were about how I would cope, knowing full well that I've been in situations – mostly when there have been steep cliffs and dangerous drops – when I haven't coped at all. It wasn't the mountain that I feared, but the fear of the mountain. It had amplified this ride into something much bigger and more dangerous than it probably was and it was the not knowing that made me fear it. I was on my own and didn't have the supporting presence of Lizzy. Normally, in cases where we were cycling down steep hills or doing things out of our comfort zones, it would be me who was the one being positive and encouraging. On the Isle of Wight, for instance, Lizzy had cried about a cliff we were halfway down while I was too busy encouraging her to be scared for myself. But here, as I rode higher and higher and the reservoir got further and further below me, I was the one who needed encouragement. I needed to find it for myself.

'You can do this.'

'It won't be so bad.'

'You've faced worse.'

I cycled on, turning the pedals continuously as I rose, reaching the top of the track and the bottom of the clouds at Blaen-y-glyn, a National Park car park. It began to drizzle as the wind whipped around me, so I didn't stay long enough to think about the next section and instead carried on, over the pass and down the hill to where the Taff Trail headed north again. The trail here was absolutely lovely, passing high on the mountainside with trees and lakes below. I noted mountain ash, birch and pine growing out of the dense undergrowth, which was mostly made up of over-exuberant bracken. I passed a few walkers on this section. I knew that soon I would come to the point where the Taff Trail headed off down the hill in a switchback and the trail to the Gap would continue. I told myself that I could just turn around if it was too hard. No pressure. Just don't stop before you reach the edge of your comfort zone. Push a little bit further, if you can.

The Gap Road was really bumpy, with plenty of large loose rocks and slippery slabs. As the path left the relative safety of the wooded mountain it headed out over open moorland, traversing a slope that was probably no more than 30 degrees. I rode it carefully and slowly as it rose gently. I was relieved that this section was hard, but the drop wasn't too steep. I arrived at a steep gorge and walked the bike down and up the other side. Things were fine. I was feeling fine.

I rode on to the Gap itself. Cribyn, at 795m (2,608ft), rose up steeply to my left and Fan y Bîg, at 716m (2,351ft), steeply to my right, 100m (328ft) higher than me. I got off my bike and walked the last bit of the trail to see what the route was like. Walking through the Gap itself was like walking through a door to another world. In front of me I could see, in the distance, the forests and fields of mid-Wales. The back sides of the two peaks – the north face of the Brecon escarpment – made a horseshoe in front of me as they tapered off into the forest. The path turned sharp left and then traversed the lower slopes of Cribyn, quite steeply at first and then levelling out to follow the contours.

I realised then that I would be able to make it. It wasn't so hard. I could see the path was rocky with some rock steps, but nothing more than I'd encountered before. The drop at the top would be nasty if I went over, but I wouldn't fall to my death. I'd probably just roll for a few hundred metres and end up in a stream at the bottom. I walked my bike to the edge and sat down to have my lunch.

I was in a celebratory mood so I spent a while trying to get a selfie by balancing my phone on a rock and taking pictures of myself sitting on another rock, my legs hanging over the drop. All the time, I was alone on the mountain. At least I felt alone. Behind me, over the ridge, I knew people would be climbing Pen y Fan, but they were out of sight and earshot. For all intents and purposes I could be the last person up here. Instead of feeling afraid and alone, I felt fantastic. I didn't need help and I had got here on my own. One might have described the moment as a 'peak' experience, but I was just happy to be here, achieving something that had scared me.

The downhill was tricky, steep and rocky, but I didn't mind. I knew I wouldn't fall off and that was the main thing. I bounced and shook my way down the hill, my arms absorbing the juddering of the handlebars. I stood up in the saddle for most of the descent until I got to the road – almost 2 miles (3.2km). The further I got down, the better the path became, until I reached soft, forgiving grass just above the treeline and the path ran though a beautiful grassy gully. I let the brakes off and flew as fast as I dared. I was flying. At the bottom I met a couple who were lost.

The ride back to Brecon took me down some steep, leafy lanes, lined with uncut hazel, and then on to a bridleway that crossed meadows and streams, downhill all the way until it hit the road at Llanfrynach, just a short pedal from Brecon.

I was elated, beyond buoyed up by the ride. I had 'conquered' a classic, and, in doing so, had found a little slice of heaven on the mountainside. I'd discovered that my comfort zone is limited by fear and fear alone, not by ability or reality. I also found out that if you want solitude it's not so tough to go and find it.

I can do this.

I did.

DO IT THE HARD WAY

The Gap is a black graded mountain bike trail of about 19 miles (30km)-plus with about 500m (1,640ft) of vertical climbing that starts and ends in Brecon. It follows the Taff Trail for a lot of its length and also takes you on a section of the Mon and Brec Canal. Once high in the hills above Talybont Reservoir the trail veers off from the Taff Trail to go over the Gap. When you come down off the mountain you can follow the fantastic Three Rivers Ride back into Brecon. Exhilarating in the extreme. www.mbwales.com/listings/the-gap

You will need:
- a bike
- wet weather gear
- OS maps
- food and drink

DO IT THE EASY WAY

Driving: The Brecon Beacons are stunning and there are plenty of routes to follow. Don't miss the A4069 or the A470 and enjoy the views on the A4059. If it opens, it's well worth driving Gospel Pass too. Drive past the Talybont Reservoir from Talybont to Pant and Merthyr Tydfil.

Cycling: The Brecon Beacons have long been known for mountain biking and there are easier routes than the Gap. The Mon and Brec Canal is flat for its entire length, so you could cycle as far as you want, and then back again. www.breconbeacons.org/things-to-do/activities/cycling-mountain-biking

DO IT THE REALLY EASY WAY

BikePark Wales have all grades of singletrack, along with an uplift service, so you could spend the whole day whizzing down mountains and 'never' have to pedal, almost. The 'Kermit' green run is 3.1 miles (5km) of fabulously smooth and flowing downhill. Book early. www.bikeparkwales.com

CAMPING

Pentwyn Farm Caravan Site, Cantref: A really nice, basic Certified Location just down the mountain from the Gap. www.caravanclub.co.uk/certificated-locations/wales/powys/brecon/pentwyn-cantref

Cwmcynwyn Farm Camping, Cantref: A rather rough and ready site on a working farm just as you come down from the Gap. Basically, it's at the end of the road. Stay here and ride straight off the mountain and into your van. https://breconbeaconsholidaylets.co.uk

Brecon Beacons Caravan Club Site, Brecon: A standard C&MC site, adjacent to the A40 and just about 20 minutes' walk along the Mon and Brec Canal from Brecon. www.caravanclub.co.uk/club-sites/wales/powys/brecon-beacons-caravan-club-site

Hay-on-Wye Motorhome Overnight, Hay-on-Wye: I like Hay-on-Wye for this. You can park your moho or van in their huge car park overnight for just

a few quid. www.hay-on-wye.co.uk/visithay

Llanthony Camping, Llanthony: In an absolutely idyllic spot below the Gospel Pass, by a river, near a pub, up an Elysian vale, miles from anywhere. Pray for sun. www.llanthony camping.co.uk

INDEX

Entries in **bold** refer to
featured routes

A

Adnams Brewery Tours 165
Afon Artro 274
air, travelling by 13
Aldeburgh 160, 164, 167, 169
Alnmouth 213, 216
Alum Bay Chine 97, 105, 107
Alwinton 219, 225, 227
Amble 213, 215, 216
The Angel on the Bridge 129,
    131
Anthorn Radio Station 244
Aqueduct Trail 59
Areas of Outstanding Natural
    Beauty (AONB) 10, 159, 163,
    167, 258–69
Ash Bridge 44–5
Aunemouth Camping 70
Aveton Gifford 65, 70
Avon River 60–71
Axbridge 81

B

Badbury Rings 26, 29, 32, 36
Bake Farm 29, 34
Bala Lake 286, 289
Bala Lake Railway 287
Baltic Centre for
    Contemporary Arts 198, 202
Bamburgh 208, 211, 214, 216
Bamburgh Castle 213
Bantham Swoosh 60–71
Barmouth 274, 280, 281
Barnstaple 83, 85, 87, 92, 94
The Barrel at Bude 56
Bawdsey 159, 163, 169
Beadnell 214, 216
Beadnell Bay Camping and
    Caravan Club Site 216–17
Beamish Open Air Museum
    202
Beggar's Bridge 187, 191
Bempton Cliffs RSPB 176, 178,
    180
Berwick Caravan and
    Motorhome Club Site 238, 9
Berwick St John 30

Berwick Seaview Caravan Club
    Site 217
Berwick-upon-Tweed 209, 210,
    215, 216, 229, 230, 231, 234,
    236, 238, 239
Bexhill-on-Sea 133–4, 135, 144
Bigbury-on-Sea 62, 66
Bikepark Wales 307, 314
Black Horse Farm Caravan
    Club Site 145
The Black Mountain 303, 304
Black Sail Youth Hostel 251
Blackgang Chine 97, 102
Blackshore Quay, Southwold
    167–8
Blaen y Glyn Uchaf 306
Blakey Ridge 184, 185, 191, 194
Blyth, River 167
Borrowdale 253, 257
Boulter's Lock 129, 131
Bourne End 128
Bowness-on-Solway 242, 245,
    247
Brecon 312, 313
Brecon Beacons 303–15
Brecon Beacons Caravan Club
    Site 314
Brendon 40–1, 44, 47, 53
Brennand Farm 263, 268
Brennand Fell 265–7, 268
Brit Stops 15
Bude Canal Trust 53
Bude Sea Pool 51, 56, 57
Bude's Lost Waterway 7,
    49–59
Budle Farm Campsite 216
Bundu Camping and Caravan
    Park 94
Burgh by Sands 246, 247
Burgh Island 62, 63, 66, 69
Buttermere 252, 253, 254
Bwlch Llyn Bach 284, 288
By the Byre Caravan Site CL 59

C

Cae Adda 280
Camber Sands 135, 136, 143,
    144
Cambrian Mountains 291, 301
Campaign to Protect Rural
    Britain (CPRB) 33
Camping and Caravanning
    Club 15

Campra 14
campsites 15
Cann Orchard 54
Canterbury 147, 149–50, 151,
    155, 157
Canterbury Cathedral 150,
    151–2, 153, 154
Caravan and Motorhome Club
    CLs 15, 269
Cardigan 291–3, 297, 298
Carlisle 242, 243, 247
Castleton 184, 185, 191, 194, 195
Caversham Lock 126
Centre for Alternative
    Technology 284, 287
Cerist Valley 285
Certified Locations (CLs) 14, 15
Chainbridge 209, 211, 239
Chainbridge Caravan Site 239
Charmouth Heritage Coast
    Centre 76
Chartham 151, 155, 157
Charton Bay 78
Chesil Beach 137
Cheviot Hills 219, 225, 238
Chew Green 227
Chilham 155
Chilton Chine 106
Cilgerran Castle 298
Cilgerran Gorge 297–8
Clennell Hall Riverside
    Holiday Park 227
climate, travel and 20–1
Clitheroe 261, 264
Clitheroe Camping and
    Caravanning Club Site 269
Cliveden House Gardens 129
Coast to Coast (C2C) cycle
    197–205
The Cobb, Lyme Regis 76
Cockermouth 250, 256
Cocklawburn Beach 210–11
Coed y Brenin Visitor Centre
    279
Coed-y-Llwyn Caravan Club
    Site 280
Cogra Moss 251, 254–5
Coldstream 230, 238
Coleridge Way 43, 47
Compton Beach 99, 100–2, 107
Compton Chine 106
Consett 200, 202, 203, 204,
    205

Consett Steelworks 200
Coombe Bissett 29, 33
Coquet Island 216
Coquet Valley 219–20
Cragside 223–4, 226
Cranborne Chase 31, 32
Craster 213, 216
Cribyn 305, 311
Cross of Greet 264
Crummock Water 252
**Cwm Bychan and the Roman
    Steps 273–81**
Cwm Porth 306
Cwmcynwyn Farm Camping
    314

D

Daleacres Caravan Club Site
    145
Danby 187, 191
Dark Sky Parks 260, 264, 307
Dartmoor 16, 83–8, 266, 278
De La Warr Pavilion 133–4, 142
Deben, River 163
Derwent Reservoir 203
Derwent valley 201, 203
Derwent View Camping 205
Derwent Walk Country Park
    201
Derwent Water 253
Devon Coast to Coast 83–95
Dick's Field 37
Dinas Caravan Park and
    Camping 280
Dockray Meadow Caravan
    Club Site 257
Donald McGill Museum 102
Doone Valley 42
Doone Valley Camping 47
Dorchester 26, 28
Dorchester Museum 32
Dorset Cursus 26
Druridge Bay 215, 216
**Dungeness Desolation
    133–45**
Dunsop Bridge 262, 268, 269
Dunsop River 263, 268
Dunstanburgh Castle 213
Dunwich 166
Durham 198, 204
Durham Grange Caravan and
    Motorhome Club Site 205
Dyfi Valley 283, 285

E

e-vehicles 20
Easington 175
East Arncliffe Wood 187
East Combe Wood 33
The East Lyn River 39–47
East Lyn River path 43–5
East Yarde 90, 92
Ebbesbourne Wake 33
Ebble, River 33
The Eel's Foot Inn 169
Efford Camping 59
Egton Bridge 187, 193, 195
Elan Valley 301
England 9–10, 22–269
    getting to 12–13
    where and how to stay
        overnight 14–16
Ennerdale 251, 252, 257
equipment, essential 17–19
Esk, River 191, 194
Esk Valley 183–95
Esk Valley Railway 192–3
Esk Valley Walk 194
Eskdale 256, 257
Eurostar 13
Exmoor 39–47

F

Fairlight Cove 143
Fairlight Wood Caravan Club
    Site 145
Fangs Brow 252
Farley Mount Country Park 34
Farne Islands 216
Fawnog Valley 284–5
Felixstowe Ferry 163
Ffair-Rhos 299, 301
firelighting 19
Fishing Breaks 111, 118
Flamborough Head 176
Folkestone Creative Quarter
    and Art Installations 143
Forest of Bowland 259–69
Fremington Quay Café 90,
    92, 93
Freshwater 99, 107

G

Galloway 242, 244
Gap Road 302–15
Gateshead 201, 202
Gisburn Forest MTB 264

Glaisdale 187, 191
Glen Lyn Gorge 42
Go North East 202–3
Goat Island 78–9
Goring 123, 130
Goring to Maidenhead 121–31
Gospel Pass 305
the Granary Gallery 234
Granite Way 85–92, 94
Grwyne Fawr 305
Gwersyll Pen y Bont Touring
    Park 289

H

Hadrian's Wall 242, 247
Halsteads Farm 269
Hardknott Pass 250, 257
Harlech 280
Harlech Castle 279
Hastings 134, 144
Hay Bluff 303, 305
Hay-on-Wye 11, 305, 307
Hay-on-Wye Motorhome
    Overnight 314
Hele Bridge 55, 59
Henley-on-Thames 122, 127,
    130–1
Highview, Little Firs Farm 119
Hobbacott Down 54, 58, 59
Hodder, River 262
Hodder Valley 261
Holmes Mill 264
Holsworthy 50, 53
Holy Island 209, 211–14, 216
Honister Pass 250, 252,
    253–4, 257
Honister Slate Mine 254
Hooper's Rule 152–3
Horseshoe Walk 305
Hownsgill 200
Hull 171, 175
Humber Bridge 180, 181
Humber Bridge Country Park
    176
Humber Estuary 171–5
Hurley 126, 127–8, 130, 131
Hurley Riverside Park 131
Hythe 135, 138, 144, 145

I

Inn at the Bush 244, 247
Isle of Wight 97–107, 137,
    310

J

Jurassic Undercliff 73–81

K

kayaking 56, 59, 71, 229–39
Kent's Pilgrims' Way 147–57
Kielder Forest 219
Kirkbride 244, 246

L

Lake District 16, 248–57, 259
The Lake District Coast
  Aquarium 243
Lake Viaduct 86
Lampeter 293
Lamplugh 252, 254, 256, 257
Lealholm 187, 195
Leeford Farm Riverside
  Camping 47
Lindisfarne 211–14
Lindisfarne Castle 214
The Lion Inn 184, 191, 194
Llanbedr 274, 278, 280
Llanddewi-Brefi 299
Llandysul Angling Association
  293
Llanidloes 283
Llanthony Camping 314
Llyn Clywedog 283–4
Llyn Teifi 299–300
Longshoreman's Museum 102
Lower Tamar Lake 52, 56, 59
Loweswater 251, 252, 257
Lydd-on-Sea 135, 136
Lydford 83–5, 86
Lydford Castle 83
Lydford Gorge 90
Lyme Regis 73, 74, 79, 80, 81
Lyme Regis Museum 76
Lyme Regis Sculpture Trail 76
Lynmouth 40, 41–3, 44, 46
Lynton and Lynmouth Cliff
  Railway 42

M

Machynlleth 284, 287
Maiden Castle 25–6, 32, 36
Maidenhead 128, 129, 130, 131
maps 18
Marhamchurch 54, 58, 59
The Mayfly 117
Meldon Viaduct and Reservoir
  90, 92

The Milk Race 288
Millshield Picnic Area 203, 205
Minsmere RSPB reserve 164,
  165, 166, 169
Monmouth Beach 76
Monmouthshire & Brecon
  Canal 307, 308, 313, 314
Moors National Park Centre
  191
Morn Hill Caravan Club Site 37
motorhome stopovers 16
Mottisfont Abbey 117
Muncaster Castle 254, 256

N

National Nature Reserves
  72–81
National Parks 16
National Trust 90, 99, 102, 117,
  129, 160, 214, 257
the Needles 99, 105, 107
Nether Wallop Mill 118
New Dover Road Park and
  Ride 150, 157
Newcastle 197, 198, 200, 201–2,
  203, 204, 205
Norham Castle 234, 235, 238
North Downs 147, 148, 149,
  152–6, 157
North Downs Way 150, 156, 157
North Upton Camping 70
North York Moors 183–95,
  259
North Yorkshire Moors
  Railway 191
Northumberland Coast
  207–17
Northumberland National
  Park 225

O

Old Hartley Caravan and
  Motorhome Club Site 217
The Old Post Office Campsite
  257
Old Sarum 26, 32, 34, 36
Old Shaftesbury Drove 30
Old Station House 197, 198,
  203, 204
Orford 163
Orford Castle 165
Orford Ness 160, 163, 164, 165
the Otterburn Ranges 219–27

Outdoor Swimming Society
  63
Ox Drove 27, 31, 33

P

Packman's Trod 187, 188
Paddleboard 71, 121–31
Paddleboard Maidenhead
  130, 131
Pangbourne 125, 130
The Parsonage 113, 118
Parsonage Mill 112
The Pass of the Cross 283–9
Pen y Fan 303, 305, 306, 311
Pennine Way 221
Penrhiw Campsite 301
Pentwyn Farm Caravan Site
  314
Peter Tavy Inn 90
Pett 143
Pett Level 144
The Pier, Totland 102
The Pilchard Inn 63
Pilgrims Way 149, 150, 151–7
Planekeepers Path 54, 58
Plym Valley Railway 90
Plym Valley trail 94
Plymouth Hoe 85, 94
Polhampton Farm 110
Port Lympne Safari Park 143
Postgate Inn 193
Prospect Cottage, Dungeness
  138, 140–1, 145
Pub to Pub swim 63
The Puffing Billy Trading Co. 92

R

rail, travelling by 13
Ravenglass 256
Ravenglass Steam Railway 254
Reading 126, 130
Reculver Country Park 153, 157
Red Kite Touring Park 289
Rhaeadr Nantcol Waterfalls
  274–8, 279
Rhinogs 280
Rhododendron Mile 28
the River Avon 61–71
River Beach 70, 71
the River Test 109–19, 293,
  295
road, travelling by 13
Rodd's Bridge 57, 59

Roman Steps and the Cwm Bychan 273–81
Romney, Hythe and Dymchurch Railway 142
Romney Marsh 135, 143, 144
Rothbury 223, 227
Royal Military Canal 143
Rye 135, 142, 144
Rye Castle 142

S

Sailor's Path 169
St Catherine's Point, Niton 102
St David's 11
Salisbury 26, 29, 32, 33
Salisbury Campsite 37
Salisbury Cathedral 32
Saltram House 90
Sandalwood Certified Location 181
Scafell Pike 255, 256
Scarborough Cinder Track 189
sea, travelling by 13
Seahouses 208, 211, 214
Search For Sites 14
Seaton 79, 80
Senhouse Roman Museum 243
Shaftesbury Drove 31, 34
Shelley Oaks Farm 113, 119
Shepherd's Chine 106
Shingle Street 163, 169
Shiplake Lock 127
Silloth 246–7
The Sloop Inn 63, 64, 66, 71
Smeaton's Tower 85, 94
Smiddy Shaw 199
Snape Maltings 165, 169
Snook 214–15
Snowdon 11, 242
Snowdonia 273, 280, 285
the Solent 97
the Solway Firth 241–7
Solway Wetlands Centre 243
Sonning Lock 126
South Downs Way 150
South West Coast Path 73, 75
Southampton 109
Southwold 159, 160, 165, 166, 167–8, 169
Southwold Camping and Caravan Site 169
Spittal 209

Spurn Head and the Humber 171–81
Stanhope 197, 198, 204
Stanhope to Newcastle 197–205
Stanhope Open Air Pool 202
Stoats Farm 98, 107
Stockbridge 34, 110, 111, 117
Stour Valley 150, 157
Stour Valley Way 150–1
Strata Florida 298
The Suffolk Coast 159–69
Suffolk Coast Path 169
Sugar Loaf Mountain 305
Summerleaze Beach 50, 57
Sunderland 197, 200
SUP 71, 121–31
Sutton Hoo 161, 163, 165

T

Taff Trail 310, 312
Talybont Reservoir 306, 308, 313
Tamar Lakes 51–2, 56, 58, 59
Tamar Lakes Water Park 56
Tamar River 52–3, 58
Tarka Line 85, 94
Tarka Trail 92, 94
Tarr Steps 42
the Teifi 291–301
Teifi Pools 291, 298–300
Tennyson Down 105, 107
Test Way 117, 119
Thames, River 120–31
Three Rivers Ride 313
Tinside Lido 90
Top Gear (A4069) road 11, 306, 307
Totland 98, 102
touring parks 15
travel, and the climate 20–1
Trough of Bowland 262, 264
Tunstall 177
Turner Contemporary 153
The Tweed Valley 209, 229–39
Ty Gwyn Caravan and Camping Park 301
Tyllwyd Campsite 301

U

UK Motorhomes 16
Upper Coquet 220
Upper Tamar Lake 51–2, 56

V

Vale of Ewyas 305
Valley of the Rocks 42
Vallum 243, 245–6
vans, renting 19
Ventnor Botanic Garden 102
The Village Hall, Butley 169
visas 13

W

Walberswick 167, 168
Walbury Hill 117
Wales 11, 270–315
    getting to 12–13
    where and how to stay overnight 14–16
Wargrave 127, 130
Warkworth Castle 213
Wasdale Head 255, 256
Waskerley 199
Wastwater 255, 256
Waterfall Country 306
Watersmeet 45, 46, 47
The Weir 56
Welsh Wildlife Centre 297, 298
Wessex Wandering 25–37
West Devon Way 94
the Western Lakes 249–57
Whin Fell 263, 268
Whitby 184, 189–90, 191, 192, 194
Whitehall Meadows Nature Reserve 151
Whitendale Hanging Stones 266, 268
Whitstable 153
the Wight Chines 97–107
wild camping 16
Wild Slack Farm 194
Win Green 27, 31, 32, 33
Winchelsea 135, 144
Winchester 25, 26, 34
Winchester Cathedral 32, 36
Withernsea 175
Withernsea Lighthouse 176
Wood Farm Caravan Park 81
Wooda Farm Holiday Park 59
Woodbridge 161, 169
Wye 151, 157

Y

Yarde Orchard Cafe 90, 92, 93
Yorkshire Wildlife Trust 175
Yr Wyddfa (Snowdon) 11, 242

ACKNOWLEDGEMENTS

With grateful thanks, as ever, to the following people,
without whom this book would have been an awful lot harder,
and much less enjoyable, to research and write.

Lizzy, the botanist, a wild woman swimming.
Elizabeth, Jenny, Kathryn, Brittani and everyone at Bloomsbury Publishing.
Tim and the team at Peter Fraser Dunlop.
Andy, the fisherman's friend.
Simon Cooper at Fishing Breaks.
Bob and Ian, our incredible fishing guides.
Cath and Giz, great company on the river.
Nikki and all at the Caravan and Motorhome Club.
Mark Sutcliffe at Salar Media.
Heritage Canoes at the Welsh Wildlife Centre.
Tara at Paddleboard Maidenhead.
The Bluefin SUP Co.